Landscaping for Wildlife

Tom Mangelson

About the Author

Carrol L. Henderson

Carrol L. Henderson grew up on a farm near Zearing, Iowa. He received a B.S. degree in zoology from Iowa State University in 1968 and a Master of Forest Resources degree in ecology from the University of Georgia in 1970. He has been the supervisor of Minnesota's Nongame Wildlife Program in the Department of Natural Resources since its beginning in 1977. Prior to that, he was the assistant manager of the Lac Qui Parle Wildlife Refuge near Milan, Minnesota from 1974 to 1976. During the past eighteen years, he has developed a statewide program for the conservation of nongame wildlife and has been personally involved with efforts to bring back bluebirds, bald eagles, peregrine falcons, river otters, and trumpeter swans. His awards include the 1993 Chuck Yeager Conservation Award from the National Fish and Wildlife Foundation, the 1994 Minnesota Award from the Minnesota Chapter of The Wildlife Society, and the 1990 National Chevron Conservation Award. Henderson has also served as president of the Nongame Wildlife Association of North America, the Minnesota chapter of the Wildlife Society, and the Minnesota Fish and Wildlife Employee's Association. His writings have included the books "Woodworking for Wildlife" and "Wild About Birds: The DNR Bird Feeding Guide," and numerous articles in *The Minnesota Volunteer* magazine.

Foreword

There is little reason to doubt that if we took a properly designed poll of the great body of our citizens, we would find them more idealistic, more artistically inclined, more outdoor minded than anyone has given them credit for. In fact, that is easy to prove, because in Minnesota, and in increasing numbers of other states, we have had such a poll. It is the check-off device on your income tax form by which you can make a modest contribution in support of the state's Nongame Wildlife Program. This voluntary kind of fund-raising has had unmistakable public approval, and it has helped to develop a system of management for everyday, dooryard, "environmental" wild things that is one of the best in the nation.

People who see their surroundings being extensively paved-over, plowed-up, and artificialized sometimes speak of "getting back to nature." The author of this book — the person immediately responsible for that non-game effort — talks about bringing nature back to people. He knows that all living things depend for survival on a community of plants and animals. There is no life without habitat and no habitat without life. He also knows that his big challenge of creating pleasant and productive environments for creatures and people is not exclusive to such things as dickeybirds and butterflies. It includes every species in the out-of-doors. The pheasant, sharptail, mallard and deer are nongame for most of the year.

I have read Carrol Henderson's book with interest and pleasure. He brings together a world of good information on the needs of common (and some not so common) animal life and the select greenery in which they all must live. In making plans for high-quality habitats he has a logical preference for native — even regionally adapted — kinds of trees, shrubs and other vegetation. However, he knows about and uses the good ones from far-away places.

Amid this useful detail, there probably is a thread of down-home philosophy; that each of us technology-oriented moderns is at heart a citizen of the natural world; and that there are easy and practical things we can do to keep it that way.

Durward L. Allen
Professor Emeritus of
Wildlife Management
Purdue University
August 11, 1986

Acknowledgments

This publication has been made possible by donations made in memory of conservationists and nature lovers Lance Thoen of Eden Prairie and Carl W. Curtis of Minneapolis and by donations to the Nongame Wildlife Check-off on Minnesota's income tax and property tax forms.

The Department of Natural Resources gratefully appreciates the involvement and suggestions of the following people who have contributed their expertise to the writing of this book:

Dr. Durward Allen
Dr. Alfred Berner
Robert A. Blackbourn
Dr. Walter J. Breckenridge
Sue Brokl
Barbara Coffin
Carmen Converse
Robert Dana
Bob Djupstrom
Joan Galli
Fred Glasoe
Meg Hanisch
Bonnie Harper
Arthur S. Hawkins Sr.
Tex Hawkins
Katie Haws
Bob Hess
Rudy Hillig
Roger Holmes
Laura Jackson
Sarma Jatnieks-Straumanis

Doug Keran
Dr. Jim Kitts
Ann McNitt
Jack Mooty
Steven Mueller
Bill Oemichen
Pam Perry
Lee Pfannmuller
Larry Pollard
Doug Reeves
Jay Rendall
John Scharf
John Schladweiler
Dr. Harold "Scotty" Scholten
Dave Shaffer
Welby Smith
Koni Sundquist
Dr. Dan Svedarsky
Dr. Gustav Swanson
Darlyne Thoen

Special appreciation is extended to Lynn Reinhardt and Kim Bottolfson for typing this manuscript and to Janice Orr and Margaret Dexter for editing the manuscript. Appreciation is also extended to Bachman's in Minneapolis, Pine Cone Nursery in Coon Rapids and Bergman's Nursery in Stillwater for permission to photograph plants referred to in the text.

Table of Contents

Carrol Henderson

Appendix

Talented artists like Catherine McClung of Dexter, Michigan create beautiful paintings of wildlife. Landscaping to attract wildlife is also a form of art.

Landscaping for Wildlife

Chapter 1

The Midwest has an abundance of talented wildlife artists — people who can paint beautiful images of cardinals, bluebirds, deer and ducks. While you may not be skilled as an artist, there is a living canvas which you can personally adorn with real cardinals, bluebirds, deer and ducks — the landscape. You can develop the land to support an abundance of wildlife — starting with your own backyard. Instead of using paints and brushes, your tools are trees, shrubs, grasses, flowers and structures like bird houses and feeders. You may find that being a "wildlife landscape artist" will be one of the most delightful and rewarding hobbies you have ever known.

This book is about landscaping for wildlife. It is designed to take a habitat-oriented look at landscaping concepts in the Midwest — primarily Minnesota, Iowa, Wisconsin, Michigan and northern Illinois, Indiana and Ohio. It focuses on providing the components necessary to support diverse native wildlife populations. It also provides other ecological, energy and soil conservation benefits. The recommendations apply to urban areas, backyards, farms and woodlots.

Landscaping for wildlife is not as difficult as it might seem. This book is designed to simplify the process of designing and managing the landscape so you can double the abundance of wildlife on your land through landscaping (5, 22, 42, 44).

The introduction of wildlife habitat requirements into the

This painting by Catherine McClung portrays how a backyard with the necessary habitat components will attract a variety of wildlife.

landscaping process means additional criteria must be considered during the design process for "wildlife landscape artists." Those requirements are explained on the following pages.

This book is written to satisfy the needs of a broad audience — homeowners, farmers and woodlot owners as well as professional wildlife managers, soil conservation specialists, foresters, landscape architects, horticulturists and nursery managers.

The first four chapters are a general introduction for all readers to the benefits and principles of landscaping for wildlife. It includes a systematic explanation of 16 wildlife habitat components. Chapter 5 includes advice for

homeowners who wish to develop their yards for wildlife. Chapter 6 includes advice to farmers for farmland development and management. Chapter 7 includes suggestions to woodlot owners for wildlife habitat enhancement in woodlots.

Much technical wildlife information relating to these chapters has been placed in the appendices where important or relevant information can be reviewed in depth. The appendices are loaded with information and you are encouraged to become familiar with their contents. Literature cited in the text is referred to by a number or numbers in parenthesis. These numbers refer to the appropriate number in the "Literature Cited"

Carl R. Sams II

section where the full literature citation occurs.

The French philosopher Voltaire once said "If you would converse with me, define your terms." Wildlife can be many things to many people. To a hunter it might mean deer, ducks and pheasants. A person who maintains a backyard bird feeder would think of cardinals, blue jays, chickadees and evening grosbeaks. In this book, wildlife includes birds, mammals, reptiles, amphibians, fish and insects not generally regarded as pests.

Traditionally "landscaping" has been defined as the modification of a tract of land — usually for aesthetic purposes. Frequently, these artistic effects are incorporated into landscape designs with more complex and functional goals such as energy conservation, recreation, soil stabilization, food production or restoration of natural communities. A contemporary definition of landscape architecture is:"The manipulation and management of outdoor space to bring harmony between living things and their environment." This concept includes planning, design and management activities in this book. Emphasis has been placed on native plant species from the Midwest.

Benefits of Landscaping for Wildlife

Chapter 2

There are many added benefits to well-conceived landscape designs. A diverse landscape with many plant species supports an abundance of wildlife. Such habitats are less vulnerable to large scale destruction caused by insect pests or diseases that can devastate a single plant species. For example, a woodlot comprised of 5 percent American elm trees and 10 other tree species would be less disrupted by Dutch elm disease than a woodlot consisting of 95 percent American elms and one other tree species.

Humans often tend to simplify the landscape by creating large areas that contain a single species — monocultures. These are vulnerable to environmental problems. By increasing the number of plant species used in a landscape plan you can increase the ecological stability of your property (68).

Raymond Dasmann (25) made an eloquent plea for the preservation of natural diversity in "A Different Kind of Country":

"There is a trend toward uniformity in environment, people, and ways of life over all the earth. This trend is in the long run inimical to life, including human life . . .

Diversity has always characterized the biosphere to which man belonged. In living systems, complexity brings stability and ability to withstand change. The future survival of man may well depend on the continuing complexity of the biosphere. . ."

Carrol Henderson

Wildlife Benefits

By planting certain plant species on your property you can increase wildlife abundance on your land. Creatures ranging from white-tailed deer to hummingbirds and monarch butterflies will respond to your landscaping plan if it includes the habitat components they need for survival.

Energy Conservation

Landscaping for wildlife has an economic dimension. It presents an opportunity to save heating and cooling costs for your home. Conifers on the north and west side of your home will reduce the cooling effect of harsh winter winds on your house and concurrently provide shelter for wintering songbirds.

Hardwoods such as oaks, basswood, green ash, white ash, sugar maple, soft maple or hackberry can be planted on the south side of a home to shade it in the summer and reduce cooling costs. They provide nesting sites and wildlife food, and when they drop their leaves they allow the home to receive the sun's rays during the winter.

Soil Conservation

One of the greatest responsibilities shared by rural landowners is the need to conserve the soil. Field windbreaks are not relicts left over from the dust bowl days of the 1930s — they are important landscape features that help farmers conserve their soil. Some field windbreaks need to be renovated and new ones planted.

Lynn Rogers

Eastern Chipmunk

Prairie grasses provide excellent erosion control and nesting cover. Combinations of grasses and legumes protect soils while providing nectar for bees and butterflies. Raspberries, sumacs, coralberry, gray dogwood, red-osier dogwood, bearberry, highbush

Don Henderson shows his son Michael a bluebird house on their farm near Zearing, Iowa.

cranberry and snowberry all protect erodable slopes while creating important food and cover.

Habitat for Kids

Don't forget to look at your property through the eyes of a child. Is it diverse, exciting and filled with different habitats that support a multitude of wildlife? Or is it a monotonous sea of bluegrass, corn or red pines? A young and growing mind will thrive in an environment that contains much wildlife. You can expose your children to the wonders of the natural world on your property by landscaping for wildlife. This process can become more meaningful by allowing children to help plant trees, shrubs and flowers for wildlife. This opportunity exists on your own property and on local school grounds as well.

Natural Beauty

Some of the most desirable and beautiful plants for landscaping also provide significant benefits for wildlife. Conifers like white spruce, Black Hills spruce and eastern white pine all provide good winter cover and summer nesting cover. Nanking cherry, American elderberry, sugar ma-

Backyard wildlife can be enjoyed by children from the comfort of their homes.

ple, cockspur hawthorn and 'red splendor' crabapple are highly regarded by horticulturists for both their beauty and wildlife benefits.

Photography and Birdwatching

If you enjoy photography, imagine the opportunities that exist in a backyard that is regularly visited by butterflies, cardinals, hummingbirds, chickadees and squirrels. Appendix C includes a listing of useful references on wildlife photography.

Did you know that over the years you could see more than 100 species of birds in your backyard? Don and Wynne Mahle of Wabasha, Minnesota have

Attracting wildlife is even more popular for kids today than it was in 1886 when this drawing appeared in *Harpers Weekly*.

10

counted 191 bird species in or from their backyard! You too can make a hobby of recording a list of the wildlife seen in your yard. The best way to start is to buy a pair of good binoculars and a good bird field guide, as well as guides for butterflies, mammals, reptiles and amphibians. Appendix C is a list of some commonly used field guides. You might try documenting the increase in wildlife populations that occurs as you improve backyard habitat. You can also compare the relative attractiveness of different plants to wildlife in your yard.

One way to enhance your viewing opportunities in an area heavily used by wildlife is to build an observation blind as shown in Appendix D (113).

Wildlife photography can be an immensely rewarding hobby. (Birds don't always cooperate as well as this red-breasted nuthatch.)

Natural Insect Control

Insects like mosquitoes and grasshoppers can be a nuisance around your home or garden. By providing the right habitat components, you can encourage insect-eating predators like bats, purple martins, dragonflies, tree swallows or bluebirds. Many people dislike bats until they learn that a single bat can eat 3,000-7,000 insects per night. Bats can be accommodated by building

Bats eat large numbers of insects, including mosquitoes.

bat houses. Details are explained in the Department of Natural Resources booklet "Woodworking for Wildlife (53)." This is ecologically more compatible with the environment than placing too much emphasis on solving insect problems with "bug zappers" or chemicals that could be harmful to the environment.

Windbreak and Shelterbelt Benefits

A multi-row farmstead shelterbelt to the north and west side of a cattle feedlot can help protect cattle during blizzards and increase their rate of gain by reducing the effect of windchill. This is because more livestock food is converted into meat and less energy is needed for production of body heat.

A well-placed farmstead shelterbelt can also help reduce snow accumulations in your yard and driveway, reducing the time and fuel costs necessary to keep your yard and driveway clear of snow.

An evergreen shelterbelt between a road and a home can be very attractive and can help reduce highway noise and dust problems if it is at least 30 feet wide. It is especially valuable near freeways.

Food Production

Plants that provide some of the best wildlife foods are also excellent for human consumption. Herbs like parsley, anise, spearmint and thyme provide food for butterflies. Scarlet runner beans

provide nectar for hummingbirds and an abundance of edible beans. Cherries, chokecherries, strawberries, raspberries, elderberries, wild plums, blueberries, cranberries, grapes, juneberries, apricots and crabapples can all be shared with wildlife. When you harvest your fruit, consider leaving some for wildlife to eat (98).

Property Value

Don't forget the increase in property value that occurs on a "well landscaped" area! Proper harvesting practices in woodlots can also improve wildlife habitat while providing timber income and/or fuelwood.

Soil conservation practices can help prevent dust storms.

This rose-breasted grosbeak, like all wildlife, needs food, water, shelter, and space in which to live and raise its family.

Principles of Landscaping for Wildlife

Chapter 3

"Landscaping for Wildlife" involves some new principles which are beyond the scope of traditional landscape practices. This is because some traditional landscaping criteria for plants are not related to wildlife needs. A landscaping strategy that incorporates wildlife, however, adds new criteria based on wildlife benefits.

There are essentially nine principles involved in landscaping for wildlife.

1. Provide the four basic needs of wildlife — food, water, shelter and space.

Wild animals have four basic needs for survival: food, water, shelter and space. If you keep those needs in mind as you develop a landscape plan, you will have an excellent chance for success.

Food

Every species has its own unique food requirements. Food requirements change as an animal grows older and from one season to another. Food includes obvious nutritional parts of an animal's diet as well as supplements like salt. Grit or gravel is required by many birds for grinding up food in their gizzards. Several types of foods can be provided in a landscaping plan:

fruits and berries, grain and seeds, nectar sources, nuts and acorns, browse plants (woody twigs and buds), forage plants (grasses and legumes) and aquatic plants.

Many insects and other invertebrates are attracted to trees and shrubs. They also provide a food source for wildlife.

Water

Water! The importance of water for wildlife cannot be overemphasized. Springs, beaver ponds, marshes, creeks, swamps, lakes, and rivers are vital components of our environment. Species ranging from deer to ducks to dragonflies depend on water for survival. One of your biggest challenges in developing a landscape for wildlife is to preserve and manage watery habitats where they still exist, to create ponds where they are absent, and to restore wetlands where they have previously been destroyed.

Shelter

Shelter, or cover, is necessary for protection from adverse weather and for hiding from predators. Shelter is particularly critical while animals are nesting and raising their young. It is also necessary when animals sleep or rest.

Shelter can come in many forms. It can be trees, shrubs, grasses, flowers, or structures like rockpiles, brushpiles, cut banks, hollow trees, bird houses, burrows, bridges and abandoned buildings.

Space

Every wildlife species has a unique pattern of space or territorial needs. By understanding how much territory is defended by a pair of house wrens, bluebirds, ruffed grouse and other species you can learn how much wildlife can reasonably be expected to occur on your property. Loons and trumpeter swans will defend up to 100 acres of lake or wetland for their nesting territory. A ruffed grouse pair needs about 10 acres. Bluebirds need about 5 acres per pair. In contrast, wood ducks and purple martins do not defend territories around their nests, so many pairs can nest within a limited area.

Additional statistics on home range requirements are presented in Appendix E.

2. Function

The "function" served by plants and structures is more important than their appearance. Don't base your planting decisions solely on whether or not a plant is pretty. Find out if it provides good nesting cover, winter cover, edible fruits, butterfly nectar, grains, nuts, acorns or other factors of value to wildlife. Think in terms of providing the four basic requirements of wildlife.

Water is essential for the survival of creatures, including the Blanchard's cricket frog.

3. Diversity

High species diversity is an integral part of a good landscaping plan. A high diversity of plant species helps protect against drastic changes caused by plant disease and insect pests. It also attracts a higher diversity of wildlife for you to see and enjoy.

Three kinds of diversity are important — plant diversity, structural diversity and vertical diversity.

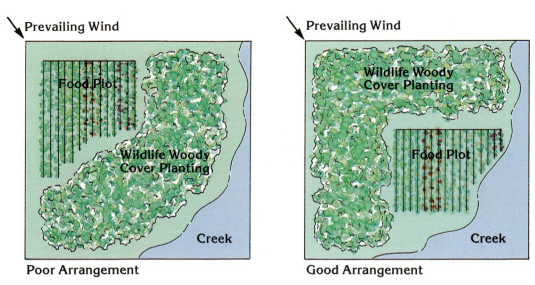

Figure 1. Good and poor arrangements for a wildlife woody cover planting and food plot.

Plant diversity includes providing a wide array of living trees, shrubs, perennial flowers, annual flowers and grasses. For the purposes of this book, structural diversity includes non-vegetative structures and/or dead plant materials which complement the living plants. This includes wildlife feeders, nest and roost boxes, dead trees, logs, brush piles, rock piles, salt licks, dust, grit and water sources. Vertical diversity refers to "levels" of habitat that may occur in various habitats. For example, some species live underground, some live at ground level, some live in low, bushy cover and others live in tree tops. A good landscape plan will consider providing these various levels of vertical diversity.

4. Seasonality

It is necessary to provide the four basic needs of wildlife through all four seasons of the year if you want year-long wildlife activity on your property. Planting a variety of trees, shrubs and other plants will be necessary to accomplish that objective.

For example, a backyard landscaping plan might include this combination of plants for songbirds: Black Hills spruce and white spruce provide winter cover and summer nesting sites; nanking cherry and American elderberry provide summer fruits; red-osier dogwood and mountain ash provide fall fruits; and 'red splendor' crabapple and American highbush cranberry provide fruits in winter and spring.

5. Arrangement

Habitat components need to be properly arranged or interspersed to maximize the value to wildlife. A food plot with no nearby winter cover serves little purpose. It may even cause extra mortality for pheasants by forcing them to cross open country to reach the food plot. This increases their chance of being preyed on or exposed to blizzard conditions.

Food, water and cover need to be close together. When planning their arrangement you also need to consider the direction of prevailing winds, snow drifting characteristics and soil erosion control techniques.

Figure 1 contrasts an example of a good arrangement with a

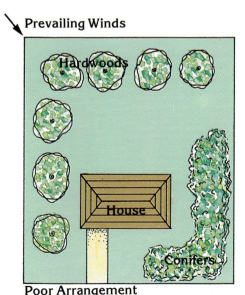

Figure 2. Examples of a good arrangement and a poor arrangement for a backyard planting.

poor arrangement for a wildlife woody cover planting and food plot. The good arrangement has a woody cover planting on the northwest corner of a farm where it will help prevent snow from filling in the corn food plot. The poor arrangement has a corn food plot in the northwest corner of the farm where it will fill with snow during the winter's first blizzard. The woody cover planting along the creek does not help shelter the food plot because of the prevailing northwest winds.

Figure 2 compares an example of a good arrangement to a poor

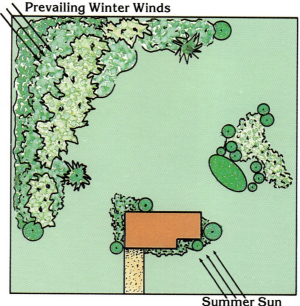

Figure 3. Example of a naturalized yard design. Plants are not arranged in rows.

Hardwoods on the south and east side of the house provide shade in summer, sunlight in winter, and wildlife habitat.

arrangement for a backyard landscaping plan. The good arrangement has a row of conifers on the north and west side of the property to shelter the home from prevailing northwest winter winds. Hardwoods on the south and east side of the house provide shade in the summer and sunlight in the winter to facilitate energy conservation. In contrast, the poor arrangement has hardwoods on the north and west where they provide little protection from northwest winds. The conifers on the east and south shade the house in the winter, minimizing the natural solar heating effects on the home.

Another facet of arrangement is to use nature as a model — think crooked! Trees in forests don't grow in rows! Look for opportunities to design naturalistic clumps or arrangements of plants that are not in rows. Where cultivation with machinery is necessary in farm shelterbelts or wildlife woody cover plantings, rows are necessary, but they don't need to be straight. Gentle curves in the rows will add to their visual appeal. The same concept applies in designing openings or cutting blocks in woodlands. Instead of square or rectangular plots it is esthetically more appealing to design curving or irregular edges to management tracts. Figure 3 is an example of a naturalized yard design in which straight lines and rows have largely been avoided.

A final aspect of arrangement is spacing of certain habitat components like bird houses. Wood duck and purple martin houses can be grouped together while tree swallows will nest 25 yards apart and bluebirds will nest 100 yards apart. This factor is discussed more fully in "Woodworking for Wildlife" (53).

6. Protection

A good landscaping plan considers how to protect wildlife from unnecessary mortality. Predation by natural predators is a fact of life and should not be considered a problem in most circumstances. In contrast, predation by free-ranging dogs and cats is unacceptable. Your cats can be rendered more harmless by having them de-clawed, by putting bells on them or by keeping them indoors. They should not be allowed to roam at large. Dogs can also cause problems and should be kept under control.

Structural hazards like picture windows or reflective windows can kill songbirds that have been attracted to your property. They will see the reflection of vegetation or sky in the glass and break their necks on striking the glass. This problem is particularly acute where buildings occur in woodland habitats. You can minimize this problem by placing a falcon silhouette on the outside of the window. A sample falcon silhouette is shown in Appendix F. Other techniques to keep birds from hitting problem windows include stretching parallel strings on the outside surface of the window at 4 inch intervals or placing a dead branch perch or a mobile of pine cones close to the window.

Two birds of foreign origin are particularly devastating to our native songbird populations— house sparrows and European starlings. House sparrows can kill bluebirds and tree swallows by scalping them and piercing their skulls with their bills. They will also go into bluebird nests and kill the young. Starlings will kill or drive away native songbirds from nest boxes or natural cavities in trees. Both species are unprotected by law and should be controlled where they are a problem. Starlings can be prevented

An immature goshawk has just killed a bluejay. Predation by natural predators is a fact of life and should not be considered a problem in most circumstances.

Chip Clark

from using most bird houses, except those made for purple martins and wood ducks, by using entrance holes less than 1 3/4 inches in diameter. Sparrow problems can be minimized by removing their nests whenever they occur and by using an elevator-type sparrow trap to remove high concentrations of sparrows. Elevator-type traps can be purchased from the Cumberland Hide and Fur Co., P.O. Box 408, Owatonna, MN 55060 phone number (507) 451-7607.

Finally, wildlife — and humans — need protection from dangerous, persistent or non-specific chemicals in the environment. Fertilizers can leach into wetlands and cause deadly algal blooms or eutrophication. Some pesticides can kill earthworms and other important bird foods. We need to be cautious about the amounts and kinds of herbicides and insecticides we use. Whenever fertilizer and pesticides are used, they should be used only when necessary and applied strictly according to the label instructions. However, some pesticides are lethal to birds, fish, and small mammals even when used according to the instructions.

There are many natural and relatively harmless techniques for controlling plant, insect or other pest problems where wildlife is a consideration.

For example, "Dipel" Crop

The House sparrow is an exotic pest bird that can kill native songbirds. It is unprotected by law and should be controlled where it is a problem.

Saver is a bacteria called **Bacillus thuringiensis** which kills leaf-eating caterpillars but will not harm wildlife. It can be used to protect many common garden plants. Marigolds can be planted in gardens to control nematodes. Safer's Insecticidal Soap is also a naturally occurring compound that can be used on flowers, vegetables and fruit trees. It is not harmful to people, pets, ladybugs or honey bees, but will control many common insect pests. The pests controlled by these compounds are listed in Appendix G.

7. Native Plants and Seed Origins

There are significant benefits to using native plants in a land-scaping plan. Native plants help perpetuate our natural heritage and are adapted to the climate of an area, so winter kill is not a serious problem. Native plants generally require a minimum of maintenance once they are established. You may find it particularly rewarding to develop part of your property as a native prairie plant garden, or as a native woodland flower garden . Prairie grasses provide excellent ground nesting cover for birds, and certain prairie wildflowers attract hummingbirds and butterflies. Some native flowering shrubs also produce berries used by birds.

If you try using native plants for landscaping, some "homework"

will be necessary. Identify the origin of seeds or planting stock you plan to use. Consult companies that sell prairie or woodland plants that are derived from your region as well as the Soil Conservation Service (SCS) or Department of Natural Resources (DNR). Prairie plant seed stock and woodland planting stock have the best chance for survival if they are planted in the same state or at the same latitude. For example, big bluestem is a native prairie plant in Minnesota, but if seeds are brought north from Texas they will not survive because they need a longer growing season to develop seeds. The SCS recommends that seed be transplanted no more than 200 miles north, 100 miles south or 250 miles east or west of its original source. Ideally, the seed source should originate within 25 to 50 miles of where it is to be planted.

If you wish to consider natural, local sources for obtaining native plants, good ecological sense dictates that you do not move entire plants out of the wild. Instead, consider the limited removal of a few seeds from these plants so natural plant communities are not disrupted. You may be able to salvage entire plants, however, from natural sites in your area that are scheduled for destruction by housing developments, creation of parking lots, road construction or expansion of farm fields.

Probably the best way to understand what native vegetation should be included in your landscaping plan is to know what native plant community originally occurred on your land. Within the Midwest are 13 different plant communities that are shown in Figure 4 (67). Identify your native plant community. Then contact your nearest arboretum, the botany department at a nearby college or university, your DNR Natural Heritage Program or your local DNR area office to learn what original plant species are characteristic of your area. These species can provide a basis upon which to build your landscaping plan (28). It can also help you avoid the mistake of trying to make plants grow which are not appropriate or adapted to your property.

17

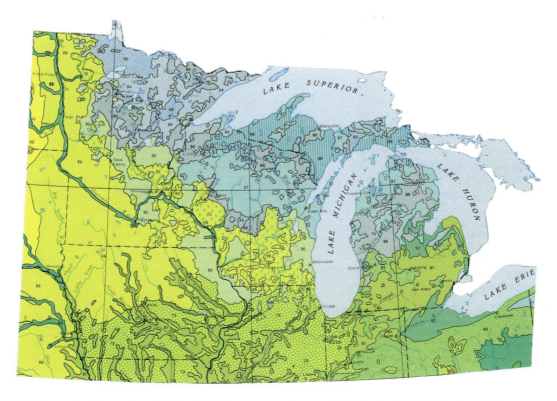

GRASSLAND AND FOREST COMBINATIONS
- **Oak Savanna**
  (Quercus-Andropogon)
- **Mosaic of Numbers 66 and 91**

NEEDLELEAF FORESTS
- **Great Lakes Spruce-Fir Forest**
  (Picea-Abies)
- **Conifer Bog**
  (Picea-Larix-Thuja)
- **Great Lakes Pine Forest**
  (Pinus)

EASTERN GRASSLANDS
- **Bluestem Prairie**
  (Andropogon-Panicum-Sorghastrum)

BROADLEAF FORESTS
- **Northern Floodplain Forest**
  (Populus-Salix-Ulmus)
- **Maple-Basswood Forest**
  (Acer-Tilia)
- **Oak-Hickory Forest**
  (Quercus-Carya)
- **Elm-Ash Forest**
  (Ulmus-Fraxinus)
- **Beech-Maple Forest**
  (Fagus-Acer)

BROADLEAF AND NEEDLELEAF FORESTS
- **Northern Hardwoods**
  (Acer-Betula-Fagus-Tsuga)
- **Northern Hardwoods-Fir Forest**
  (Acer-Betula-Abies-Tsuga)

Figure 4.   Native plant communities in the Midwest.

8. Climate and Plant Hardiness Zones

An exotic plant is one that originated in another region or country. There are many exotic plants which will survive in the Midwest and some provide excellent wildlife benefits. They should be used with discretion because some are too aggressive and become "weeds." To use exotic plants, it is necessary to understand the concept of "hardiness zones."

Trees, shrubs and perennial forbs are rated by horticulturists according to the northernmost climate zone in which they normally are winter hardy. Four different hardiness zone maps may be encountered as you review plant lists and garden catalogs. Note which hardiness zone map is being referred to as you use a garden catalog or plant reference. Zones 1,2,3,4 and 5 are different in each map.

For purposes of this book, the United States Department of Agriculture (USDA) Zones of Plant Hardiness are used, with two modifications as shown in Figure 5. First, the southeastern region of Minnesota along the Mississippi River is Minnesota's "banana belt." It is listed by the USDA as Zone 4, but here Zone 5 has been modified to extend northward from northeastern Iowa into southeastern Minnesota. Second, Zone 3 has been split into north and south halves — Zone 3 North (3N) and Zone 3 South (3S). This corresponds to the hardiness differences that have been portrayed in the maps developed by the Minnesota Horticultural Society and the Agricultural Extension Service (72).

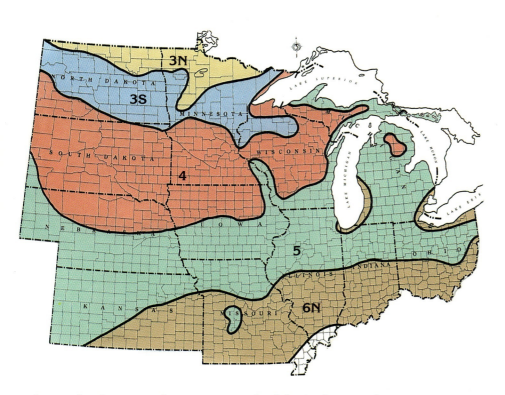

Approximate range of average annual minimum temperatures.

☐	-40° to -35°	Zone 3N	☐ -20° to -10°	Zone 5
☐	-35° to -30°	Zone 3S	☐ -10° to -0°	Zone 6N
☐	-30° to -25°	Zone 4		

Figure 5.   Plant hardiness zones.

9. Soils and Topography

Know your soils and topography. Topography refers to the natural slope and contour of the land as it affects water drainage and sun exposure. Consult with your county extension office, the SCS or local garden center to learn about your soils. Are they clay, loam, silt or sand? Are they acidic or alkaline? Notice what areas are on the warmer, sunny south-facing slopes and which areas are on the cooler, more shaded north-facing slopes. Are there deficiencies in nitrogen, sulphur, phosphorus or potassium that will require fertilization? Do you have areas that are shaded, wet or poorly drained? Learning these soil facts is absolutely vital to the success of your landscaping efforts. A good knowledge of your soils is the foundation of your decision-making process as you plan how to match plants to specific sites on your property. Your local County Extension Service can perform inexpensive soil tests for you.

A published Soil Survey Report can be obtained from your county SCS, Soil and Water Conservation District (SWCD) office or County Extension Service offices. It gives information on soils in the county. This information is generalized or detailed depending on the purpose and specific site in mind. The information describes the topographic, physical and chemical properties of the soils but more importantly, there are various interpretations for land uses and management. Interpretations are made for: recommended species to plant; growth and yield response of forest, herbaceous or landscape materials; engineering properties; natural vegetation that can be expected and other management needs.

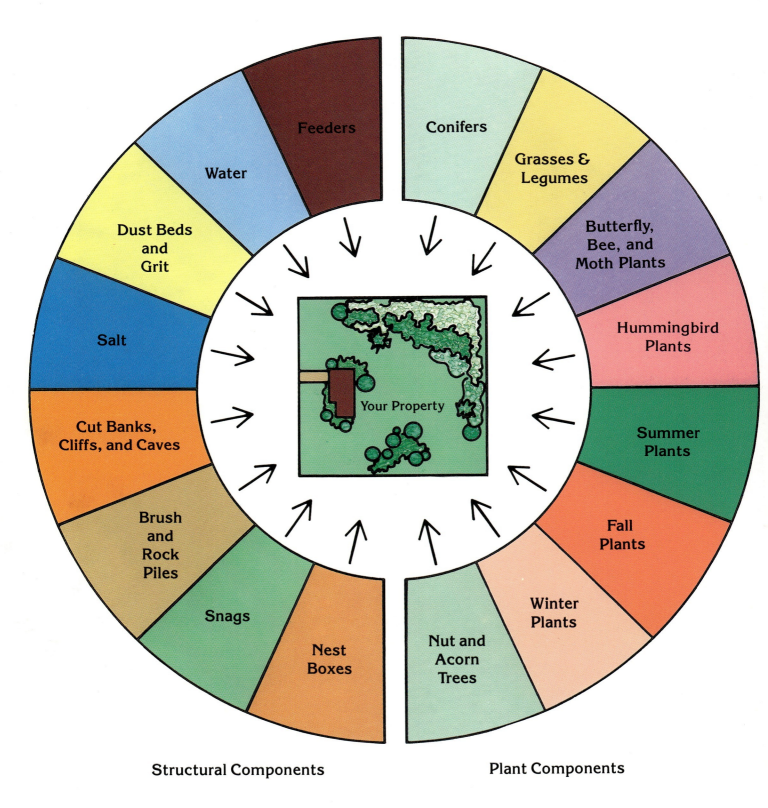

Figure 6.   Sixteen components of wildlife habitat.

Habitat Components for Wildlife
A New Approach to Landscaping

Chapter 4

There are basically 16 landscape components necessary to fulfill the major habitat needs of our wildlife — eight living plant components and eight structural non-living components. These are portrayed in Figure 6 and are the building blocks of your landscaping plan.

The plant components are organized primarily by the season in which they provide major food and cover values. Because of their popularity in backyard landscaping plans, butterfly, bee and moth nectar plants and hummingbird nectar plants are separately identified. A landscape which includes plants from all these categories will provide year-round benefits to an enormous variety of wildlife.

VEGETATIVE COMPONENTS OF WILDLIFE HABITAT

There are eight vegetative components of wildlife habitat 1) conifers which provide protective winter shelter, summer nesting cover and some food; 2) grasses and legumes which provide nesting cover, winter cover, and food; 3)

This field sparrow, a native songbird, is nesting in a spruce tree.

Gregory K. Scott

plants which provide nectar for bees, moths, and butterflies and food for caterpillars; 4) plants which provide nectar for hummingbirds and orioles; 5) plants which provide summer wildlife foods and some shelter value, including aquatic plants; 6) plants which provide fall foods and some

shelter; 7) plants which provide winter wildlife foods and some shelter; and 8) hardwood trees and shrubs which produce nuts and acorns.

1. Conifers

(See Appendix A, Part 1)

Conifers, also called evergreens, include trees and shrubs which generally do not lose their needles in winter. They include pines, spruces, firs, arborvitae, junipers, cedars and yews. Exceptions are bald cypress and larch (tamarack) trees which lose their needles in winter. These plants are critically important as escape cover and winter shelter and serve as summer nesting sites. Also the sap, needles, twigs, buds and seeds are eaten by wildlife. They also provide the visual enjoyment of staying green all year.

The eastern white pine is used by 48 bird species. Yellow-bellied sapsuckers eat the sap, spruce grouse and turkeys eat the needles, and many other birds eat the

Missouri Department of Conservation

The eastern red cedar is an excellent conifer for wildlife.

seeds. The branches are heavily used as nest sites, and cavities are also used for nesting.

Other conifers which provide exceptional food and cover value are balsam fir, eastern red cedar, all spruces and eastern hemlock. Common juniper and red (Norway) pine are used to a moderate extent by wildlife. Scotch pine and northern white-cedar are used by a few species. Canada yew is so highly preferred by deer that it is generally wiped out wherever significant numbers of deer are present.

Appendix A, Part 1 includes a list of conifers which can be used for landscaping in the Midwest (27, 31, 69, 71).

2. Grasses and Legumes
(See Appendix A, Part 2)

Grasses and legumes provide habitat needs in rural areas or large yards for many ground nesting birds like pheasants, mallards, blue-winged teal, meadowlarks, dickcissels, bobolinks, and vesper sparrows. Grasses and legumes also provide forage for plant-eating animals — whitetailed deer, cottontail rabbits, woodchucks, meadow voles and others. Grassy habitats can be important in forest openings. In the early spring the grass greens up when deer need good forage to improve their body condition after being stressed by winter. Grassy cover provides summer cover for ground-nesting birds

A native prairie can be an outstanding feature of the landscape that also benefits wildlife.

accompanied by young. This habitat also provides hunting sites for red foxes, red-tailed hawks, kestrels, northern harriers, short-eared owls, coyotes, long-tailed weasels and striped skunks. Grasses like switchgrass provide winter cover for pheasants and deer, and also provide food for seed-eating winter birds like redpolls.

The planting of grassy nesting cover is undergoing a dramatic transition in the Midwest. Formerly such nesting cover consisted almost entirely of exotic species like bluegrass, brome grass, orchard grass, alfalfa and sweet clover. Often these species lose their vigor after several years. They are difficult to rejuvenate.

The use of native grasses and legumes has increased in the past

10 years. Native prairie stands will maintain their vigor indefinitely by being burned about every three to five years. Switchgrass is also an excellent species for providing nesting cover. Appendix H is a map with an accompanying table that portrays which commercially available prairie grass cultivars are best suited for use in the Midwest (37). Also included in Appendix H is a variety of grass and legume combinations which can be used to establish grassy nesting cover. Legumes are important in those plantings because they convert, or "fix," atmospheric nitrogen in their roots. This nitrogen subsequently becomes available to other plants as a source of natural fertilizer.

A solid stand of switchgrass is not a prairie, nor does it provide habitat diversity for a diversity of wildlife. Some people prefer to recreate a prairie habitat on their land by using a variety of native grasses, legumes and flowers. A restored prairie can provide beautiful aesthetic benefits as well as wildlife benefits (35). Prairie Restoration, Inc. of Princeton, Minnesota, can provide advice and recommendations on prairie restoration with specific advice on seed origins. Other excellent sources of prairie plant seeds and planting advice are the Prairie Moon Nursery of Winona, and Landscape Alternatives of Minneapolis, Minnesota.

Appendix A, Part 2 includes a list of grasses and legumes suitable for use in the Midwest. Persons interested in seeding prairie grasses should order the publica-

The meadowlark nests in Midwestern grasslands.

The black-eyed susan is an attractive wildflower and a good nectar source for butterflies.

tion "Establishment of Seeded Grasslands for Wildlife Habitat in the Prairie Pothole Regions" United States Department of Interior — United States Fish and Wildlife Service Special Scientific Report — Wildlife Number 234, from the Superintendent of Documents, U.S. Government Printing Office, Washington, D.C. 20402 (66, 79, 112).

3. Butterfly, Bee and Moth Plants

(See Appendix A, Part 3)

One of the greatest opportunities for enhancing your yard for wildlife is to provide the plants that will attract butterflies, bees, and moths. A butterfly garden can quickly become the pride of anyone's yard. You may wish to develop a butterfly garden around a theme like native prairie wildflowers or native woodland wildflowers.

There is an incredible variety of beautiful butterflies in the Midwest — at least 200 species. Among the most common butterflies are the monarch, painted lady, comma, red-spotted purple, tiger swallowtail, several fritillaries, red admiral, sulphurs, cabbage butterflies and several species of blues. Honeybees and bumblebees are common nectar feeders as are hummingbird clearwing moths and sphinx (hawk) moths (1, 30, 54, 60, 82).

Butterfly Plants

Two types of food are necessary for butterflies — food for caterpillars and nectar sources for adult butterflies.

At least 175 plants are used by different butterfly caterpillars in the Midwest. Among the most used trees are birches, aspens, willows, hackberry, cherries and oaks. Other well used plants are composites, legumes, grasses, herbs, blueberries, sedges and docks. Examples include asters, alfalfa, vetches, clovers, Kentucky bluegrass, little bluestem and violets. Other good larval food sources are hollyhock, milkweed, lupines, black-eyed susan, sedum and marigolds.

Appendix I shows some of the best butterfly nectar sources. In general, the best plants are dogbanes and milkweeds. Other outstanding plants are asters, thistles, goldenrods, Joe Pye-weed, ironweed, fleabane, red clover, winter cress, selfheal, vetches, peppermint, globe thistle, purple coneflower and blazing stars. Members of the carrot family are very good, including Queen Anne's lace, dill and parsley. Plants with a flat-topped flowering head, like stiff goldenrod, are usually excellent butterfly plants. "Single-flowered" plants are better for butterfly and bee use than double-flowered plants because the nectar is richer and more accessible. Examples are peonies and marigolds. Canadian and Korean varieties of lilac are generally excellent for butterflies because they bloom in June after many butterflies have emerged. May-blooming French lilacs are of less value for butterflies except in zones 3N and 3S where they don't bloom until June. Good varieties of Canadian and Korean lilacs are Maiden's Blush, Royalty, Palabin, Miss Kim, Miss Canada, Minuet, James MacFarlane, and Donald Wyman. Miss Canada and Minuet are also good because they also do not sucker. Appendix A, Part 3, includes a listing of butterfly, bee and moth plants (1, 23, 24, 65, 76, 77, 82, 83, 84, 85, 89, 96, 97, 115, 116).

Bee Plants

There are nearly 50 plants that rate as "excellent" for attracting bees in Appendix A, Part 3. Among the most significant bee plants are those which are available when bees first emerge in the spring. These include grape hyacinth, jonquil, daffodil, sweet mock orange, cherry, apple, plum, peach, apricot, almond, pussy willow and lilac.

Other good bee plants are evening primrose, penstemons, petunia, phlox, moss rose, salvia, sedum, goldenrods, globe thistle, obedient plant, coralberry, wolfberry, snowberry, marigolds, clovers, garden verbena, broccoli and Mexican sunflower.

Many of the best bee and butterfly plants are herbs. Therefore, you can create many wildlife benefits by planting an herb garden that includes borage, hyssop,

The monarch butterfly depends on the common milkweed as nectar source and caterpillar food.

lavender, lovage, mint, spearmint, peppermint, applemint, lemon balm, sweet marjoram, wild marjoram, Cretan dittany, rosemary, sage, dill, winter savory and thyme. Obviously you can benefit from the use of the herbs in your kitchen as well (38, 52, 57, 95).

Moth Plants

Several kinds of moths can regularly be attracted to a flower garden. Hummingbird clearwing moths resemble bees and are attracted to Sweet William, fireweed, dame's rocket, bergamot, showy evening primrose, petunias, sweet mock orange and phlox. Coralberry and snowberry provide larval food for hummingbird clearwing moths.

Night flying sphinx (hawk) moths resemble hummingbirds in flight and are attracted by night-flowering plants including Sweet William, heliotrope, dame's rocket, madonna lily, white lilies, marvel of Peru (or four o'clock), flowering tobacco and petunia.

Day-flying sphinx moths like the white-lined sphinx moth are attracted by trumpet creeper, dwarf blue gentian, standing cypress, madonna lily, white lilies, cardinal flower, phlox and old-fashioned weigela. Spicebush provides larval food for the promethea moth, and boxelder trees are used by caterpillars of the cecropia moth.

The ruby-throated hummingbird is a popular visitor to Midwestern flower gardens.

4. Hummingbird and Oriole Plants
(See Appendix A, Part 4)

Hummingbird Plants

Ruby-throated hummingbirds are like a crackling campfire at night. As you watch them you are drawn to them, entranced and fascinated. They are one of the most popular visitors to flower gardens.

The hummingbird is our smallest native bird and is famous for its incredibly rapid wingbeat — up to 200 beats per second. Because of the high rate of metabolism, a hummingbird may eat more than one-half its weight in food and eight times its weight in fluids daily. Flower nectar and tiny insects are the preferred diet. Tubular red flowers are especially attractive to hummingbirds.

A good strategy is to provide some plants that bloom in early summer and some in late summer. Early blooming plants include American columbine, petunia, foxglove, hardy fuchsia, and 'firebird' penstemon. Later blooming flowers include red (scarlet) bergamot, cardinal flower, dwarf blue gentian, scarlet trumpet honeysuckle, plantain lily (Hosta), scarlet runner beans, salvia and trumpet vine. The best flowers for attracting hummingbirds are listed in Appendix A, Part 4.

Oriole Plants

Most people do not realize that the beautiful northern oriole (formerly Baltimore oriole) can be attracted to feed on the nectar or blossoms of several red or orange flowers, including hollyhock, trumpet vine, daylily, lemon daylily, tiger lily, turk's cap lily, wood lily, scarlet trumpet honeysuckle and cherry, plum, apricot and almond trees.

5. Summer Fruit, Berry and Cover Plants
(See Appendix A, Part 5)
This landscape component is comprised of trees, shrubs,

The chokecherry is an excellent summer fruit.

Bluebirds will eat pin cherries and choke cherries in summer as well as insects.

aquatic plants and vines which provide food and nesting cover from June through August, with emphasis on plants that produce fruits and berries in the summer.

These fruit and berry plants attract the brown thrasher, blue jay, gray catbird, American robin, eastern bluebird, wood thrush, cedar waxwing, northern oriole, scarlet tanager, northern cardinal, indigo bunting, rufous-sided towhee, dark-eyed junco, woodpeckers, deer, grouse, squirrel, raccoon, red fox, pheasant, cowbird and many butterflies (27). Bluebirds particularly like pin cherries.

Several offer an additional benefit for wildlife — they spread by suckering to create dense thickets that create ideal nesting cover for shrub-nesting species like catbirds and brown thrashers. These thickets can also comprise important winter pheasant cover. Thicket-forming plants include wild plum, scarlet Mongolian cherry, chokecherry, lilac-flowered honeysuckle, black raspberry, red raspberry, blackberry, and Juneberry (serviceberry). Ginnala (amur) maple does not spread by suckering but its dense

branches also provide excellent nesting cover for birds.

Grapes and other vines can be used to enhance the value of fences or dead trees. By planting vines at the base of a fence or dead tree, the vines can climb the fence or tree and subsequently create nesting cover and summer fruits.

Among the best summer fruit trees for wildlife are the red mulberry, amur chokecherry and black cherry. Excellent tall shrubs (15' - 25') include Manchurian bush apricot, chokecherry, birdcherry, and Alleghany serviceberry. The best medium shrubs (10' - 15') include American plum, Siberian plum, pin cherry, 'meteor' cherry and Nanking cherry. The best low shrubs (1'-10') include 'Scarlet' Mongolian cherry,

sand cherry, lilac-flowered honeysuckle, raspberry, elderberry, blackberry, Juneberry and blueberry. The top choices for vines are grapes (Beta and riverbank) and the best forb is the strawberry (8, 11, 12, 18, 41, 103).

The best shelterbelt species for summer benefits are American elderberry, scarlet elder, American plum, 'Scarlet' Mongolian cherry, Nanking cherry, chokecherry, sand cherry, and Alleghany serviceberry. Red mulberry and Russian mulberry are excellent for birds but they can be messy in yards. They also can invade areas where they are not wanted.

Plants that are particularly well adapted to use in backyards with limited space are elderberry, 'Beta' grape, ginnala maple, sugar maple, ninebark, 'meteor' cherry, Nanking cherry, pin cherry and downy serviceberry. The Nanking cherry is hardy statewide and is an excellent choice as a summer fruiting shrub. It is used by 49 bird species and is outstanding for its overall landscape qualities.

Included in the summer plant category are aquatic plants and moist soil plants. These species provide extremely important foods for many wetland wildlife species. Included are smartweed (used by 66 species), bulrush (used by 52 species), pondweed (used by 40 species), wigeon grass (used by 33 species), wild millet (used by 29 species), spike rush (used by 29 species), wild rice (used by 23 species), northern naiad (used by 19 species), cattails (used by 17 species), wild celery (used by 16 species) and duckweed (used by 16 species).

American elderberry is an excellent native fruiting shrub for wildlife. The gray catbird shown here has a bill full of elderberries.

These plants are dispersed naturally by wind and on the legs and feathers of waterfowl. Germination can often be stimulated on managed wetlands by lowering the water level in summer to expose mud flats, allowing the mud flats to dry, and subsequently reflooding the area in the fall.

Two of the few commercial sources of moist soil and wetland plants are Wildlife Nurseries, P.O. Box 2724, Oshkosh, Wisconsin 54901 and Game Food Nurseries, P.O. Box V, 4488 Hwy. 116, Omro, Wisconsin 54963.

Appendix A, Part 5 includes a listing of plants best adapted to provide food and shelter for wildlife from June to August in the Midwest.

6. Fall Fruits, Grains and Cover Plants
(See Appendix A, Part 6)

This landscape component is comprised of shrubs, vines and grain crops which are primarily of value in the fall. Their food value for wildlife may extend into the winter if they are not immediately consumed by wildlife or covered by snow.

Wildlife foods are extremely

Sudex is an excellent grain for use in wildlife food plots.

important in the fall. They allow migratory birds to build up fat reserves prior to migration. Resident non-migratory wildlife species also need fall food to build up food stores or fat reserves that allow them to survive the winter.

Fruits of red-osier dogwood, gray dogwood, mountain ash, winterberry, cotoneasters, and buffaloberry are important foods for gray catbirds, brown thrashers, American robins, wood thrushes, cedar waxwings, cardinals, purple finches, dark-eyed juncos, and black-capped chickadees. Also benefitting are white-breasted nuthatches, evening grosbeaks, ruffed grouse, bluebirds, wood ducks, pheasants, and northern orioles.

Grains are also extremely important. Corn, for example, is used by 100 wildlife species in the United States. Wheat is used by 94 species and oats by 91 species (71). Sudex is also excellent.

Appendix A, Part 6 lists plants that are primarily of value to wildlife in the fall.

7. Winter Fruits and Cover Plants
(See Appendix A, Part 7)

Many of the best winter wildlife foods are characterized by two important qualities: persistence and low appeal to wildlife when they first mature. Obviously, winter fruits must remain (persist) on trees or shrubs until they are needed as food. Examples of persistent foods are glossy black chokeberry, Siberian and

"red-splendor" and "prairie fire" crabapple, common snowberry, staghorn and smooth sumac, bittersweet, American highbush cranberry, eastern and European wahoo (Euonymus species), and Virginia creeper (woodbine).

Second, many of these fruits are not immediately desirable as wildlife foods. Some summer and fall fruits like American elderberry and Nanking cherry are eaten as soon as they are ripe and are frequently referred to as "ice cream plants" for wildlife. On the contrary, many of the winter fruits could be termed "spinach" plants for wildlife. Some are bitter when they first ripen. Others must freeze and thaw several times until the fruits break down and become more palatable. Plants like bittersweet may not be eaten until late winter or spring. Bluebirds eat bittersweet berries when they first return in the spring.

Examples of "spinach plants" are bittersweet, dwarf hedge rose, sumacs and highbush cranberries. These plants are extremely important for late winter survival when other food supplies are limited or exhausted. If space is severely limited on your property, winter foods are probably the most important category plants you can provide for because natural foods are most limited at that time of year (7, 9, 59,102).

Appendix A, Part 7 shows a list of plants that are primarily of benefit to wildlife in winter.

European mountain ash has berries in fall that are eagerly consumed by cedar waxwings.

8. Plants That Produce Nuts and Acorns (Mast)

(See Appendix A, Part 8)

Nut-and acorn-producing plants are another extremely important landscape component for wildlife. Nuts and acorns, collectively referred to as "mast," are significant foods in the fall and winter for white-tailed deer, wild turkey, wood duck, pheasant, gray squirrel, fox squirrel, red squirrel, ruffed grouse, bobwhite quail, mallard, black bear, raccoon and other species.

Among important mast producers in the upper Midwest are white oak, bur oak, northern red oak, American hazel, beaked hazel, black walnut, shagbark hickory and butternut.

Appendix A, Part 8 shows a list of mast-producing hardwoods which are recommended for use in the Midwest.

Perhaps one of the greatest benefits of planting these hardwoods is they are a wonderful long-term investment in wildlife production. Many of the fruit-producing shrubs are relatively short-lived, whereas oaks may produce acorns for up to 400 years. These trees also contain natural cavities that are used by up to 96 species of wildlife. Northern red oak and beaked hazel are two native species which deserve special mention as being hardy in northern climates. Their acorns and nuts are eaten by black bears (15, 81).

STRUCTURAL COMPONENTS OF WILDLIFE HABITAT

There are also eight structural components of wildlife habitat: 9) nest boxes and nest platforms; 10) dead trees, fallen trees and perches; 11) brush piles and rock piles; 12) cut banks, caves and cliffs; 13) salt; 14) dusting beds and grit; 15) water; and 16) feeders. (See Figure 6). In contrast to the vegetative components that are comprised of living plants, these structural features of habitat are not living. Examples are nest boxes, rock piles, and dead trees.

9. Nest Boxes

Nest boxes and nest platforms are used by at least 46 species of northern wildlife. These structures are fully discussed in "Woodworking for Wildlife" (53). In most woodlands, management of trees to preserve natural cavities is the best way to provide cavity nest sites. Nest boxes are a supplement to natural cavities.

10. Dead Trees (Snags), Fallen Trees and Perches

A "snag" is a dead or dying tree. To many people, a snag is just firewood waiting to be cut. To many wildlife species, a snag is a bird's version of a fast food restaurant — a valuable habitat component filled with fast food. Snags are used by 43 species of birds and at least 26 mammal species in the Midwest (64). Snags

Snags provide woodpeckers a place to feed and raise their young.

are used as nesting sites, for perching sites, for territorial establishment, and as a food source. Insect larvae commonly occur under the bark and in the soft wood of snags.

Appendix J shows lists of Midwestern birds and mammals that use snags (64). The table includes species which have the ability to create cavities — like woodpeckers — and species which use cavities created by other animals, like screech-owls and wood ducks.

There are two kinds of snags — hard and soft. A hard snag is a dead or partially dead tree with at least some limbs remaining and fully sound wood (not punky). A soft snag is a standing dead tree in an advanced stage of decomposition, with few, if any, limbs and advanced heart rot (punky). Both kinds are used by wildlife.

A snag should be at least six inches in diameter and 15 feet tall. However, the larger the snag, the greater will be its value for wildlife. Snags are good locations for placing suet feeders.

Some people attract woodpeckers to their yards by cutting down a soft snag and setting it up in their yard where it can be watched from the house (Swanson, pers. comm). Even the shy pileated woodpecker is known to visit backyards where such snags are provided.

Perches are another integral habitat component. The belted

Rock piles and brush piles are important habitat components for cottontail rabbits and woodchucks.

kingfisher and green-backed heron use branches overhanging water as perches from which they can spot fishes which serve as prey. Snags also serve as perches from which flycatchers fly out to catch insects. Snags or tree branch perches can be provided over backyard ponds, on the edge of hayfields or at bird feeders to stimulate additional bird use. Logs can also be anchored to concrete blocks in small ponds to provide secure loafing sites for ducks and turtles. These logs are relatively safe from predators.

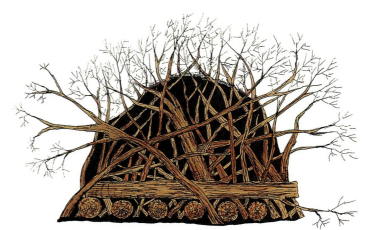

Figure 7. Diagram of a brushpile.

11. Brush Piles and Rock Piles

Brush piles and rock piles are worthwhile components of wildlife habitat. They provide escape cover, nesting sites and den sites for cottontail rabbits, long-tailed weasels, woodchucks, striped skunks, northern prairie skinks, red foxes, garter snakes and many other species.

Brush piles can provide important reptile and amphibian habitat if placed on the edge of a small pond so part of the brush is submerged. Similarly, rock piles or rock riprap can be placed along the north side of ponds larger than one acre. Such rocks can be football-sized up to three feet in diameter. They can be dumped along the water's edge, up the bank three or four feet, and below water level to depths of two to three feet. These sites provide both aquatic shelter for frogs and

toads and sunny basking sites for turtles, skinks and snakes.

Rock piles are excellent duck and turtle loafing sites if they are placed out in the water. Rock piles near shore make animals more vulnerable to ambush by predators.

Rock or brush piles can be located in larger backyard lots or scattered throughout woodlots, meadows or farm groves. Since they may attract skunks and woodchucks, you may not want them too near your house or garden.

Brush piles should be placed in sheltered areas along the edges of fields and woods and in cutover forest lands with shrubby cover and second growth vegetation. Rural brush piles should be a minimum of 12 to 15 feet in diameter and five feet high. The brush pile shown in Figure 7 should have a

foundation of big rocks, stumps, and logs to keep it from decomposing too quickly. Several heavy logs can also be placed on top of the pile to keep it from blowing apart. Old sections of culverts, field tiles, or sections of hollow logs placed within the foundation of a brush pile can serve as animal den sites.

Sometimes, however, large brush piles are created by clearing aspen brush in the prairie pothole region. They have frequently been pushed into or adjacent to wetlands. This creates predator cover that contributes to high duck mortality.

12. Cut Banks, Cliffs and Caves

While "cut banks," cliffs and caves are neither normal features of backyard habitats nor features that homeowners should attempt to create, they are important features of the landscape for several species ranging from peregrine falcons to belted kingfishers, bats and bank swallows. Peregrine falcons, ravens and turkey vultures nest on cliffs. Exposed soil, gravel and even limestone banks along creeks and rivers are used as burrow sites by rough-winged swallows, belted kingfishers and bank swallows. Exposed cut banks in gravel pits are also used by these species and as den sites by badgers, red foxes, coyotes and woodchucks.

Gravel pits are also used as rendezvous sites for gray wolves in northern Minnesota. The reason for highlighting this unique habitat component is that reclamation of gravel pit sites has often called for leveling and reseeding cut banks that have been created by

Carrol Henderson

Bobwhite quail and many other birds control external parasites by dusting. Dust beds are, therefore, an essential habitat component.

quarrying. Preservation of those cut banks is actually a good habitat management technique, but make sure they do not pose a safety hazard to humans. Gravel quarrying can also provide water by excavating down to the water table and gently sloping the banks.

Caves are another habitat feature important primarily for bats and a variety of specialized invertebrates. Caves may need to be protected or sealed with a gate to prevent entry by vandals who would disturb hibernating bats.

13. Dust and Grit

Both dust and grit are used by many wild birds to satisfy special needs. Birds ranging from pheasants and turkeys to small songbirds will squat into beds of dry soil and take a dust bath to help control external parasites. Dusting beds of fine soil can be provided in backyards or woodlots. A backyard dusting site can be simply a circle of finely pulverized soil no more than 1 1/2 to 2 feet across. In most rural areas there is no shortage of dusting sites because birds can use soil on gravel roads, in cultivated fields, or in pocket gopher mounds..

Grit is another important habitat component. Grit is fine to coarse sand that is needed in a bird's gizzard to grind up seeds and other food. Most birds are mobile enough that finding grit is not a problem in woodland and farmland areas. If you are trying to increase the number and variety of birds in your yard, however, you can provide a tray or bed of sand near your bird feeder. Sand can even be mixed into the contents of a bird feeder.

14. Salt

Salt and some other trace elements are other essential components of wildlife habitat. For some species, the salt requirements are met as a trace element in their food, but other animals like white-tailed deer, moose, pine grosbeaks and even crossbills will actively seek out salt deposits. This is particularly true for deer in the summer. You can create a "salt lick" on your land either by placing a salt block in good deer habitat or on the edge of a meadow where deer could be seen from your home. It is legal to place salt

This young white-tailed buck has been attracted to a salt block.

licks in Minnesota. Consult your local game warden or conservation officer before placing them in other states. Another way to create a salt lick is to fill a burlap sack half full with granular salt and hang it from a tree where rain can leach the salt into the soil. Eventually deer will locate the salt lick and benefit from its presence. In turn, the deer can provide much viewing enjoyment. This practice could eventually kill the tree, so don't hang a salt sack from a tree that you wish to preserve.

15. Water

Water is an essential component of wildlife habitat. It will attract a wonderful variety of wildlife — from songbirds to small mammals, small reptiles, amphibians, and insects. Planning to provide water is an integral step in landscaping for wildlife. Water

can be provided in many forms, from a dripping source of water in a mud puddle for butterflies to bird baths, backyard ponds, springs, creeks, marshes, ponds, lakes, and rivers. **Dripping or flowing water is more attractive to wildlife than still water.**

Birdbaths, Waterfalls and Sprays

A birdbath can be as formal as a plastic or concrete structure or as informal as an upside down garbage can lid. The birdbath should be located at least 15 feet from trees and shrubs because they provide cover from which cats can catch the birds. Birdbaths can also be shallow depressions in concrete at ground level. Dripping water from an overhanging bucket or hose will increase the attractiveness of such a ground-level birdbath. A birdbath should be no more than three

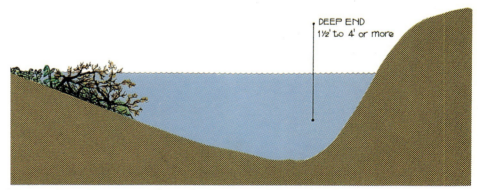

Figure 8.   Cross section of a backyard frog pond.

inches deep with gently sloping sides and bottom. The surface of the edge should be roughened to provide a good perching surface. Robins frequently are attracted to a fine spray of water like a lawn sprinkler in hot weather. The moist soil in such sites brings earthworms to the surface of the ground. Birds need water in winter as well as summer. A dog water dish or poultry water heating element can be placed in a birdbath and the resulting open water can attract birds all winter.

Backyard Frog Pond

A small frog pond in your backyard can be a delightful addition to your property. It can reveal the private lives of songbirds, ducks, frogs, toads, and salamanders.

The pond can be lined with concrete or a plastic liner. The pond need be no more than 8 or 10 feet across and one or two feet deep. Flat stones can stabilize the pond edge and be highlighted with various native rock garden plants. Soil should be placed over the pond liner so you can seed some native aquatic plants into the pond — like cattail, water lily, arrowhead, marsh marigold, or duckweed. Or pots with aquatic plants can be placed on the pond bottom. Seeds from most of these plants can be collected locally from wild sources. (Be sure to obtain the landowner's permission before collecting such plants on someone else's property.) To provide a variety of depths for various wildlife uses, one edge could be vertical to a depth of from 1 1/2 to 2 feet and the opposite edge could have a shallow gradient as shown in Figure 8. You may need to provide more water for the pond with a garden hose during periods of low rainfall or to freshen up the water if it becomes stagnant in late summer. Ideally, the pond should receive five hours or more of sunlight daily to stimulate the growth of aquatic plants. The pond should be within reach of your garden hose. Another alternative for creating flowing water is to use a submerged pump to push the water up into a miniature waterfall that flows back into the pond. The flowing water in the stream will be well-used by birds for bathing and drinking.

This backyard pond has attracted a pair of mallards. A submerged pump causes water to flow from the pond and trickle over the rocks.

Bob Djupstrom

A backyard frog pond can be a great place to discover wildlife.

Ohio DNR

Instructions for creating a backyard pond can be obtained for 50 cents by writing to the National Institute for Urban Wildlife, 10921 Trotting Ridge Way, Columbia, MD 21044. Ask for "Urban Wildlife Manager's Notebook, #2, A Simple Backyard Pond" by Louise Dove.

If your goal is to benefit amphibians, keep your pond fishless since fish normally eat frog, toad, and salamander eggs and young. In a fishless pond, they have a better chance for survival.

If you wish to attract fish-eating birds like kingfishers and green-backed herons to your property, you may wish to stock your pond with sunfish or fathead minnows. These fish will also help control algae growth in the pond.

Small Ponds

Where space and topography allow, a somewhat larger pond can accommodate dozens of wildlife species. These ponds, if fishless, will be used by crayfish, blue-spotted salamanders, central newts, American toads, cricket frogs, spring peepers, chorus frogs, green frogs, wood frogs, pickerel frogs, leopard frogs, garter snakes, birds, and painted turtles. The pond should be 30 to 40 feet across and at least four feet deep.

Another alternative for this type of pond is to stock it with mosquitofish, mud minnows, and fathead minnows to help feed on algae and to provide a prey base that will attract green-backed herons, great blue herons, and belted kingfishers. A branch or post should be placed in or by the pond to serve as a perch for these fish-eating birds. The minnows will need to be stocked annually. Be sure to check with your nearest DNR fisheries office to learn what laws apply to trapping, transplanting and stocking minnows.

A small pond should have at least one-third of the bank constructed with a very gradual incline toward the deep point. Brush piles should be placed in the shallow water (two feet or less) as sites where frogs, toads, and salamanders can lay their eggs. At least one-fourth of the pond's edge should have submerged brush.

About five to ten logs, at least six inches in diameter and five to eight feet long, should be placed on the pond margin. Part of each log should be in the water with as much of the underside of the log touching the ground as possible. This is especially good habitat for salamanders. Figure 9 portrays a small pond.

Rock piles or riprap can be placed along the water's edge on the north side of the pond to serve as sunning sites for harmless snakes and turtles (62).

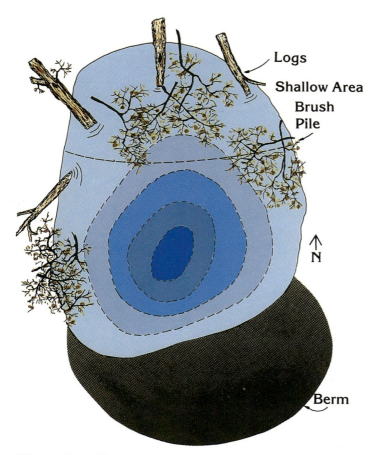

Figure 9.   Diagram of a small pond.

Labels on figure: Logs, Shallow Area, Brush Pile, N, Berm

If you have a small pond that is used by wood ducks, mallards, or Canada geese, try keeping one side of the pond mowed. This creates a safe loafing and sunning area where they can readily see predators approaching.

Wood duck populations have increased significantly in recent years and may be attracted to small ponds and marshes.

Gregory K. Scott

Marshes

Marshes are one of the most valuable types of wildlife habitat. These priceless areas provide food, cover and water for dozens of native species — ducks, geese, grebes, herons, yellow-headed blackbirds, black terns, marsh wrens, Forster's terns, muskrats, minks, raccoons and many others. Marshes capture eroding soil from surrounding fields, thereby purifying water draining into downstream areas. Some agricultural fertilizers and herbicides can also be neutralized by the organisms in a marsh because it serves as a natural "kidney." Marshland also provides exceptional opportunities for bird watching, photography, hunting, and trapping. Hunting leases and trapping revenue can generate significant income for marshland owners. Some persons are fortunate enough to own land where marshes are already present. For most agricultural landowners, however, there is nothing more than a drained marsh basin left where wetlands once existed. Marshes can be restored on such sites through coordination and

cost-sharing with the DNR, SCS, and Agricultural Stabilization and Conservation Service (ASCS). Both state and federal water bank subsidy benefits may be available to qualified landowners who preserve or restore wetlands. Marshes can also be created in areas with favorable topography and soils by building dikes and installing water control structures.

There should also be at least two to four acres of adjacent or nearby grassy nesting cover for each acre of marsh. Waterfowl like mallards and blue-winged teal need upland nesting cover near marshlands. It is not enough just to preserve marshes for wildlife. The nearby nesting cover is also essential for some species.

16. Feeders

The finishing touch to a wildlife landscaping plan is an assortment of wildlife feeders which supplement the foods already provided by trees, shrubs, flowers, and food

Carrol Henderson

Marshes are a vitally important type of wildlife habitat.

plots. "Wild About Birds: The DNR Bird Feeding Guide" was published in 1995 by the Minnesota Department of Natural Resources. It is the third book in this series that explains how to attract wildlife. "Wild About Birds" contains natural history information and photos of 68 bird species that visit feeders in the Midwest. It includes sections about raptors at feeders, unusual visitors at feeders and problem animals. There are also sections describing 44 different kinds of wild bird food and 55 different feeders. Designs are included for making 26 bird feeders.

Many songbirds can be attracted to feeders stocked with sunflower seed and beef suet.

Bird feeding continues to evolve as a hobby from scattering table scraps for the birds in winter to a well-planned procedure involving a variety of foods and feeders for use in all four seasons. It is most successful if the feeding is done as part of a comprehensive plan to provide wildlife with plantings, water, and nest boxes.

For best results, provide feeding areas with "clusters" of four or five different feeders that have different kinds of foods. See "Wild About Birds" for detailed information on this fascinating hobby.

Backyard Feeding

More than two dozen birds as well as rabbits and squirrels can be attracted to your feeders. The

The northern oriole will feed on orange halves, grape jelly, and nectar feeders.

best all-around bird food is black oil-type sunflower seed. It can be used in open tray feeders, in self-feeders which can be purchased commercially, in home-made feeders which can be easily constructed, or spread on the ground or snow. Appendix K shows a diagram for a home-made bird feeder for sunflower seeds.

Cylindrical Feeders

Goldfinches will use this feeder all year-around and are especially striking as they cluster around the feeder in midsummer. Thistle feeders are cylindrical tubes which can be purchased commercially or made at home from a plastic quart pop bottle. Niger thistle is an exotic type of seed used in cylindrical feeders that is extremely popular among goldfinches and pine siskins. This seed will not grow into Canadian thistle.

The design for that feeder is shown in Appendix K. Another type of bird food which is popular with goldfinches, redpolls, pine siskins, and chickadees is a commercial mix comprised of sunflower hearts coated with beef suet and corn protein. It also is fed in cylindrical feeders.

Suet Feeder

Suet is animal fat generally derived from beef, pork, or deer. It is a high energy food that is extremely popular among chickadees, downy woodpeckers, hairy woodpeckers, red-bellied woodpeckers, white-breasted nuthatches and even pileated woodpeckers. Suet can be purchased at most supermarkets and is usually derived from fat that surrounds

the kidneys of cattle. Suet can simply be placed in an onion or potato string bag and suspended in a tree, but it may need to be protected from squirrels. It can be fastened on a feeder tray or non-metallic suet feeder. If a metal like hardware cloth is used to hold suet, a bird's tongue can freeze to the metal while it is feeding. Suet can also be pushed into shallow 1 1/2-inch diameter holes that have been bored into small logs to form a natural-looking feeder. Suet can also be melted and mixed with various grains and dried fruits to form suet cakes.

Squirrel Feeder
(Spike Ear Corn Feeder)

Squirrels can be fed by pushing ears of corn onto long spikes that are fastened onto trees or feeders. They will carry away any ears that are not attached. They are also extremely messy when they scatter and waste bird food from a bird feeder that is not squirrel-proof. The best way to eliminate this problem is to use a squirrel-proof feeder like the Hylarious Bird Feeder. It has a counterweight on the back that causes the feeder to close whenever a squirrel stands on the feeder. It costs from $45 to $50 and can be purchased at many bird feed supply stores.

A spike feeder featuring ear corn will also be used by pheasants, deer, prairie chickens, jays, and other species.

Summer Feeding

Summer feeding of oil-type sunflower seeds can be very enjoyable and rewarding because many birds will come to a summer bird feeder.

Summer feeding is not as essential for bird survival as in the winter. It is also likely to attract birds that you may not wish to attract — house sparrows, starlings, cowbirds, red-winged blackbirds, and grackles. One way to solve this problem is to use a thistle feeder for goldfinches and nectar feeders for hummingbirds. Orioles are attracted to nectar feeders as are hummingbirds but need a larger perch to stand on. They will also eat grape jelly in small trays and orange halves. Red-bellied woodpeckers, catbirds, and red squirrels also like orange halves.

The ruby-throated hummingbird will feed at nectar feeders.

Dick Peterson

Hummingbird Feeder

Many commercial hummingbird feeders are available. The large plastic flowers are not necessary on these feeders and may be removed. Several feeders scattered around a porch or yard are better than a single feeder because hummers are very combative and will spend much time chasing each other away from a single feeder.

Try placing one feeder near your "hummingbird flower garden" to attract the attention of hummingbirds. Place the others near your porch or windows so you can then enjoy hummingbirds around your house. The feeders must be kept filled and clean. The most common homemade hummingbird nectar recipe is four parts of boiling water to one part cane sugar. Let it cool before filling the feeders. Red food coloring is unnecessary because most feeders are red. Honey is not recommended. It spoils too easily and attracts bees. Commercial nectar mixes are also available.

The sugar water solution will spoil within two to three days in warm weather. This causes the water to become cloudy and a black fungus will develop. To clean the feeder, soak in a dilute solution of chlorine bleach for one hour. Then allow the feeder to dry out before refilling it.

Bees and wasps may be a nuisance at these feeders, but most commercial feeders have bee guards to prevent this problem (78).

Moth Feeding

If you want to add some variety to your backyard wildlife watching, try feeding moths. There is a fascinating technique called "sugaring" that will allow you to attract and photograph moths. Several "brews" will attract moths. One recipe calls for four pounds of sugar, one bottle of stale beer and some cheap rum. A second recipe consists of mashed peaches that have been left out to ferment then mixed with white sugar. The third recipe is comprised of fermented bananas and dried apricots mixed with brown sugar.

Shortly before dusk, paint your moth brew onto the trunk of several trees that are convenient. The edge of a wooded area is best. After dark, check the trees periodically with a flashlight. As a moth laps the juice through its proboscis it can be photographed using a flash unit on your camera. A hot, humid night before a thunderstorm is ideal for moth watching. Few moths will be seen after a rain or when the moon shines brightly. A field guide to moths will help you identify the many different moths attracted to these unusual brews (55, 60).

Where ear corn is available, a simple "hog fence" feeder can be constructed for deer and pheasants.

MN/DNR

Pheasant and Deer Feeders

Several homemade pheasant and deer feeders can improve chances of winter survival in severe winters where there is adequate cover but a lack of natural foods or food plots. Such feeders can also be used in winter to reduce the chance of deer being hit on highways where they have been crossing highways to reach a corn field or corn crib. If feeders are placed on the same side of the road as their cover, you can improve their chances of survival. Shelters or lean-to covers as shown in Appendix L can be placed over ground-level pheasant feeders to keep them from being covered by snow.

The Olson deer feeder is efficient and effective feeder for white-tailed deer.

MN/DNR

Olson Deer Feeder

The Olson Deer Feeder is an excellent feeder for deer and pheasants. It is made from one whole and one half 55-gallon metal barrels. Instructions for making the Olson Deer Feeder are given in Appendix K.

Hog Fence Feeder

Figure 10 shows a simple ear corn feeder made of woven wire

Figure 10.   Hog fence deer and pheasant feeder.

The beautiful cedar waxwing is welcome visitor in Midwestern yards. In spring it may eat crabapple flower petals and in fall it eats mountain ash berries.

hog fence. All it requires is a four to five foot length of hog fence (new or old) that is fastened into a cylinder. It is placed on a pallet on a clear, windswept, high spot with a southern exposure and adjacent to a large marsh, shelterbelt, or other secure winter cover. A protective shelter of poles, brush, and grass can be built to enhance a potential feeding site. This type of feeder is used mainly for pheasants and will handle up to a dozen birds for two months. Squirrels may try to carry off the ears of corn, so another piece of hog fence should be wired onto the top of the cylinder to keep the ears from being removed. The feeder should be placed and filled by November and **maintained all winter.** Larger flocks of pheasants can be accommodated by using a larger cylinder made from a 12-foot length of hog fence. The pallet should be four feet by four feet and should be set onto four concrete foundation blocks or any other objects that will raise it four to eight inches above the ground.

If shelled corn is available to feed pheasants but not ear corn, a cylindrical hardware cloth feeder about 12 inches in diameter can be used. If one-half-inch mesh hardware cloth is used, the corn kernels may flow out too freely. If this is a problem, two layers of hardware cloth can be used to form the cylinder. It is shown in Appendix K.

Automatic Feeders

Hanging feeders that have a time-release mechanism also work well for feeding pheasants, turkeys, and deer. Most hold about two bushels of shelled corn, but some can be adapted to hold enough for the entire winter. Although they may cost about $100, they are quite maintenance-free and reliable.

Other Feeders

Several other ideas for "side-hill" feeders, open field shelters, brush shelters, and hopper feeders for pheasants, bobwhites, prairie chickens, turkeys and gray partridge are shown in Appendix L (105).

Landscaping Your Yard for Wildlife

Chapter 5

One of the greatest opportunities that exists for homeowners to help wildlife is within the boundaries of their own yards! In most yards that have been landscaped in the past, wildlife benefits were accidental or incidental. Only the most adaptable species like robins, house sparrows and European starlings thrived in such habitats. More than 100 wildlife species, however, may use a well-planned backyard habitat at one time or another. Appendix P contains a list of summer resident wildlife species which may be seen in backyards.

It is possible to transform your yard into a wonderful habitat for wildlife and a delightful environment for you and your family. The key is to develop and implement a plan according to the following steps. The steps also apply to the development of farms and woodlots.

Please don't let this list overwhelm or intimidate you. Remember, keep this project fun.

A butterfly flower garden is a special feature in some yards.

Carrol Henderson

Missouri Department of Conservation

Landscaping for wildlife in your yard can become a delightful hobby.

1. SET YOUR OBJECTIVES AND PRIORITIES.

Decide what species or groups of animals you wish to attract. Examples include butterflies, hummingbirds, shrub-nesting songbirds, winter songbirds, pheasants, grouse, reptiles and amphibians, and deer. Then you can build your plan around those species. Learn what native plant community you are in and consider featuring native prairie or woodland plants as part of your plan.

2. DRAW A MAP OF PROPERTY.

Identify existing features, including buildings, power lines, buried cables, septic tank fields, trees, shrubs, or other features. Make the map roughly to scale using graph paper. Consider how much space you have to work with. Also consider natural features on adjacent property.

Identify and map special conditions including shady or sunny areas, low and wet poorly-drained sites, sandy and well-drained sites, areas of native vegetation that will be preserved as is, and soil types. Also map views that you enjoy or that you would like

to screen. Consider what needs your family has in the yard like areas for pets, benches, picnics, storage, playing, sledding, vegetable gardens, and paths.

Your SCS, local garden center or county extension office can help you identify soil types. They can also test your soil to see if there are any nutrient deficiencies. Your soil types and conditions are extremely important and will provide the criteria by which your plan will proceed. The soils will dictate the species of vegetation to be planted and how they will need to be managed.

3. REVIEW THE 16 VEGETATIVE AND STRUCTURAL COMPONENTS NEEDED FOR GOOD WILDLIFE HABITAT.

Decide what vegetative and structural components are already present, what undesirable plants may need to be removed, and identify what components need to be enhanced or added. Then review the plant lists in Appendices A and B to learn what plants you may wish to include in your plan.

Please understand that most yards will not be large or diverse enough to include all 16 habitat components. However, try to include as many components as possible. Learning to recognize these components in your neighbors' yards and in your neighborhood will also benefit wildlife. It may be possible for several neighbors to combine their efforts to create a "block" for wildlife. Try to select "excellent" category plants. Avoid plants in Appendices M and N that could cause problems for you.

4. CONFER WITH RESOURCE PEOPLE AND CHECK REFERENCE BOOKS

Check with your local resource people if you are developing a plan for a farm or woodlot. Check with your local wildlife/soil conservation/forestry/horticultural resource persons to obtain advice on your plan. A variety of farm and woodlot conservation projects can be cost-shared with these agencies. They can also direct you to public or private lands that demonstrate successful landscaping and planting projects. Check the literature for current information on landscaping for wildlife. Review the references listed in the "literature cited" section of this book and consider subscribing to *The Minnesota Horticulturist,* 1970 Folwell Ave., 161 Alderman Hall, University of Minnesota, St. Paul, MN 55108. *The Minnesota Horticulturist* contains up-to-date information on

This butterfly garden is a special feature of this yard plan.

Decide which wildlife species you wish to attract so you can provide the appropriate plants. This red admiral is feeding on a purple coneflower.

plants, plant care, landscaping, and control of insect and disease problems for northern gardeners.

Other excellent references include *The Wildlife Gardener* (30), supplements to the *Urban Wildlife News* by Louise Dove (32, 33, 34, 35, 36), *Trees and Shrubs for Northern Gardens* (101), *Flowers for Northern Gardens* (104), *American Wildlife and Plants* (71), and *Natural Landscaping: Designing with Native Plant Communities* (28).

You may wish to participate in the "Backyard Wildlife Habitat Program" of the National Wildlife Federation by purchasing a "Gardening with Wildlife Kit." Write to them at 1412 Sixteenth St. N.W., Washington, D.C. 20036. The kit includes booklets, landscape plans, a landscaping template and graph paper, designs for a bird feeder, packets of seeds for plants with blossoms that will attract butterflies and hummingbirds, a record book for keeping track of your project, and an application for certification to register your yard in the National Wildlife Federation's registry of certified Backyard Wildlife Habitats.

Visit a local arboretum to examine plant species that may have potential on your land.

5. DEVELOP PLANTING PLAN

Sketch on your map the plants you intend to put on your property. Trees should be drawn to scale at a diameter that represents three-fourths of their mature width and shrubs at their

full mature width. See Appendix A, Snyder (101) or Olson (80) to learn plant diameters. This will help you calculate how many plants you need and how much expense will be involved.

Decide how much money you can afford to spend and the time span of your development. Don't try to do too much at once. An example would be to develop a five year schedule for landscape development. Develop a budget to coincide with your development schedule.

Observe your neighbors. Tour your neighborhood to see which plants thrive in your area and which don't. This will give you an excellent idea of which plants are winter hardy and capable of growing on soils similar to those in your yard. It can also alert you to plant problems that may affect the survival of your plantings.

6. IMPLEMENT YOUR PLAN

Learn where to obtain plants or seeds you will need. For some approved farmland or forestry conservation practices, plants or seeds can be obtained by contacting your local DNR wildlife manager or forester or the county SCS or SWCD office. Appendix O contains a list of sources of seeds, plants, and garden catalogs. Plants are also available from local nurseries or garden centers. You may wish to contact the Nurseryman's Association in your state to learn what nurseries are in your area. You may also be able to obtain free seeds or seedlings from friends who already have mature plantings on their property. Then implement your project.

Document your expenses and actions, both on paper and with photography. By taking pictures of your land from exactly the same location every year you can dramatically document the success of your habitat project and share it with others.

7. MAINTAIN YOUR PLAN.

New tree and shrub plantings in a yard can be maintained relatively weed-free by using polyethylene landscaping film and a layer of four to six inches of shredded bark mulch. Plants in a yard will need to be watered regularly in their first year after planting to aid them in becoming established.

Plants obtained from nurseries are already fertilized. If plants are well-adapted to their site, no future fertilization is necessary. In grass plantings, fertilization favors growth of agricultural weeds. Pruning of trees and shrubs should be unnecessary although touchups for esthetic reasons may be desirable. In new wildflower plantings, some mowing or hand pulling of grass and woody plants will help suppress weed and woody plant invasion. Rural prairie sites can be maintained by prescribed burning. Information on weed control is given in Appendix G.

8. ENJOY!!

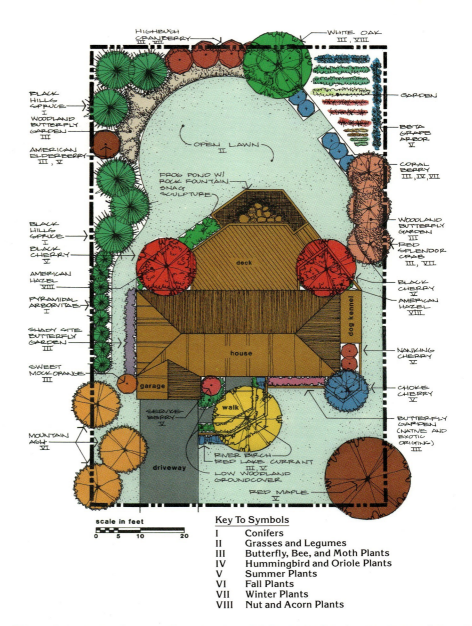

Key To Symbols

I	Conifers
II	Grasses and Legumes
III	Butterfly, Bee, and Moth Plants
IV	Hummingbird and Oriole Plants
V	Summer Plants
VI	Fall Plants
VII	Winter Plants
VIII	Nut and Acorn Plants

Figure 11. A plan for a medium-sized yard(80' x 140') showing landscape features.

Carrol Henderson

Native prairie perennials like purple coneflower are desirable species for a yard planting.

Bruce Edinger

Sometimes the best way to get started with landscaping your yard is to look at some examples.

Figure 11 is a plan for a medium-sized yard that is 80 ft. x 140 ft.

A small urban lot (50 ft. x 125 ft.) is shown in Figure 12. Even in a lot of this size, it is possible to include all eight vegetative components of wildlife habitat and some structural components like bird feeders and bird houses.

Conifers are planted on the north and west margin of the property and hardwood trees are present on the south side of the house.

Notice the various yard features that are included: a boulevard tree, large shade trees, several small ornamental lawn trees, foundation plants, an herb garden, and a container garden. See Appendix B for examples of

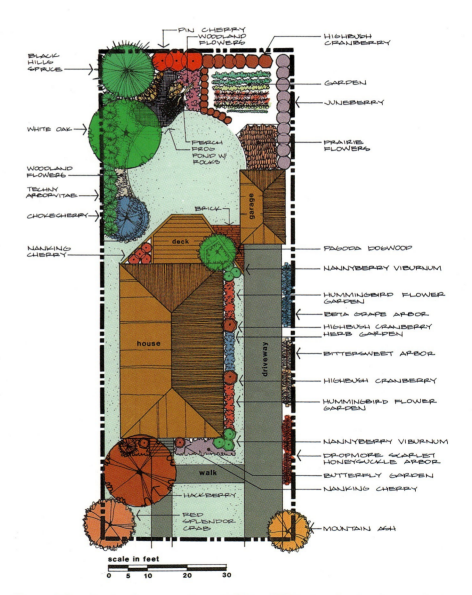

Figure 12. A plan for a small yard (50' x 125') showing landscape features.

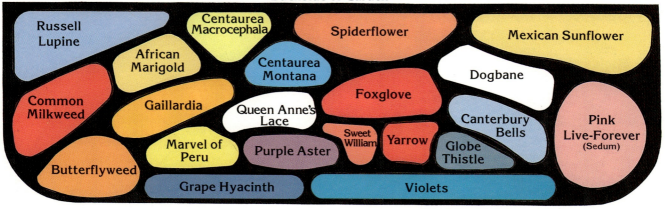

| | | |
| Russell Lupine | Centaurea Macrocephala | Spiderflower | Mexican Sunflower |

Figure 13. Butterfly, bee, and moth garden for full sun to partial shade. Native and exotic origins.

2'
Scale

plants that are suitable for each feature. The wildlife ratings of each plant are also shown. If you see a species that interests you, check its characteristics in Appendix A to determine if it is suited to your yard conditions.

For example, suppose you wish to include a crabapple as a small ornamental lawn tree in your yard. See Appendix B for the section on "small ornamental lawn trees." Among the crabapples listed are *red splendor, radiant, profusion,* and Siberian crabapples. The *red splendor, prairie fire* and Siberian crabapple rate excellent both for attracting butterflies and as winter foods for wildlife. By checking those two crabapples in Appendix A you can decide which

Bruce Edinger

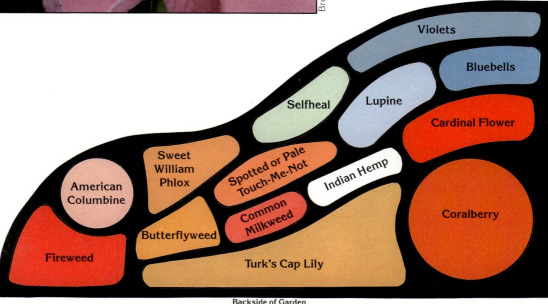

2'
Scale

Figure 14. Native woodland wildflower garden for butterfly, bee, moth, hummingbird and oriole use for sunny to partially shaded sites.

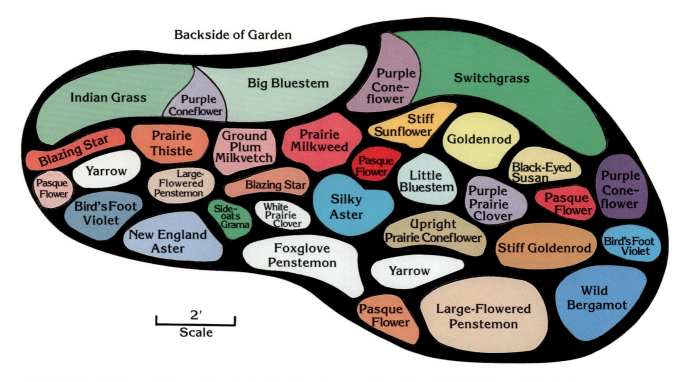

Backside of Garden

Indian Grass · Purple Coneflower · Big Bluestem · Purple Coneflower · Switchgrass · Stiff Sunflower · Goldenrod · Blazing Star · Prairie Thistle · Ground Plum Milkvetch · Prairie Milkweed · Pasque Flower · Black-Eyed Susan · Yarrow · Large-Flowered Penstemon · Blazing Star · Little Bluestem · Purple Prairie Clover · Pasque Flower · Purple Coneflower · Pasque Flower · Bird's Foot Violet · Side-oats Grama · White Prairie Clover · Silky Aster · Upright Prairie Coneflower · Bird's Foot Violet · New England Aster · Foxglove Penstemon · Yarrow · Stiff Goldenrod · Pasque Flower · Large-Flowered Penstemon · Wild Bergamot

2′ Scale

Figure 15.   Native prairie garden for butterflies, bees and moths.   Full sun to partial shade.

one you prefer. Since the ***red splendor*** crabapple grows to a height of 18 feet and the Siberian crabapple grows to a height of 30 feet, you may decide that your space is more suited to a ***red splendor*** crabapple.

If you wish to develop a butterfly garden, see Appendix A, part 3, and review the plants listed. They are grouped by categories:

BUTTERFLY, BEE AND MOTH PLANTS
Excellent Plants
1. Trees and Shrubs
2. Annuals
3. Biennials and Perennials

Good Plants
1. Trees and Shrubs
2. Annuals
3. Biennials and Perennials

For each butterfly, bee or moth plant species or cultivar listed, check the column entitled "Wildlife Value" to determine how the plant is used by wildlife. The letter "B" means use by butterflies, "E" indicates use by bees, and "M"

refers to use by moths. An "L" means that the plant is a food source for caterpillars (larvae) of moths or butterflies.

The column "No. Wildife Species" identifies how many species use that plant.

Several plans are presented on

the following pages to illustrate yard features designed to attract wildlife. Several butterfly, bee, and moth gardens are shown. Figure 13 portrays a general butterfly garden for sunny to partially shaded sites that includes flowers of both native and exotic origins.

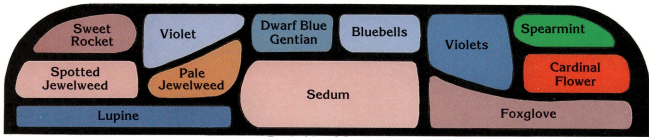

Backside of Garden

2'
Scale

Figure 16. Butterfly, bee, and moth flower garden for shady sites, including west and north sides of houses.

The cecropia moth caterpillar feeds on boxelder leaves and other plants.

Bruce Edinger

Figure 14 is a native woodland wildflower garden that will attract butterflies, bees, moths, and orioles. Figure 15 is a prairie grass and wildflower garden that will attract butterflies, bees, and moths. Both gardens are intended for sunny to partially sunny sites.

Figure 16 is a butterfly, bee, and moth garden for shady sites, and Figure 17 is a wildlife garden for sites with moist to wet or poorly drained soils.

A moist soil butterfly garden can be created even in well-drained soils in a manner similar

Backside of Garden

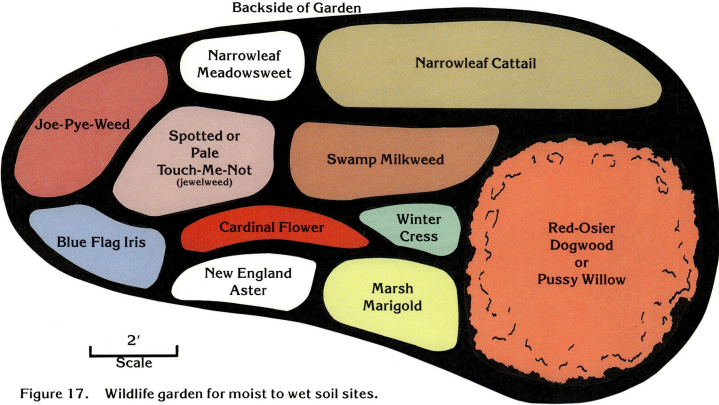

2'
Scale

Figure 17. Wildlife garden for moist to wet soil sites.

41

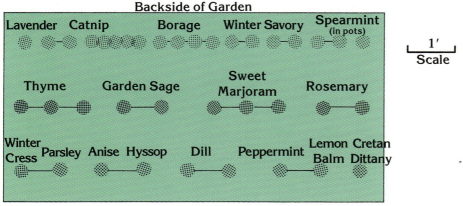

Backside of Garden

Lavender Catnip   Borage   Winter Savory   Spearmint
                                                  (in pots)

Thyme   Garden Sage   Sweet   Rosemary
                             Marjoram

Winter
Cress Parsley Anise Hyssop   Dill   Peppermint   Lemon Cretan
                                                      Balm Dittany

1'
Scale

Figure 18. Herb garden for butterflies and bees for neutral to slightly alkaline soils which are average to well-drained.

to the procedure for creating a small backyard frog pond. Dig out a pond basin to a depth of approximately 14 to 18 inches. Line the bottom of the basin with a double layer of polyethylene landscaping film. Then refill the pond basin with soil. The moist soil garden will support a variety of attractive plants that require saturated soil. If the soil is too wet for the plant species chosen, poke several small holes in the polyethylene film to allow a small amount of drainage.

An herb garden is featured in Figure 18. It is designed for average to well-drained soil that is neutral to slightly alkaline. It is mainly attractive to bees.

Finally, a hummingbird garden is shown in Figure 19. It provides

an irresistible combination of plants that will attract ruby-throated hummingbirds throughout the spring and summer.

Apartment dwellers do not have the option of developing a yard for wildlife, but they too can attract butterflies, bees, moths, hummingbirds and orioles to a container garden on their deck or patio. Figure 20 shows a simple

plan for attracting wildlife to a deck, balcony or patio. Bird feeders, perches, and a wren house could also be placed on a deck (49). A list of plants suitable for use in a container garden is given in Appendix B.

One topic of special interest to northern gardeners is knowing what perennial flowers are most hardy for backyard use in extreme

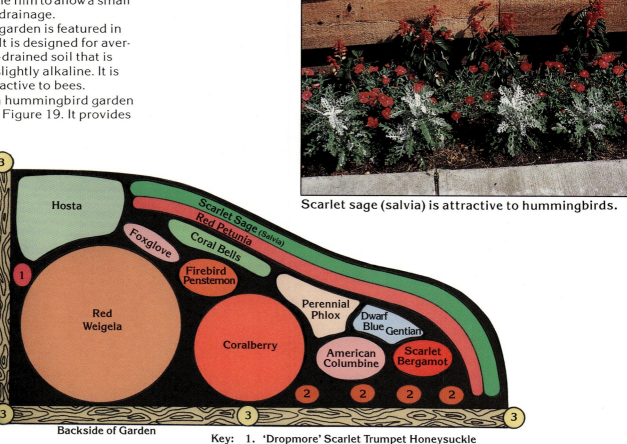

Carrol Henderson

Scarlet sage (salvia) is attractive to hummingbirds.

Hosta

Scarlet Sage (Salvia)
Red Petunia

Foxglove   Coral Bells

1

Firebird
Penstemon

Red
Weigela

Perennial
Phlox

Dwarf
Blue Gentian

Coralberry

American
Columbine

Scarlet
Bergamot

2   2   2   2

Backside of Garden

Key: 1. 'Dropmore' Scarlet Trumpet Honeysuckle
      2. Scarlet Runner Bean
      3. Split Rail Fence Support For Vines

2'

Figure 19. Hummingbird garden for sunny to partially shaded sites.

Gregory K. Scott

The dun skipper, feeding at a milkweed, is one of over 200 butterfly species found in the Midwest.

northern areas, including hardiness zone 3N. Ruth Masters from the Grand Rapids, Minnesota, Garden Club has compiled a list of such hardy perennials, and from that list has been extracted a partial list of plants which attract butterflies, bees, hummingbirds, and orioles: delphinium, oriental poppy, peony, daylily, primrose, hosta, bergamot, daisy, phlox, violet, columbine, lupine, hollyhock, rudbeckia, sedum, rock cress, alpine and other asters, balm melissa, coral bells, foxglove, and allium.

Regardless of which plans you adopt, patience is necessary. A backyard wildlife landscaping project will develop dramatically over the period of a few years.

As you develop a yard for wildlife in an urban area, it will be necessary to comply with municipal ordinances regarding lawn care and weed control. In some areas, it may not be legal to let grassy areas grow unmowed. An excellent reference on designing naturalized landscapes in an urban setting is Diekelmann and Bruner (29).

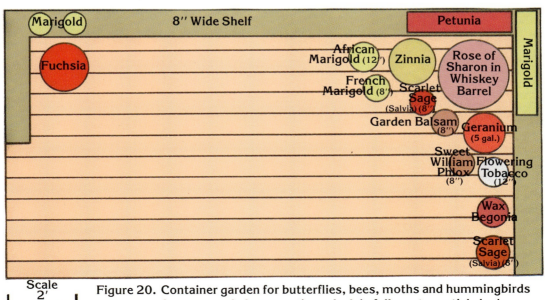

Figure 20. Container garden for butterflies, bees, moths and hummingbirds for use on a balcony, patio or deck in full sun to partial shade.

Scale 2'

The American kestrel is typically found in farmland habitat.

Landscaping Farmland for Wildlife

Chapter 6

Farmland that contains essential components of wildlife habitat will support a diverse community of wild creatures — a continuing source of beauty, inspiration and recreation for rural residents. Farmland that contains only a farmhouse and rowcrops planted road to road or fence to fence will be nearly devoid of wildlife. Appendix P contains a list of typical wildlife species that occur in farmland areas of the Midwest. There are generally four types of habitat that occur in farmland: 1) open cropland areas, 2) farmstead and wooded sites, 3) grasslands, haylands and prairies, and 4) wetlands. If any or several of these latter habitats are missing, the species diversity will be significantly decreased. This is especially true if wetlands are missing.

A study by Graber and Graber (43) in Illinois showed that rowcrop areas of corn and soybeans support only two or three nesting bird species and a total of only up to 88 birds per 100 acres. Pasture and haylands support seven to eleven nesting species and a total of up to 386 birds per 100 acres. Marshland supports 13 nesting bird species and up to 702 birds per 100 acres.

Farmland offers many opportunities for enhancement of wildlife habitat and concurrent soil conservation benefits. Often these opportunities can be incorporated as part of state or federal conservation reserve programs or cost-shared with public agencies.

An excellent example of a farm that has been developed for crop production while providing soil conservation benefits and wildlife production is the 259-acre Ridge Lake Farm in Swift County, Minnesota. The farm, owned and managed by Bill Oemichen, is a

Ridge Lake Farm in Swift County, Minnesota, is an outstanding example of a farm with conservation features.

living example of a modern conservation-era farm. It is not drained, plowed, and planted from boundary to boundary. On the contrary, the soils, drainage, topography, and productivity of the land have all been used to design a farm landscape that produces crops and concurrently reflects a conservation ethic. Figure 21 portrays an aerial view of the farm and includes a diagram that identifies the crops and conservation features present.

Among the features of significance to wildlife on Oemichen's farm are grassy waterways, a food plot, wildlife woody cover plantings, field windbreaks, upland grassy nesting cover, restored wetlands and wood duck nest boxes.

Following is an explanation of several features of farmland habitat that each offer potential for wildlife benefits on your land if they are properly managed, preserved, or developed.

Roadsides

In many rural areas, roadsides are the only significant grassland wildlife habitat. Roadsides are used by at least 40 wildlife species, including pheasant, gray partridge, mallard, goldfinch, bobolink, meadowlark, mourning dove, dickcissel, grasshopper sparrow, vesper sparrow, common yellowthroat, cottontail, woodchuck, thirteen-lined ground squirrel and many others. While the acreage of roadside along a mile of road may seem small, there are 525,000 acres of roadside habitat in Minnesota's farmland area alone. Unfortunately, that habitat becomes a death trap for many nesting birds and mammals because an estimated 70 percent is disturbed by burning, mowing, or spraying. In agricultural areas roadsides may comprise only two percent of the land area but if protected will produce 25 percent to 50 percent of the pheasants raised. Protected road-

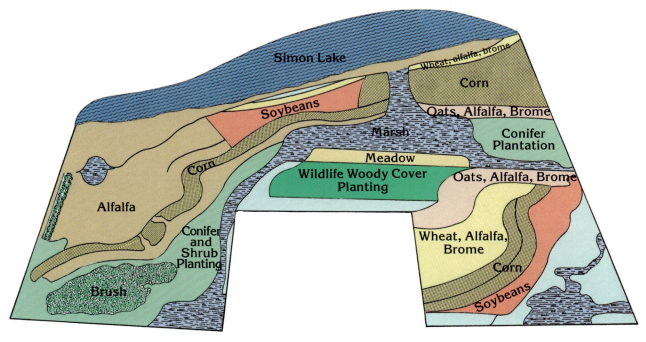

Figure 21. Landscape design for Ridge Lake Farm in Swift County, Minnesota.

sides will also be used by one to five nesting songbirds per acre (3).

Roadsides should be undisturbed whenever possible. When weed control is necessary, use spot mowing or spot spraying. Highway shoulders may be mowed to one or two mower widths when necessary to improve visibility. Clip the grass at a height of 10 to 12 inches to leave nesting cover for the next year. When more extensive mowing is necessary, it should be delayed until after August 1.

One way roadside habitat in prairie regions of the Midwest can be improved is by seeding prairie grasses and wildflowers. For further information on the latest roadside vegetation management techniques, contact the Roadside Habitat Specialist, DNR, Box 756, New Ulm, MN 56073.

Fence Rows

Fence rows can provide grassy nesting cover, winter cover, wildlife travel lanes, and perching sites for songbirds. Scattered trees and shrubs provide nesting sites and fruits for birds. Unfortunately, high-quality fencerow habitats are becoming very rare. Among birds using fence rows are vesper sparrows, eastern kingbirds, dickcissels, loggerhead shrikes, meadowlarks, song sparrows and ring-necked pheasants.

There are several kinds of fence rows: herbaceous cover only, herbaceous cover with scattered trees and shrubs, and fence rows with continuous trees and shrubs. Research along fence rows in Iowa has shown summer counts of 12.7 birds per mile along herbaceous fence rows, 16.5 birds per mile along herbaceous fence rows with scattered trees and shrubs, and 28.5 birds per mile along fence rows with continuous trees and shrubs (16).

High-quality fence rows should be preserved whenever possible. They can be enhanced by planting a few scattered vines or shrubs,

constructing rock piles, and placement of nest boxes for bluebirds, tree swallows, house wrens, deer mice, kestrels, and flickers.

Shalaway (94) recommended that wildlife benefits in fence rows will be greatest where they are at least nine feet wide or wider and characterized by two or three large dead trees per mile of fenceline.

Grassy Waterways

Waterways are drainage courses that are normally dry but sustain water flows during moderate to heavy rains. These waterways need to be protected from

Farmland can be managed for crop production as well as soil conservation and wildlife production.

soil erosion by permanent grassy cover. This can be done with brome grass or alfalfa, but it may be a better long-term investment to use prairie grasses like switchgrass, big bluestem, Indiangrass, and little bluestem. The prairie grasses will form an excellent protective sod and generally provide better wildlife food and cover.

Concurrently, waterways can provide nesting cover and good fall and winter shelter for pheasants and deer.

Don't make a grassy waterway too narrow or water will simply divert around the edges. The width of a good waterway will vary depending on hydrology and the topography. The local SCS office can provide assistance in planning a grassy waterway.

Food Plots

Food plots are an excellent way to enhance the survival of wintering wildlife. Food plots can include corn, grain sorghum, sorghum - sudangrass (sudex), buckwheat, soybeans, sunflowers, or any combination of those crops. Even rutabagas can be

planted as a food plot for deer. A typical food plot is up to 10 acres in size.

A grain sorghum and cane sorghum food plot provides excellent winter food and cover for pheasants as well as wintering songbirds. Corn food plots are better for both pheasants and deer. Excellent food plots can be created by planting corn in one direction (i.e. rows are east-west) and by planting cane sorghum in the same food plot at a right angle to the orientation of the corn (sorghum rows are north-south). If a corn food plot is not entirely consumed in its first winter, it can be left standing a second year. The herbaceous vegetation that grows up in the rows provides wonderful pheasant food and cover and abundant seeds for other wildlife. Grain sorghum, sudex, and buckwheat food plots can be disked down in the spring, and the residual seed will sprout for the second year. In northwest Minnesota, sunflower food plots are well-used by wildlife.

A food plot should be sheltered on the north and west by natural

features that will prevent drifting winter snows from covering the grain. Farm shelterbelts, wooded creek bottoms, or wetlands can help shelter a food plot. Figure 1 shows an acceptable design for food plot location.

Food plots for wildlife can generally be paid for in part through participation in USDA cropland set-aside programs. They are also known as CRP—Conservation Reserve Programs. Check with the local ASCS office or area wildlife manager for details. Pheasants Forever is an organization which can also provide free seed for food plots (10).

Farmstead Shelterbelts

One technique for improving farmland consists of planting trees and shrubs around the farm buildings — creating a farmstead shelterbelt. This was a strong tradition among pioneers who first settled on the prairies of the Midwest.

Willa Cather, in "My Antonia," conveyed the sense of safety and peace that good farmstead plantings provided our early farmers.

Table 1. Suggested species arrangements using tall trees on the outside of an 8-row farm shelterbelt (99).

	SPECIES			
Row	Example No. 1	Example No. 2	Example No. 3	Example No. 4
1 (outside)	Silver Maple Hybrid Poplar	Silver Maple Hybrid Poplar	Silver Maple Hybrid Poplar	Silver Maple Hybrid Poplar
2	Hybrid Poplar Male Boxelder	Hybrid Poplar Male Boxelder	Hybrid Poplar Male Boxelder	Hybrid Poplar Male Boxelder
3	Hybrid Poplar Hackberry (Wildlife option #1)	Green Ash Male Boxelder (Wildlife option #1)	Hybrid Poplar Hackberry	Green Ash
4	Norway Spruce	Green Ash Norway Spruce	Green Ash Hackberry (Wildlife option #1)	Hackberry (Wildlife option #1)
5	Douglas Fir Norway Spruce	Douglas Fir Norway Spruce	Douglas Fir Norway Spruce	Douglas Fir Norway Spruce
6	White Spruce Black Hills Spruce	White Spruce Black Hills Spruce	White Spruce Black Hills Spruce Douglas Fir Norway Spruce	White Spruce Black Hills Spruce Douglas Fir Norway Spruce
7 (inside)	E. Red Cedar White Spruce Black Hills Spruce	E. Red Cedar White Spruce Black Hills Spruce	White Spruce Black Hills Spruce	White Spruce Black Hills Spruce
8	Shrub row either 70 feet to the windward of the outside tree row or 30 feet to leeward of the inside conifer row. If wildlife option #2 is used, the second alternative should be selected. Wildlife option #2 should be placed inside row 8.			

In one instance, the Czech farm girl Antonia was showing her friend Jim Borden her farmstead (114).

"At some distance behind the house were an ash grove and two orchards: a cherry orchard, with gooseberry bushes between the rows, and an apple orchard, sheltered by a high hedge from the hot winds. . . As we walked through the apple orchard, grown up in tall blue-grass, Antonia kept stopping to tell me about one tree or another. 'I love them as if they were people,' she said rubbing her hand over the bark. There wasn't a tree here when we first came. We planted every one and used to carry water for them too — after we'd been working in the field all day . . . In the middle of the orchard we came upon a grape arbour. . . There was the deepest peace in that orchard. It was surrounded by a triple enclosure; the wire fence, then the hedge of thorny locusts, then the mulberry hedge which kept out the hot winds of summer and held fast to the protecting snows of winter."

Farmstead shelterbelts also provide valuable nesting habitat and winter cover for birds. DNR surveys in southwest Minnesota have shown a range of three to 52 bird nests in a shelterbelt, with an average of 22. The surveys revealed 13 species. Among the bird nests discovered were those of grackle, mourning dove, robin, gray catbird, chipping sparrow, blue jay, black-billed cuckoo, Brewer's blackbird, indigo bunting, brown thrasher, goldfinch, yellowthroat and red-winged blackbird.

Since these shelterbelts average 1.86 acres in area, they provide an average density of 13.1 bird nests per acre. Jackson (58) in Clay County, Minnesota, discovered a density of 17.6 nests per acre in a 2.5-acre conifer plantation comprised mainly of white spruce.

The design recommended for farmstead shelterbelts has undergone a dramatic change recently. Older designs, which had tall hardwood trees in the central rows, were referred to as "hip roof" designs. This characteristic and the close spacing of the trees and shrubs contributed to unnecessary drifting in the farmyard and a relatively short lifespan for the shelterbelt. The new design explained here (99) is designed to minimize snow drifting in the farmstead **and to last about 100 years or more.** The main difference is that the tallest trees are in the outside row of the shelterbelt and the trees are more widely spaced.

Table 1 is a list of suggested arrangements for trees and shrubs in an eight-row farm shelterbelt. Figure 22 shows the general layout of a farmstead shelterbelt and Figure 23 shows a side view of a shelterbelt.

Male boxelder trees are included as an option to hybrid poplars. Hybrid poplar has negligible value for wildlife, whereas boxelder is used by five species and is an important food for cecropia moth caterpillars. Boxelder is a native, fast-growing species that is characterized by many cavities for wildlife nesting when it is mature. Boxelder bugs are characteristic only on female boxelder trees, so only male trees are recommended. Female trees can be recognized by the presence of female flower structures in the spring.

This type of farm shelterbelt accomplishes its intended purposes of snow drift control and will provide nesting cover and winter shelter for wildlife, but it does not provide an adequate amount of wildlife food.

This deficiency can be corrected by either of the following two "wildlife options" by adding two more rows to the eight-row design.

1. Place two additional rows of the following deciduous trees in the central rows of the shelterbelt between rows 3 and 4 as explained in Table 1 (Examples 1 and 2); or between rows 4 and 5 as explained in Table 1 (Examples 3 and 4): black cherry, black walnut, butternut, Amur chokecherry, cockspur hawthorn, sakhalin corktree, bitternut hickory, bur oak, scarlet oak and white oak. Trees should be spaced 20 feet apart in rows 20 feet apart. See Figure 24.

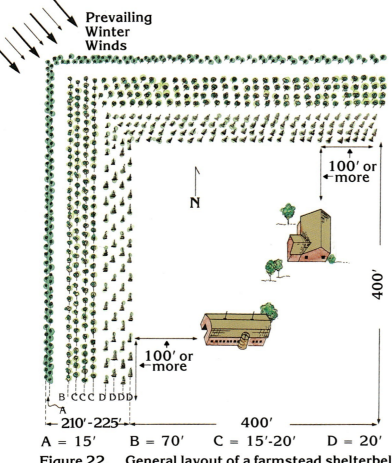

Prevailing Winter Winds

100' or more

N

400'

100' or more

B C C C D D D

A

210'-225'

400'

A = 15' B = 70' C = 15'-20' D = 20'

Figure 22.   General layout of a farmstead shelterbelt.

2. Place two additional rows of shrubs or small trees inside the single shrub row that is recommended to be 30 feet inside the innermost conifer row. Then there will be three rows of shrubs. Excellent species are American plum and chokecherry in the outermost row. The two innermost rows can include Nanking cherry, red-osier dogwood, gray dogwood, Juneberry, highbush cranberry, elderberry, *red splendor* crabapple, pin cherry, *meteor* cherry, Siberian crabapple and American or beaked hazel. You can increase the diversity of these rows by having the east-west portion of a row comprised of one species, like chokecherry, and the north-south portion of the same row comprised of another species, like American plum.

These rows should be 15 feet from each other, and the plants should be spaced at least four to six feet apart, depending on the species. Therefore, the first shrub row will be 30 feet from the conifer row; the second shrub row will be 45 feet from the conifers, and the third shrub row will be 60 feet from the conifers. American plum and chokecherry are recommended primarily for their qualities as suckering shrubs which will create excellent thickets for songbird nesting. Don't place these 2 species in the innermost shrub row where they would sucker into your lawn.

Figure 25 is a top view of the trees and shrubs in a 10-row farmstead shelterbelt with wildlife option #2.

Several features should be kept in mind as you develop a farmstead shelterbelt.

• The innermost row of a farmstead shelterbelt should not be too close to the house, barn and feedlot. Close spacing can cause drifting problems. Consult with the SCS or ASCS office regarding proper spacing for your situation and general planting advice.

• Rows of trees should be spaced 20 feet apart (30 feet for silver maple and cottonwood rows).

• Farmstead shelterbelts should extend at least 50 feet and preferably 100 feet beyond the last main building at the east and south ends of the farmstead to provide maximum protection from snow drifting.

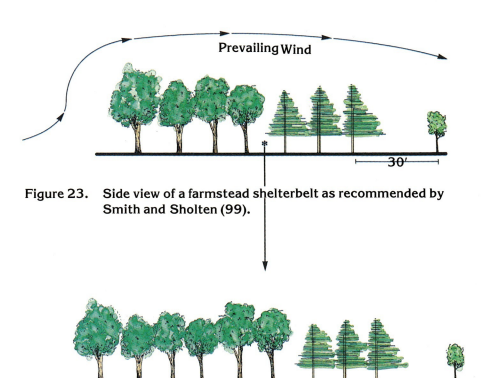

Figure 23.   Side view of a farmstead shelterbelt as recommended by Smith and Sholten (99).

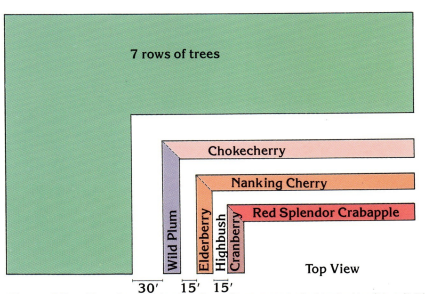

Figure 24.   Side view of a farmstead shelterbelt with wildlife option #1 — two additional rows of hardwood trees.

7 rows of trees

Chokecherry

Nanking Cherry

Red Splendor Crabapple

Wild Plum

Elderberry

Highbush Cranberry

Top View

30'   15'   15'

Figure 25.   Top view of design for a farmstead shelterbelt with wildlife option #2 — two additional rows of shrubs.

• Farmstead shelterbelts may require an area from 210 to 225 feet wide.

• You can simplify the process of establishing a new farmstead shelterbelt by maintaining your new *conifer* trees in plastic containers at your farmstead for a couple years until they are at least two feet tall. You can regularly water the trees with a garden hose. The larger size of your conifers when eventually planted will help them compete better with weeds and save about two years of herbicide costs (Scharf pers. comm). Container stock normally grows two to three times faster than bare root stock when planted properly.

• Order about five percent more trees and shrubs than are needed to replace trees that die. Any excess plants can be planted elsewhere and transplanted back into the shelterbelt later if needed.

• Be sure to consult your county SCS office for advice on planting a field windbreak or farmstead shelterbelt on your land. They can tell you what tree and shrub species are best suited to the soils and special conditions on your land. They can also advise you on proper spacing of trees and shrubs.

• Avoid planting windbreaks or shelterbelts under or near powerlines or other utilities. If this isn't possible, discuss using shorter species with the affected utility company.

• Do not create driving hazards or other obstructions that will deposit snow on highways or blind corners. Locate the leeward (downwind) row of a windbreak or shelterbelt no closer than 100 feet north or west of a road or right-of-way. Finally, weed control in **new** shelterbelts is **absolutely** essential. Information on weed control techniques for shelterbelts is included in Appendix G. After about five or six years a shelterbelt can be permanently seeded down between the trees. Herbicides or mulching provide adequate vegetation control directly adjacent to your trees and shrubs so cultivation and mowing aren't necessary.

Wildlife Woody Cover Plantings

Wildlife woody cover plantings are placed in odd corners or along edges of farms or woodlots in rec-

Many kinds of Midwestern wildlife, like this female rose-breasted grosbeak, inhabit wildlife woody cover plantings.

tangular, square, or irregularly shaped blocks rather than L-shaped blocks as are shelterbelts.

The best type of woody cover planting contains 16 rows and is 800 feet long. This occupies three to four acres. A 16-row planting should have six rows of conifers, five rows of small and large trees, and five rows of shrubs.

Figure 26 is a side view of a 16-row planting. An adequate but somewhat less beneficial woody cover planting should contain at least 10 rows of trees and shrubs and be 200 feet long. If the planting is 150 feet wide, this occupies only three-fourths of an acre but provides huge benefits to wildlife.

One or two rows of shrubs may

be planted on the south or east (downwind) side of the conifers to provide wildlife with protected loafing and sunning areas.

The effectiveness of the planting is much greater if it is near a wetland characterized by much emergent vegetation and if corn, sorghum, or sudex food plots or wildlife feeder cribs are located on the downwind side of the planting (39, 51, 88, 99, 118, 119).

Following is a description of how a wildlife woody cover planting can be designed.

Rows 1 and 2 (10-row planting); Rows 1 through 5 (16-row planting)

Rows 1 and 2 are low growing shrubs in the windward (most

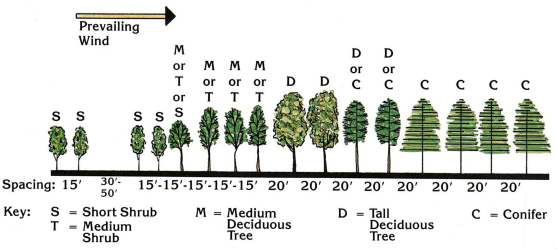

Spacing: 15' 30'-50' 15'-15'-15'-15'-15' 20' 20' 20' 20' 20' 20' 20' 20'

Key: S = Short Shrub   M = Medium Deciduous Tree   D = Tall Deciduous Tree   C = Conifer
T = Medium Shrub

Figure 26. Side view of a 16-row wildlife woody cover planting.

northerly or westerly) position of the wildlife woody cover planting. Rows 1 and 2 should be spaced 15 feet apart. Row 2 should be about 70 feet from row 3. These shrubs should be planted about six feet apart in each row. Species to consider using are lilac, coralberry, Juneberry, ginnala maple (compact cultivar), Mongolian cherry, American elderberry, ninebark, red-osier dogwood, gray dogwood, cotoneaster, American highbush cranberry, dwarf *meteor* cherry, purple-osier willow, glossy black chokeberry, common snowberry, northern bayberry, wolfberry, beaked hazel or American hazel. More than one species could be used in a row by having alternating stretches of different species.

Rows 3 and 4 (10-row planting); Rows 6, 7 and 8 (16-row planting)

Rows 3 and 4 are tall shrub or medium-height trees inside and adjacent to the shrub rows. Trees or shrubs in these rows should be at least 8 to 10 feet apart, depending on the species used. Species or cultivars to consider are: laurel-leaf willow, American plum, ginnala maple, boxelder, chokecherry, Siberian crabapple, *red splendor* and *prairie fire* crabapple, pin cherry, Juneberry, red mulberry, nanking cherry, dwarf *meteor* cherry, American elderberry, Siberian plum, silver buffaloberry, Canadian buffaloberry, northern arrowwood viburnum, wayfaring bush, American highbush cranberry, Amur chokecherry, and cockspur hawthorn. These rows should be spaced 15 feet to 20 feet apart.

Rows 5 and 6 (10-row planting); Rows 9 and 10 (16-row planting)

Tall deciduous trees are planted in rows 5 and 6. The spacing of these trees should be 20 feet between each other and between rows. Species to consider using are green ash, hackberry, cottonwood and its seedless cultivars, silver maple, black cherry, black walnut, butternut, sugar maple, white ash, black ash, Amur corktree, sakhalin corktree, bitternut hickory, bur oak, scarlet oak, and white oak. If you use cottonwood or silver maple, the trees should be spaced 30 feet apart and the cottonwood or silver maple row should be at least 25 feet and preferably 30 feet from adjacent rows to prevent them from shading out adjacent trees.

Rows 7 and 8 (10-row planting); Rows 11 and 12 (16-row planting)

Rows 7 and 8 are tall conifer trees. The following conifers can be included: red (Norway) pine, ponderosa (western yellow) pine, Eastern white pine, Norway spruce, tamarack (larch), Douglas fir from a hardy northern seed source or Siberian larch. The larch is a deciduous conifer.

These trees should also be spaced 20 feet apart, between rows and between trees.

Rows 9 and 10 (10-row planting); Rows 13 through 16 (16-row planting)

Rows 9 and 10 are conifers that include Black Hills spruce, white spruce, Norway spruce and northern white cedar. They should be spaced 20 feet apart. Alternative ideas are to use one row of spruce and one of northern white cedar or one row of spruce with an inner row of *red splendor* crabapple.

For details and further information on planting a wildlife woody cover planting consult your county extension agent, SCS, SWCD, area DNR forester or area DNR wildlife manager. Also, request Extension Bulletin 196, "Planting Trees for Farmstead Shelter," Agricultural Extension Service, University of Minnesota, St. Paul, MN 55108 and "Woody Cover Plantings for Wildlife," DNR, 500 Lafayette Road, St. Paul, MN 55155-4007. Another excellent reference is the "Minnesota Tree Handbook" (14, 17, 20, 40, 50, 56, 61, 70, 75, 86, 87, 90, 92, 100, 110, 111, 117).

Carrol Henderson

A well-designed farm shelterbelt can provide energy conservation, soil conservation, and wildlife conservation benefits.

The value of a wildlife woody cover planting for wildlife can be enhanced by planting grapes or raspberries on its margins and by placing some rock piles and brush piles within the planting after the area has been seeded down. Nest boxes appropriate for use in a wildlife woody cover planting are chickadee, house wren, flicker, kestrel, deer mouse, squirrel, and screech-owl.

Remember, a neatly mowed planting has **much** lower value to wildlife than one where the ground cover is enhanced by leaving the grass unmowed.

There are several variations to this plan if you do not have room for 10 rows. An eight-row planting would be comprised of rows 1, 3, 5, 6, 7, 8, 9 and 10. A seven-row planting should be comprised of rows 1, 2, 3, 4, 6, 7, 8, as explained previously. A six-row planting should consist of rows 1, 2, 3, 4, 7, 8. A five-row planting should consist of rows 1, 3, 4, 7, 8, and a four-row planting should contain rows 1, 2, 7, and 8. A three-row planting should contain rows 1, 7, 8, or 1, 3, and 7.

Another alternative for a woody cover planting is to use a naturalistic design with no rows. The trees and shrubs should be mulched for weed control. An example is shown in Figure 27 (21).

Field Windbreaks

A field windbreak is a one or two-row tree planting intended to reduce soil erosion and provide other benefits on open farmland. If properly designed, it causes the wind to deposit a **uniform blanket** of snow over adjacent downwind cropland. The problem with most older windbreaks is that they do not distribute snow uniformly over cropland. This is mainly because of improper spacing of trees or use of the wrong tree species. Good field windbreaks conserve soil moisture and improve crop yields. Research in northwest Minnesota suggests that the best technique is to use one row of green ash spaced 10 feet apart in an east-west orientation (93). Other species which may be used are Black Hills spruce, eastern red cedar, eastern white pine, hackberry, jack pine, northern white cedar, Norway spruce, ponderosa pine, red (Norway) pine, *"Siouxland"* cottonwood, white ash, red-osier dogwood, white spruce, golden willow, Siberian larch, and black ash. Consult with your county SCS office about the relative qualities of these species. Multiple row field windbreaks or closer spacing of the green ash trees causes too much deep drifting near the windbreak. In general, shrubs should be spaced three to eight feet apart in the row, and trees should be spaced six to 20 feet apart in the row. Consult with the SCS for specifics.

The benefits of a field windbreak extend to a distance of at least 10 and up to 15 times the height of the windbreak. A 30-foot high green ash planting will, therefore, provide soil conservation benefits out to at least 300 feet from the planting.

The value of field windbreaks for wildlife can be enhanced by planting a few beta grapes or raspberries and placing bird houses along the windbreak. Appropriate nest boxes would include bluebird, house wren, flicker, and kestrel.

Tree and Shrub Sources

Most state DNR forestry divisions sell tree and shrub seedlings for reforestation, erosion control, field windbreaks, farm shelterbelts, soil and water conservation, and wildlife woody cover plantings. Price lists and order forms can be obtained from DNR Forestry Offices, ASCS Offices, SCS Offices, County Extension Offices, SWCD offices, or in Minnesota, by contacting the DNR Division of Forestry, 500 Lafayette Road, St. Paul, MN 55155-4044.

Creek Banks and Drainage Ditch Bank Stabilization

Depending on topography, a margin of at least 50 to 100 feet should be seeded down on each side of creeks and drainage ditches to help stabilize the banks and to minimize soil erosion.

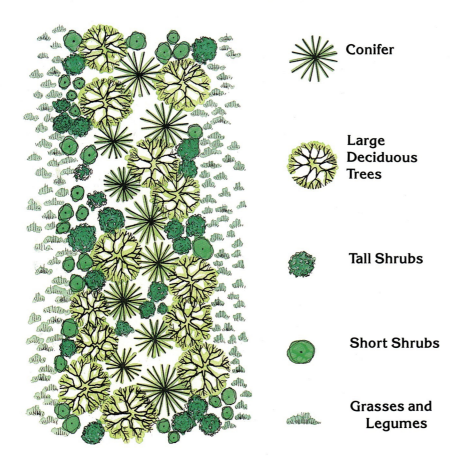

Conifer

Large Deciduous Trees

Tall Shrubs

Short Shrubs

Grasses and Legumes

Figure 27. Naturalistic planting design for a wildlife woody cover planting (No straight rows).

While exotic grass·legume combinations are acceptable, the best long-term investment in the prairie region is probably a combination of prairie grasses like switchgrass, big bluestem, and Indiangrass.

Upland Nesting Cover

For every acre of wetland on a farm, it is desirable to provide two to four acres of undisturbed adjacent grassy nesting cover for waterfowl and other associated wildlife. Otherwise, at least five percent of a farm should be retired as permanent grassy upland cover. Permanent nesting cover in prairie regions ideally would consist of native prairie grasses. Temporary nesting cover can be a grass-legume mixture like brome and alfalfa. Preserving nesting cover is essential for production of meadowlarks, dickcissels, bobolinks, pheasants, gray partridge, mallards, northern pintails, blue-winged teal, gadwalls, and other species. Reimbursement for seeding nesting cover is likely under various government land retirement or set-aside programs. Techniques for establishing prairie grass seedings are discussed by Breyer and Pollard (19) and Duebbert et al. (37). Further information is included in Appendix H.

Bruce Edinger

Raccoons are very abundant in farmland areas, especially in the vicinity of creeks and woodlots.

Marshland

Marshland is one of the most valuable natural assets on a farm. It harbors an incredible variety of wildlife and serves as a nutrient trap that filters out fertilizers and herbicides that wash into the marsh from adjacent croplands. Marshes trap rainwater and allow sediment to settle out, thereby reducing the prospects for downstream flooding and water pollution.

There are Federal Water Bank and state program incentives to promote the preservation of marshes. For more information on these programs, contact your county auditor. Marshland can be enhanced by providing adjacent grassy nesting cover. If you have a marsh, save it. Don't drain it. Cattle should not be allowed to trample entire marsh edges. Fencing may be needed to restrict their access to one area. A grazed area along part of a marsh edge may result in a useful duck loafing site that is beneficial because the unobstructed view gives them better protection from predators (63).

Potential Marshland

A survey of your property might reveal an old drained lake or marsh basin or other topographical feature that would allow the land to be impounded as a marsh. Consult with your local wildlife manager or county ASCS or SCS office to explore the possibility.

Nest Boxes

Nest boxes and nest platforms in farmland areas will be used by the house wren, mourning dove, black-capped chickadee, tree swallow, bluebird, robin, barn swallow, purple martin, flicker, bats, burrowing owl, fox squirrel, raccoon, deer mouse, white-footed mouse, and kestrel. Also the screech-owl, great horned owl, wood duck, Canada goose, and

Gregory K. Scott

Chipping sparrows regularly nest in spruce trees in farm shelterbelts. They are a native species.

Grassland habitat is important for many ground-nesting wildlife species in farmland areas.

mallard will use nest boxes or nest platforms.

For details on the construction and placement of these structures, see "Woodworking for Wildlife"(53).

Old Farmsteads/Odd Corners

There may be abandoned farmstead sites or odd corners on your farm. These are extremely important for adding diverse wildlife habitats in farmland areas that are otherwise dominated by rowcrops. Old farmstead sites are important wildlife habitat for cottontail rabbits, fox squirrels, flickers, raccoons, woodchucks, robins, brown thrashers, song sparrows, catbirds, crows, red-tailed hawks, wood ducks, screech-owls, garter snakes, goldfinches, deer, great horned owls, blue jays, red-headed woodpeckers, hairy woodpeckers, downy woodpeckers, black-capped chickadees, cedar waxwings, and gopher snakes. While it may be necessary to remove some of the old buildings, the trees and shrubs should be preserved. Additional trees and shrubs should be planted as necessary to provide maximum wildlife benefits. One special feature of old farmsteads

is that many of the older trees have natural cavities for wildlife to use. Whatever you do, don't bulldoze out the farmstead vegetation.

Odd corners of brush or grass are also important for wildlife. Preserve them, don't destroy them.

Old buildings, if preserved, may be used for nesting by barn swallows, raccoons, barn owls, rock doves, cliff swallows, and phoebes. Several years ago a turkey vulture was even found nesting in the hay loft of an abandoned barn in Aitkin County, Minnesota.

Native Prairie

If you are fortunate enough to have a remaining parcel of native prairie on your farm, preserve it. Less than 1/10 of one percent of the original native prairie in Minnesota still remains. It is one of our most rare and endangered natural habitats. You will find native wildflowers and butterflies there that grow nowhere else.

You can receive tax benefits by enrolling native prairie in the prairie tax credit program in Minnesota. A similar program is availa-

ble in Iowa. See your county auditor or DNR area wildlife manager for details.

One of the best ways to maintain the vigor and beauty of your prairie is to burn it about once every three to five years. Consult with your area wildlife manager on when and how to carry out a prescribed prairie burn. Burning permits will probably be needed from your local fire warden, and you will need to take precautions to prevent wildfires if you plan a prescribed burn.

Gravel Pits/Cut Banks

Gravel pits and cut banks are important sites for wildlife use in farmland areas. Their values have been discussed previously as structural components of wildlife habitat in Chapter 4. Cut banks should be preserved as nesting sites for bank-nesting birds and mammals.

Stock Ponds

Stock ponds are small impoundments which are dug to provide a source of water for cattle. They are usually fishless ponds no more than 50 feet across. The value of these ponds for wildlife can be enhanced by fencing part of the shoreline so that livestock cannot trample the entire shoreline. The shoreline can also be enhanced by adding loafing platforms, logs, rock piles, and brush for reptiles and amphibians as explained in Chapter 4.

Farm Ponds

Farm ponds are small impoundments from perhaps one-half up to five acres or more that are created by dikes or dams to provide fishing and soil conservation benefits. The gradient of the banks is usually rather steep so there is little emergent vegetation like cattails. Wildlife benefits are higher if livestock are not allowed to trample the entire shoreline and muddy the water. If only perhaps one-fourth of a pond's shoreline is grazed or mowed to the water's edge, however, it creates a safe loafing area for waterfowl. Floating logs or rafts will be used by eastern painted turtles and by ducks. Tree swallow nest boxes along the shoreline have a high likelihood of use.

Orchards

Fruit orchards provide desirable habitat for several types of wildlife. Nest boxes for bluebirds, flickers, and tree swallows should be well used in orchards.

Rock Piles and Brush Piles

The value of rock piles and brush piles has been discussed in Chapter 4. Look at these features as wildlife habitat assets — not eyesores. Rock piles and brush piles should be strategically placed in odd corners and in groves where they will not be in the way of storage and movement of farm equipment.

Hayfields

Hayfields normally support high populations of ground-nesting birds. However, untimely mowing will destroy the nests of these birds and frequently kills the nesting adults. South Dakota studies have shown that only 4.5 percent of all pheasant nests are successful in alfalfa fields (2). Normal alfalfa cutting usually precedes the peak of pheasant hatching by two weeks. Much pheasant mortality could be avoided by delaying mowing one week beyond the traditional point of mowing when alfalfa is 10 percent in bloom.

Kestrels (sparrow hawks) use hayfields as hunting areas where they capture small rodents and insects. Kestrel nest boxes may be placed on trees or posts adjacent to hayfields.

Pastures

The value of pastures for livestock and wildlife can be enhanced by using a rest-rotation system of grazing. The SCS should be consulted for details of pasture management. Bluebird and kestrel nest boxes can be placed along the margin of pastures.

Riparian Forest in Farmland Areas

A riparian forest is a woodland adjacent to a creek, stream, or river valley. In farmland areas, riparian forests provide linear corridors of wildlife habitat. Riparian forests provide important diversity in the agricultural landscape. Recommendations for the management of riparian forests are given in the woodland chapter. Landowners should consult with their area wildlife manager or area forester for specific advice on management of this habitat type.

Farmland Summary

The best advice for sound planning and development of your farmland is to work closely with your local SCS, ASCS, SWCD and DNR resource managers to take advantage of the latest developments in state and federal conservation programs. In conclusion, Figure 28 is a plan for a 160-acre farm that includes many of the farmland features for good wildlife habitat that have been discussed in this chapter. By reviewing this plan and the diagram of Bill Oemichen's farm, you may get some ideas for wildlife conservation projects of your own.

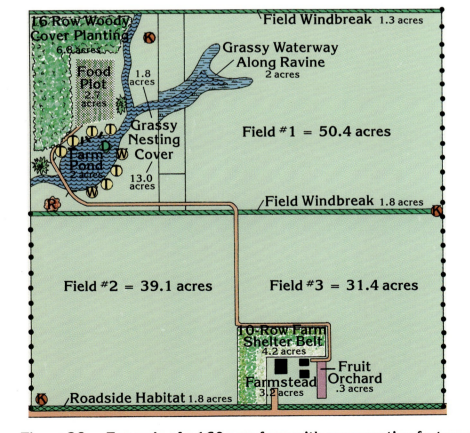

Figure 28.   Example of a 160 acre farm with conservation features.

Pileated Woodpecker

Chapter 7

Many landowners in the Midwest own woodlots of 40 to 80 acres for recreational, aesthetic, or economic reasons. The first impulse of many of these citizens is to protect their woodland from disturbance, including cutting. However, successful forest management has become a complex science which frequently requires active manipulation in order to achieve the goals for which the property was purchased. The key to successful management lies in recognizing the features of the woodland upon which a management plan can be designed. An excellent reference for woodlot management is Decker *et al.* (26).

Good forestry practices can provide additional benefits. In Wisconsin, for example, a landowner must practice good forestry management to get tax breaks.

Wildlife species typical of deciduous and coniferous woodlands are listed in Appendix P. As with other habitats, woodlands must provide food, water, shelter and space for wildlife. The greater the vegetational diversity, structural diversity, and vertical diversity of the woodland, the greater will be the diversity of the wildlife populations present.

Food is provided by mast-producing trees, snags, fruit-bearing trees and shrubs, browse, buds, grasses, food plots, feeding stations, and salt licks.

Water is provided by ponds, beaver ponds, marshes, swamps, lakes, streams, springs, and gravel pits.

Shelter in woodlands is provided by conifer stands, tree cavities, brush and rock piles, thickets, unmowed grassy areas, caves, snags, south-facing slopes, riparian vegetation, ant mounds, cut banks, unbroken forest tracts, old growth, logs, old building sites, bridges, and nest boxes. Abandoned ant mounds are used as wintering sites by small garter snakes, smooth green snakes, and red-bellied snakes. The DNR Private Forest Management (PFM) program specialist can identify your forest types and develop a plan for managing both timber and wildlife on your land. Contact your local DNR forester for more details.

Riparian Zones

A riparian zone is the area of vegetation adjacent to wetland or watery habitats. Riparian vegetation typically grows well in wet or moist soils and may include emergent aquatics, sedges, rushes, shrubs, deciduous trees, and conifers. Riparian zones support an abundance of plant and animal life and are an important source of diversity in forests (108).

Among birds found in riparian zones are the barred owl, great blue heron, broad-winged hawk, spotted sandpiper, pileated woodpecker, belted kingfisher, red-shouldered hawk, wood duck, common goldeneye and hooded merganser. Typical mammals are the black bear, fisher, otter, mink, beaver, raccoon and muskrat. Reptiles and amphibians typical of riparian zones are wood turtles, Blanding's turtles, leopard frogs and snapping turtles. These areas are especially important for cavity-nesting species.

Buffer zones 200 feet wide should be left around all wetlands over one acre in size and along all streams and rivers. Buffer zones 100 feet wide should be left around wetlands smaller than one acre. Grasslands adjacent to wetlands should be protected from mowing and grazing. Small wetlands should not be used as sites for dumping logging slash. Salvage wood cutting and fuelwood cutting should not be done in riparian zones because these trees, particularly dead trees and hollow trees, are so important for wild-

Riparian areas are important wildlife habitats.

MN/DNR

Dennis L. Flath/MT Fish & Game Dept.

The badger can be found in sandy clearings and meadows in woodland areas as well as in agricultural regions.

life. If woodcutting is necessary, single tree or small group selection is the recommended harvesting method. Riparian zones should be considered for preservation as "old growth" areas. Trail and road construction should be minimized in riparian areas because of the problems associated with increased erosion from roadways and human disturbances. Grazing should also be minimized in riparian zones.

Wetlands

Wetlands are a vital part of a forest community — springs, small ponds, beaver ponds, lakes, streams, rivers, and wet lowlands. They should be preserved. There may be opportunities for creation or enhancement of wetlands where the topography and soils allow. Preservation of riparian zones as buffer strips is an integral part of a wetland preservation plan. The DNR area wildlife manager should be consulted for recommendations about wetland management in forest lands.

Old Growth

"Old growth" is comprised of forest areas that are generally one and a half times the age of traditional forest harvesting. Table 2 shows a listing of common tree

species and the age at which "old growth" begins (74).

Wildlife species that benefit from the presence of old growth are the pileated woodpecker, gray treefrog, water shrew, heather vole, red-shouldered hawk, chorus frog, merlin, pine marten, yellow-billed cuckoo, barred owl, northern goshawk, fisher, lynx, wood warblers and bald eagle. In the Chippewa National Forest, 145 wildlife species use old growth stands during at least some part of their life. The Chippewa National Forest has a goal of reserving five percent of its forest as old growth.

The element that makes old growth such a unique and impor-

tant wildlife feature is decay. Old growth contains an abundance of hard and soft snags, fallen logs and natural cavities in mature trees. The structure of old growth is complex and is characterized by many species that are adapted to rather specific and narrow habitat niches. Many wood warblers and several woodpeckers live in old growth and feed on forest insect pests that periodically are characterized by large outbreaks. In fact, some studies have shown that commercial forests that lack tracts of old growth are more vulnerable to insect damage because of the lack of insectivorous birds that help prevent or limit such outbreaks.

Most small private woodlots will not have extensive stands of old growth. On smaller parcels, however, several types of areas should be considered for old growth designation: 1) parcels isolated by swamps or water, 2) timber of low economic value, 3) eagle and osprey nest buffer zones, 4) riparian zones, and 5) areas where aesthetics are important (71).

Northern Hardwoods and Oak Types

Northern hardwoods are characterized by about 50 to 75 percent maple and basswood mixed with oak, yellow birch, aspen, paper birch, elm, and ash. They typically have many natural cavities and diverse wildlife, including pileated woodpeckers, flying squirrels, white-footed mice, screech-owls, ovenbirds, black and white warblers, wood frogs, red-bellied snakes, black bears, chipmunks, American redstarts, chestnut-sided

Table 2. Common tree species and the age at which old growth begins.

Species	Old Growth Begins (Years)
Red and White Pine	180
Jack Pine	70 - 90
Balsam Fir	60
White Spruce	150
Swamp Conifer	150
Aspen	60 - 68
Oak	150
Birch	100 - 110
Lowland Hardwoods	150
Northern Hardwoods	150

warblers, rose-breasted grosbeaks, gray tree frogs, and common garter snakes. Trees known to have cavities should normally be preserved. Oak stands are also especially valuable because they are long-lived and produce acorn crops. Unfortunately, too many people value oak stands more as firewood than as food for wildlife. These forest types should not be used extensively for firewood cutting or for type conversion to conifers. These types are frequently best designated for old growth status.

Whenever oaks are cut, they should be cut during dormancy and low to the ground to encourage sprouting. Grazing should be avoided. When cutting trees in a predominately oak woodlot, consider leaving some relatively uncommon tree species for the unique benefits they provide. Examples would be white pine, hickory, or black cherry. Logging slash can be used to create brush piles.

The DNR PFM specialist should be consulted for specific management guidelines.

Aspen Forest Type

Aspen forest types are vital to the survival of ruffed grouse, woodcock, snowshoe hare, and moose. White-tailed deer, black bears, and some songbirds also use this forest type.

Aspen is primarily of interest to people who wish to manage their woodlots for grouse and woodcock. Because of the difficulties of establishing aspen where it does not exist, people hoping to manage their woods for ruffed grouse or woodcock should buy woodlots that already have a good stand of aspen. Aspen management for grouse is discussed in detail by Gullion (47).

Ruffed grouse need aspen in three age classes: sapling stands from four to 15 years old for brood cover, sapling and small-pole stands six to 25 years old for fall and spring cover, and older aspen for food and as wintering and nesting cover. The buds and flowering catkins of male quaking aspen are extremely important grouse foods. All of these age classes should be accessible to each grouse territory of 6 to 25 acres.

A 40-acre woodlot is adequate to support four to five drumming male grouse territories. A cutting rotation involving 2½-acre blocks will provide optimum habitat for grouse. A timber harvesting plan for a 10-acre woodlot is shown in Figure 29 (47). Cutting plans should proceed from south to north to facilitate sunlight reaching the cut area, with cutting generally scheduled for a 40-year aspen crop rotation. On poorer sites and in colder climates, the cutting interval can be modified to allow a 60-year rotation. The best time to cut is between leaf-fall in autumn and before sap runs in the spring. Late summer cutting is also acceptable.

Grouse habitat can sometimes be enhanced by placing a drumming log in the approximate center of each anticipated drumming territory — about one every 10 acres. Pick a hardwood tree that is 10 inches in diameter or greater. Cut the log three to six feet above the ground. The tree to be cut should be eight to 10 feet from another medium-sized tree. The drumming log should be felled so

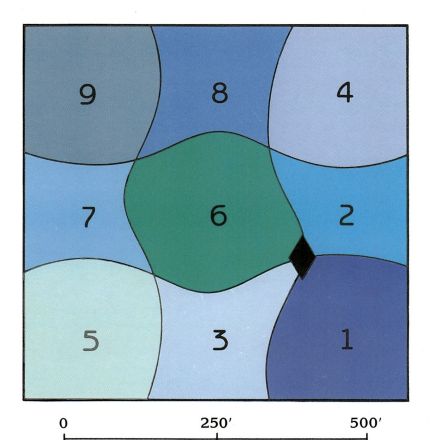

Wildlife Cutting Blocks

1 — Cut Year 1 and Year 40
2 — Cut Year 5
3 — Cut Year 10
4 — Cut Year 15
5 — Cut Year 20
6 — Cut Year 25
7 — Cut Year 30
8 — Cut Year 35
9 — Cut At Year 40

Optional: Leave one cutting block uncut as old growth.

 Expected Location of a Ruffed Grouse Drumming Site

0   250'   500'

Figure 29. A timber harvesting plan for a ten acre woodlot.

that it falls adjacent to or not more than one foot from the second tree. The entire site within a radius of 10 to 12 feet of the fallen log should have 60 to 170 sprouts of small trees or brush. This provides a protective screen of brush that prevents the approach of avian predators like goshawks while the male is drumming. There should be several mature male aspen within sight of the log. Figure 30 is a diagram of a drumming log site in which the small sprouts are not shown (4, 45, 46, 47, 48).

However, an intensive tree harvest program designed to benefit ruffed grouse will not provide for the needs of many other forest wildlife species that require older aspen stands or non-aspen habitats. While some high-quality aspen stands may lend themselves to intensive grouse management as described, most forest tracts should be managed for a diversity of wildlife and not for the maximum number of grouse that can be produced. Riparian areas, coniferous woods, old growth, oak woods, bogs, cedar swamps, and snags do not lend themselves to grouse management.

Contiguous Forest Areas

Some species of wildlife require extensive forest stands that are unbroken by openings or trails. An example would be many wood warblers, tanagers, thrushes, and flycatchers. The main reason is that cowbirds are typical of forest openings and have become more abundant. They lay their eggs in

Figure 30.   Diagram of a ruffed grouse drumming log site.

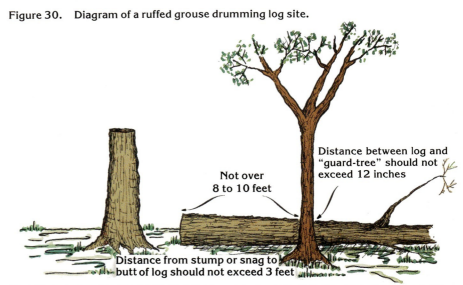

Not over 8 to 10 feet

Distance between log and "guard-tree" should not exceed 12 inches

Distance from stump or snag to butt of log should not exceed 3 feet

To make a drumming log for Ruffed Grouse, a tree can be felled or moved into a position as shown above. The drumming site will be either within a foot or two of the butt end, or within 18 inches of the "guard tree". Also, several logs 6 to 8 feet long can be piled against a snag or tree to make a drumming log. In any event the bird should be 10 to 12 inches above the surrounding terrain when standing on his "log".

the nests of forest songbirds that are in or near forest openings, and the cowbird young prevent the forest songbird young from surviving. This problem threatens some forest interior species like the ovenbird. This is not a consideration for most small woodlot owners because small woodlots are already fragmented by roads and openings. This is mainly important for large forest holdings (91).

The ruffed grouse is a common bird of northern woodlands.

Forest Openings, Gravel Pits, and Trails

A forest opening is an upland area of one-half to 10 acres with few trees or brush. Gravel pits and trails are considered types of forest openings. Forest openings are often established and maintained at log landing sites where timber has been removed. They are important because they generally contain forage grasses and legumes that are eaten by deer and other grazing animals. Small mammals in openings provide prey for predatory birds and mammals. Openings are typically provided where deer management is a primary goal. There are 158 wildlife species in northern forests that use openings at some point in their lives. The Minnesota DNR has a goal that not less than five percent of the upland area of its forest management units shall be in permanent wildlife openings. These openings are often seeded with grass and legumes and are created at the site of log landings. Native species should be used when feasible. Dutch white clover is a well-used wildlife food in openings and trails but is not native.

Wildlife openings should be on south or southeast-facing slopes. They should have a 3:1 ratio of length to width. The width should be at least twice the height of the adjacent trees. Openings should be located along the edge of hardwood cut areas and be one to 10 acres, depending on the local situation. Seeding and maintenance of openings is essential. The area should be free of logging debris. Snake hibernating mounds or clumps of fruiting shrubs may be placed on the north edge of forest openings.

Bare ground and banks are used by 21 forest species including the belted kingfisher, snapping turtle, gray wolf, red fox, woodchuck, badger, common nighthawk, smooth green snake, killdeer, bank swallow, barn swallow, cliff swallow, and common flicker.

Cut banks at gravel pits should be preserved, and at least 50 percent of the pit floor should be bare ground. The DNR area forester or area wildlife manager should be consulted about forest opening management.

One innovative structure for use along the edge of forest openings is the "snake hibernating mound." It is essentially an underground brushpile and is designed to provide burrow sites for hibernating snakes. These mounds can be built along forest openings, road cuts, timber landings, or any land clearing which has resulted in the creation of slash and stumps. Mounds should be located on the north side of a clearing where they will receive sunlight. Snake mounds are prepared in two steps: 1) site preparation and 2) mound construction. First, cut trees on the site approximately 12 to 18 inches above the ground level. Then cut the trunks into 10-foot lengths and remove all branches. Finally, remove stumps from the ground and stockpile all these materials at the location of the desired snake mound.

The mound is created by digging a trench eight feet deep and nine feet across. Excavated soil should be stockpiled by the edge of the trench. The bottom of the trench should be covered with a layer of logs and the trench should then be filled with some stumps and branches. Soil should then be pushed into the trench to ground level. Then lay the 10-foot logs side by side across the top of the trench. Place more soil onto those logs, and then deposit more stumps on top of the soil. Finally, cover the entire mound with more soil and branches to form a mound 10 feet high. A cross section of a snake hibernation mound is shown in Figure 31.

Forest Edge

The edge between a cut and uncut forest or between forest and field can be good habitat for wildlife.

Forest edges should have irregular and not straight edges. This is the way natural edges occur. When cutting along edges, save special trees like den trees and tall snags. Trees, shrubs, and vines that bear nuts and fleshy fruits are valuable along woodland edges since sunlight stimulates heavy fruiting. Hickory, serviceberry, red-osier and gray dogwood, viburnum, blueberry, and grape should be preserved along forest edges.

Bird of Prey Nests and Heronries

Nesting sites of bald eagles, ospreys, hawks, owls, and great blue heron colonies should receive special attention. These nesting sites should be reported to your local DNR area wildlife manager or regional DNR nongame specialist. They will give you advice on management of these sites.

Snags

You can allow snags to occur naturally on your woodlot or you may need to create them. Hardwood snags are preferred over conifers. However, pine and tamarack snags are long lasting and will provide good nesting and perching sites for ospreys if they are adjacent to lakes or beaver ponds.

In timber harvest areas, leave snags scattered throughout the cut area. More snags are desirable near water, oak clumps, brush piles, and windrows.

In woodlots or cut areas, preserve approximately one to six hard snags per acre and as many soft snags as possible (73).

In extreme circumstances where snags are lacking, you can create snags in a woodlot by girdling several *diseased* or *deformed* trees. The best trees for creation of snags are diseased or deformed oak, sugar maple, basswood, ash and elm. Aspen is also good, if mature. Select trees that

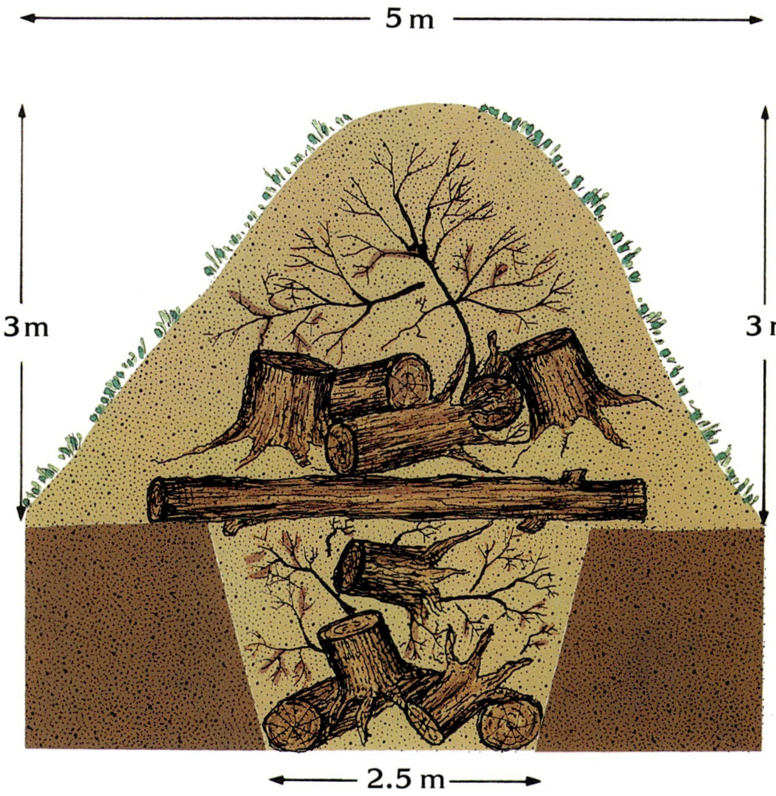

Figure 31. Cross-section of a snake hibernation mound.

are over 12 inches in diameter, when possible. Girdling involves cutting a ring around the trunk through the bark and well into the sapwood so that the cambium layer between the bark and wood is completely severed.

A good strategy for wildlife management would be to maintain a variety of snags. On a 20-acre woodlot for example, wildlife managers recommend maintaining four to five snags over 18 inches in diameter, 30 to 40 snags over 14 inches in diameter, and 50 to 60 snags over five inches in diameter (6, 13, 64, 73, 106, 107).

When snags fall down, they should be left on the ground to provide food and cover sites for birds, small mammals, reptiles, and amphibians. Logs can also provide drumming sites for ruffed grouse.

In addition to the value of fallen logs in a forest setting, logs are also important in two other circumstances. Logs can be placed on the edges of wetlands so they are partially submerged. They will be used by turtles as basking sites and by other reptiles and amphibians. Logs or platforms comprised of several logs can also be anchored in a pond to create secure sunning and resting sites for both ducks and turtles. Rotting logs also offer a smorgasbord of discoveries to children and teachers who wish to study nature (113).

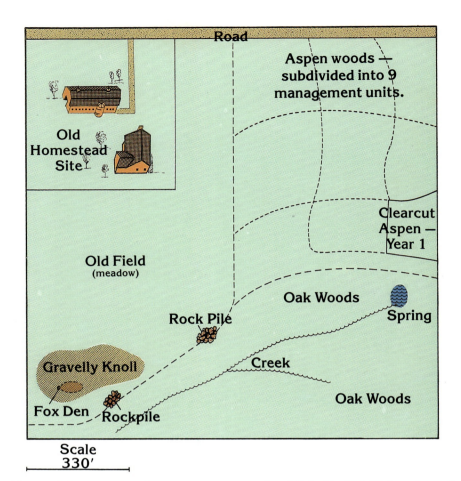

Figure 32.   A plan for management of a 40-acre woodlot — year 1.

Lowland Conifer and Bogs

The lowland conifer forest community is unique and important. It is characterized by mineral or peat soils, acid pH, and black spruce, tamarack, and northern white cedar. Rare orchids including the stemless lady slipper, dragon's mouth orchid, and calypso orchid are found in this forest type. Deer frequently use white cedar swamps as wintering areas.

This forest type is important to the gray wolf, great gray owl, pine marten, northern bog lemming, boreal owl, least chipmunk, wood frog, Connecticut warbler, northern parula warbler, yellow-rumped warbler, and yellow-bellied fly-catcher.

Snags and old growth are important considerations in this forest type. Great gray owl nest platforms are also a management option.

Other Vegetative and Structural Habitat Components

The vegetative and structural habitat components explained in Chapter 4 should be reviewed for applicability on your forest land. Planting of nut and fruit-bearing trees and shrubs can enhance the value of a woodlot. Snags, logs, rock piles, brush piles, salt licks, feeding stations, food plots, nest boxes, snake hibernating mounds, and small ponds can all be developed and maintained to enhance the value of the area for wildlife (106, 109).

The great gray owl is a northern forest species that typically hunts small rodents in forest openings.

Sample Management Plan

It may be easier to visualize how to manage a woodlot by looking at an example. Figure 32 shows diagram of a 40-acre woodlot that has just been purchased. It is an old abandoned homestead site with an old field meadow, aspen, and oak woods. The only management undertaken in that year is to clearcut approximately one acre of aspen within the first of nine aspen management tracts that have been designated for aspen management. The old buildings are also removed.

By year 5, shown in Figure 33, a five-acre white spruce planting has been made in the northwest corner of the parcel. A 6/10-acre Black Hills spruce planting and a crooked entry road provide a visual screen and barrier to the property interior.

The second tract of aspen is clearcut in year 5 and a 10-row wildlife woody cover planting is placed between the spruce planting and the aspen woods. The planting occupies 4.5 acres. Since conifers are already provided in the spruce plantings and oak and aspen are already present on the property, the woody cover planting provides 10 different woodland fruit and nut-bearing trees and shrubs: Juneberry, American elderberry, American plum, northern arrowwood viburnum, chokecherry, gray dogwood, American highbush cranberry, American hazel, Siberian crabapple, and "red splendor" crabapple.

By year 10, shown in Figure 34, a 2.4-acre corn food plot has been created, and a dike has been installed on the creek to create a three-acre pond. The oak woodland around the pond has been designated as a riparian buffer zone (old growth). Aspen management block #9 has been set aside as an aspen old-growth site, and nest boxes are set out for bluebirds, wood ducks, kestrels, and screech-owls. A loafing raft for ducks is placed in the pond, and the meadow is seeded down with grasses and legumes.

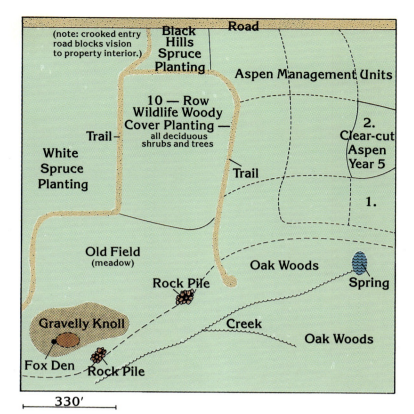

Figure 33.   A plan for management of a 40-acre woodlot — year 5.

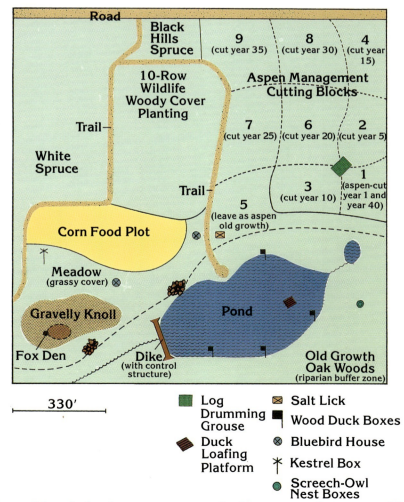

Figure 34.   A plan for management of a 40-acre woodlot — year 10

Cecropia moth

Literature Cited

1. Allenson, R. 1985. Flying flowers. Country Journal. 12(8): 32-36.
2. Anonymous. 1976. Farming and pheasants in South Dakota. Coop. Ext. Service, South Dakota State Univ. U.S. Dept. Ag. Pamphlet, 6 pp.
3. _____, 1979a. Roadsides as a natural resource. A symposium report. MN Dept. of Transportation. 24 pp.
4. _____, 1979b. Steps in managing land for ruffed grouse. U.S.D.A., S.C.S, St. Paul, MN. Pamphlet, 4 pp.
5. _____, 1979c. Urban and backyard wildlife. National 4-H Council, Chicago. Pamphlet, 12 pp.
6. _____, 1981. How to attract cavity nesting birds to your woodlot. No. Central Forest Expt. Station. U.S.F.S., U.S.D.A. St. Paul. Pamphlet.
7. _____, 1984a. A cockspur hawthorn minus thorns. The Minnesota Horticulturist. 112(7):221
8. _____, 1984b. Blueberries for Minnesota. The Minnesota Horticulturist. 112(4):125-126.*
9. _____, 1984c. Compact European cranberry bush. The Minnesota Horticulturist. 112(8):253.*
10. _____, 1984d. Sorghum plantings for pheasants. MN DNR Section of Wildlife, St. Paul. Pamphlet, 6 pp.
11. _____, 1985a. Amur chokecherry gives all-season beauty. The Minnesota Horticulturist. 113(1):28.*
12. _____, 1985b. Dart's gold ninebark, good and golden. The Minnesota Horticulturist. 113(6):190.*
13. _____, 1985c. Forest habitat management guidelines for wildlife. MN DNR Section of Wildlife, St. Paul. Pamphlet.
14. _____, 1985d. Showy mountain-ash deserves its name. The Minnesota Horticulturist. 113(3):92.*
15. Arimond, S. R. 1979. Fruit production in black bear *(Ursus americanus)* habitat of northeastern Minnesota. M.S. Thesis. Univ. of MN. 156 pp.
16. Best, L. B. 1983. Bird use of fencerows: Implication of contemporary fencerow management practices. Wildl. Soc. Bull. 11(4):343-347.
17. Blackbourn, R. A. 1985. Soils, location, establishment and early growth characteristics of important trees and shrubs grown in Minnesota. For. Tech. Note No. MN-20. U.S.D.A, SCS. 33 pp.*
18. Bodin, J. 1984. Growing garden huckleberries. The Minnesota Horticulturist. 112(7):203*
19. Breyer, D. and G. L. Pollard. 1980. Native grass establishment techniques for wildlife habitat or pastures. U.S.D.A., S.C.S. Agronomy Note No. 19. St. Paul. 7 pp.
20. Brockman, C.F. 1968. A guide to field identification. Trees of North America. Golden Press, New York. 280 pp.*
21. Canadian Wildlife Service. 1981. Wildlife habitat: A handbook for Canada's prairies and parklands. Canadian Wildlife Service. Edmonton, Alberta T5K 9Z9. 51 pp.
22. Cotton, L. 1980. All About landscaping. Ortho Books, Chevron Chem. Co. San Francisco. 96 pp.
23. Crockett, J.U. 1971. Annuals. Time-Life Books, Alexandria, VA. 176 pp.*
24. Cumming, R.W. and R.E. Lee. 1960. Contemporary perennials. The Macmillan Co. New York. 363 pp.*
25. Dasmann, R.F. 1968. A different kind of country. The Macmillan Co. New York. 276 pp.
26. Decker, D.J., J.W. Kelly, T.W. Seamans, and R.R. Roth. 1983. Wildlife and timber from private lands: A landowner's guide to planning. Cornell Univ. Ithaca, NY. 57 pp.
27. DeGraaf, R.M. and G. M. Whitman. 1979. Trees, shrubs and vines for attracting birds. Univ. of Mass. Press. Amherst. 194 pp.
28. Diekelmann, J. & R. Schuster. 1982. Natural landscaping. Designing with native plant communities. McGraw Hill. New York. 276 pp.
29. Diekelmann, J. and C. Bruner. An introduction to naturalized landscapes: A guide to Madison's natural lawn ordinance. City of Madison, Wisconsin. 25 pp.
30. Dennis, J. V. 1985. The wildlife gardener. Alfred A. Knopf. New York. 294 pp.
31. Dirr, M. 1984. All about evergreens. Ortho Books, Chevron Chem. Co. San Francisco, 96 pp.
32. Dove, L. E. 1983a. A wildlife plan for small properties. Urban Wildlife Manager's Notebook #1; National Institute for Urban Wildlife. Columbia, MD. 4 pp.

Literature Continued

33. _____ , 1983b. Feeding birds in winter. Urban Wildlife Manager's Notebook - 3. Supplement to Urban Wildlife News, Vol. VII (3). National Institute for Urban Wildlife, Columbia,MD. 4 pp.

34. _____ , 1984a. Housing for nesting birds. Urban Wildlife Manager's Notebook #4. Supplement to Urban Wildlife News, VII (4). National Institute for Urban Wildlife, Columbia, MD 5 pp.

35. _____ , 1984b. Natural landscaping - meadows. Urban Wildlife Manager's notebook - 5. Supplement to Urban Wildlife News, Vol. VIII (1). National Institute for Urban Wildlife, Columbia, MD. 5 pp.

36. _____ , 1985. Reptiles and amphibians. Urban Wildlife Manager's Notebook 1-6. Supplement to Urban Wildlife News. VIII (2):1-8.

37. Duebbert, H. F., E.T. Jacobson, K.F. Higgins, and E.B. Podoll. 1981. Establishment of seeded grasslands for wildlife habitat in the prairie pothole region. U.S.D.I., F.W.S. Sp. Scientific Rpt. — Wildlife No. 234. Washington. 21 pp.

38. Edinger, P. 1972. How to grow herbs. Lane Books. Menlos, CA. 80 pp.*

39. Farmland Committee - DNR. 1985. Woody cover plantings for wildlife. MN DNR. St. Paul. 16 pp.

40. Gill, J.D. and W.M. Healy. 1974. Shrubs and vines for northeastern wildlife. NE Forest Exp. Sta. Upper Darby, PA. 180 pp.*

41. Glasoe, F. 1984. Minnesota: A fruit garden state. The Minnesota Horticulturist. 112(6):183-186.*

42. Gleisner, D. M. 1984. Backyards for the birds. Nongame wildlife leaflet 3. Idaho Dept. of Fish and Game. Boise, ID. 12 pp.

43. Graber, R. R. and J. W. Graber. 1963. A comparative study of bird populations in Ill. 1906-1909 and 1956-1958. Illinois Natl. Hist. Serv. Bull. 28(3):376-528.

44. Graul, W.D. 1975. Cities and birds. Colorado Div. of Wild. Denver. Pamphlet. 6 pp.

45. Gullion, G.W. 1981. Integration of wildlife production into Great Lakes States forestry programs. Pages 28-35. H.C. Black, ed. Effects of forest practices on fish and wildlife production. Soc. Amer. For. Washington. 52 pp.

46. _____ , and A.A. Alm. 1983. Forest management and ruffed grouse populations in a Minnesota coniferous forest. J. of Forestry. 81(8):529-531, 536.

47. _____ , 1984. Managing northern forests for wildlife. The Ruffed Grouse Society, Coraopolis, PA 72 pp.

48. _____ , 1985. Aspen management — an opportunity for maximum integration of wood fiber and wildlife benefits. Trans. No. Amer. Wildl. and Nat. Res. Conf. 50:249-261.

49. Haapaja, M. 1986. Growing flowers in containers. Minnesota guide. Minneapolis Star and Tribune. April 13th ed. Page 2L.*

50. Harlow, W.M. and E.S Harrar. 1958. Textbook of dendrology. McGraw-Hill Book Co. New York. 561 pp.*

51. Harp, H.F. and W.A. Cumming. 1982. Hedges for the prairies. The Minnesota Horticulturist. 110(2):36-43.*

52. Hemphill, J. and R. 1983. Herbs. Their cultivation and usage. Blandford Press. Poole, England. 128 pp.*

53. Henderson, C.L. 1984. Woodworking for wildlife. MN DNR. St. Paul. 48 pp.

54. Hillstrom, J. 1982. Tithonia and the monarchs. The Minnesota Horticulturist. 110(7):216-217.*

55. Holland, W.J. 1968. The moth book — a guide to the moths of North America. Dover Pubs. Inc. New York. 479 pp.

56. Huxley, A. (Ed.). 1973. Deciduous garden trees and shrubs. Macmillan Publ. Co., Inc. New York. 216 pp.*

57. Irons, K. P. 1984. Southern living — growing vegetables and herbs. Oxmoor, Inc. Birmingham, Alabama. 272 pp.*

58. Jackson, D.A. 1976. Nesting use and success in a conifer plantation in Clay County, Minnesota. Loon 48(3):92-94.

59. Jackson, D.W. 1983. Selected vines and groundcovers for the home landscape. The Minnesota Horticulturist.* 111(6):171-173.

60. Jewell, D. G. 1982. You can catch more moths with sugar. The New York Conservationist. 37(1):36-38.

61. Johnson, G.E. 1985. Planting characteristics for trees and shrubs in southwest Minnesota. MN DNR. St. Paul. Mimeo. 6 pp.*

62.	Johnson,	T.R. 1985. Amphibian paradise — fishfree ponds. Missouri Conservationist. 46(5):28-30.
63.	Kantrud,	H.A 1986. Effects of vegetation manipulation on breeding waterfowl in prairie wetlands — a literature review. USFWS - USDI. Fish and Wildlife Technical Report 3. Washington, D.C. 1 pp.
64.	Kitts,	J.R. 1981. Snags for wildlife. Ag. Ext. Serv. Univ. of MN. Ext. Folder 581. 4 pp.
65.	Knox,	G. 1978. Annuals you can grow. Better Homes and Gardens. Meredith Corp. Des Moines. 96 pp.*
66.	Korling,	T. 1972. The prairie: swell and swale. Dundee, IL. 64 pp.
67.	Kuchler,	A.W. 1966. Potential natural vegetation. U.S. Geological Survey, Washington, D.C, Sheet No. 90.
68.	McHarg,	I.L. 1969. Design with nature. The Natural History Press. Garden City, New York. 198 pp.
69.	McKimon,	J. 1981. Choosing evergreens for the Minnesota landscape. The Minnesota Horticulturist. 109(4):115-118.
70.	McKinnon,	J. 1978. Shade trees for northwestern Minnesota. Ag. Ext. Serv. Univ. of MN. Ext. Folder No. 18 - 1978.
71.	Martin,	A.C., H.S. Zim, and A.L. Nelson. 1961. American wildlife and plants. A guide to wildlife and plants. A guide to wildlife food habits. Dover ed. New York. 500 pp.*
72.	Masengarb,	J. 1984. How hardy is hardy? The Minnesota Horticulturist. 112(5):141-148.
73.	Maser,	C., R.G. Anderson, K. Cronock, Jr., J.T. Williams and R.E. Martin. 1979. Dead and down woody material. Pages 78-95. Wildlife habitats in managed forests. Ag. handbook No. 553. J.W. Thomas, Ed. U.S.D.A. Forest Serv. Washington. 512 pp.
74.	Mathisen,	J.E. 1976. An analysis of old growth and forest land use planning — Chippewa National Forest. MN. 9 pp.
75.	Minnesota	Association of Soil and Water Conservation Districts. Forestry Committee. 1986. Minnesota tree handbook. Adventure Publ. Staples, MN. 408 pp.
76.	Moe,	S. 1985. Northern lights: Azaleas for Minnesota. The Minnesota Horticulturist. 113(5):135-143.*
77.	Moyle,	J.B. and E.W. Moyle. 1977. Northland wild flowers. A guide for the Minnesota region. Univ. of MN Press. Minneapolis. 236 pp.
78.	Newfield,	N. 1986. Advice on using hummingbird feeders. Nature Society News. 21(3):9.
79.	Nichols, S.	and L. Entine. 1976. Prairie primer. 44 pp.
80.	Olson,	J.E. 1984. Landscape plants for Iowa. Iowa Coop. Ext. Serv. Iowa State U. Ames. Pm - 212. 111 pp.
81.	Olson, K.W.	1986. Restoring the chestnut. (Editorial comment). Country Journal. 13(3):4-5.*
82.	Opler,	P.A. and G.O. Krizek. 1984. Butterflies east of the great plains. The Johns Hopkins University Press. Baltimore, MD. 294 pp.
83.	Perry,	F. 1974. Complete guide to plants and flowers. Simon and Schuster. New York. 537 pp.*
84.	Peterson,	R.T. and M. McKenney. 1968. A field guide to wildflowers of northeastern and northcentral North America. Houghton Mifflin Co., Boston. 420 pp.*
85.	Porter,	C.L. 1967. Taxonomy of flowering plants. 2nd ed. W.H. Freeman and Co. San Francisco. 472 pp.*
86.	Ray,	G. 1983. Premium trees for the northern landscape. The Minnesota Horticulturist. 111(2):36-41.*
87.	_____,	1984. Premium shrubs for the northern landscape. The Minnesota Horticulturist. 108(5):132-137.*
88.	Ray,	J. 1980. Shelterbelts for farm and town. The Minnesota Horticulturist. 108(9):264-267.
89.	_____,	1981. Meet two gentle tamers of Minnesota wildflowers. The Minnesota Horticulturist. 109(4):109-111.
90.	Ritter,	L.B., Sr. 1983. Attracting birds with woody plants. The Minnesota Horticulturist. 111(6):168-170.*
91.	Robbins,	C.S. 1984. Management to conserve forest ecosystems. Pg. 101-106. Proceedings — workshop on management of nongame species ecological communities. William McComb, ed. Univ. of KY. Lexington, Kentucky.

Literature Continued

92. Robel,   R.J. and N.G. Browning. 1981. Comparative use of woody plantings by nongame birds in Kansas. Wild. Soc. Bull. 9(2):141-148.

93. Scholten,   H. 1981. Effect of field windbreak design on snow distribution patterns in Minnesota. Tech. Bull. 329. Forestry Ser. No. 36. Univ. of MN Ag. Exp. Stat. St. Paul, MN. 22 pp.

94. Shalaway,   S.D. 1985. Fencerow management for nesting birds. Wildl. Soc. Bull. 13(3):302-306.

95. Simmons,   A.G. 1964. Herb gardening in five seasons. D. Van Norstrand. Princeton, NJ. 353 pp.*

96. Sinnes,   A.C. 1981a. All about perennials. Ortho Books. Chevron Chem Co. San Francisco. 96 pp.*

97. _____,   A.C. 1981b. All about annuals. Ortho Books. Chevron Chem. Co. San Fransisco. 96 pp.*

98. Smith,   J.R. 1977. Tree crops: A permanent agriculture. The Devon-Adair Co. Old Greenwich, Conn.

99. Smith,   M. and H. Scholten. 1980. Planting trees for farmstead shelter. Ext. Bull. 196. Univ of MN Ag. Ext. Serv. 16 pp.*

100. Snyder,   L.C. 1980a. Showy shrubs. The Minnesota Horticulturist. 108(2):56-61.*

101. _____,   1980b. Trees and shrubs for northern gardens. Univ. of MN Press, Minneapolis. 411 pp.*

102. _____,   1982. Euonymus. "Burning bush: of the autumn landscape." The Minnesota Horticulturist. 110(8):230-231.

103. _____,   1983a. Array of hardy fruits for Minnesota gardens. The Minnesota Horticulturist. 111(8):241-258.*

104. _____,   1983b. Flowers for northern gardens. Univ. of MN Press, Mpls. 385 pp.

105. Swenson,   S.B. 1930. Winter feeding of birds. Fins, feathers, and fur. (81): 8-13.

106. Thomas,   J.W., Ed. 1979. Wildlife habitats in managed forests — the Blue Mountains of Oregon and Washington. Agriculture Handbook No. 553. U.S.D.A. Forest Serv. Washington. 512 pp.

107. _____,   R.G. Anderson, C. Maser, and E.L. Bull. 1979. Snags. pp. 60-77. Wildlife habitats in managed forests. Ag. handbook No. 553. J.W. Thomas Ed. U.S.D.A. Forest Serv. Washington. 512 pp.

108. _____,   C. Maser, and J.E. Rodiek. 1979. Riparian zones. Pages 40-47 in Wildlife habitats in managed forests. Ag. Handbook No. 553. J.W. Thomas Ed. U.S.D.A. Forest Serv. Washington. 512 pp.

109. U.S. Dept.   of Ag., Forest Service. 1979. Management of northcentral and northeastern forests for nongame birds — Workshop Proc. Gen. Tech. Rpt. NC-51. U.S.D.A. Forest Service. North Central Forest Expt. Station. St. Paul. 268 pp.

110. _____,   1984. Annual Technical Report (2 parts). Soil Conservation Service. Bismarck Plant Materials Center. Part I, 156 pp. Part II, 308 pp.*

111. U.S. Dept.   of Interior. 1966. Landscape development. Field Tech Office. Bur. of Land Management. Bur. Indian Affairs. Littleton, Colorado 128 pp.

112. Van Bruggen,   T. 1976. Wildflowers of the northern plains and Black Hills. 2nd ed. Badlands Nat. Hist. Assn. Interior, S.D. 85 pp.*

113. Vogt, C.   and D. Thompson. 1974. Planning an awareness environment. Minnesota Environmental Sciences Foundation, Inc. Mpls, MN. 102 pp.

114. Welsch,   R.L. 1982. Of trees and dreams: The fiction, fact, and folklore of tree-planting on the northern plains. Nebraska Forest Service. U of Nebraska, Lincoln. 18 pp.

115. Wilson,   W.H.W. 1984. Landscaping with wildflowers and native plants. Ortho Books. Chevron Chem. Co. San Francisco. 96 pp.

116. Wright,   M. 1981. Domesticating the wildflower. The Minnesota Horticulturist. 109(4):100-108.

117. Wyman,   D. 1977. Shrubs and vines for American gardens. Macmillan Publ. Co. Inc. 613 pp.*

118. Yahner,   R. 1980a. Avian winter abundance patterns in farmstead shelterbelts: Weather and temporal effects. 29 pp. Mimeo.

119. _____,   1980b. Breeding bird records for Minnesota shelterbelts. Amer. Birds 34(1):71-73.

* All references marked with an asterisk were used in the preparation of Appendix A.

Glossary

Acre	A unit of land containing 43,560 square feet.
Annual	A plant that lives for one year or one growing season, including some frost-sensitive biennials and perennials which only live for one year in northern climates.
Aquatic Plant	A plant that grows in water.
ASCS	Agricultural Stabilization and Conservation Service. A federal agency in the U.S. Department of Agriculture. County level offices administer federal cost-sharing on conservation practices.
Biennial	A plant that grows from seed and produces leafy growth the first year. In the second year, the plant produces flowers, sets seed and dies.
Browse	Wildlife food comprised of woody material including twigs and buds.
Buffer Zone	A management area around a sensitive environmental site, like a bald eagle nest, in which human activities are prohibited or limited.
Conifer	Trees and shrubs that include pines, firs, spruces, and other cone-bearing plants as well as yews and plants related to yews that produce drupe-like seeds.
Conservation	Wise use of the environment that results in the greatest good for the greatest number of people and wildlife species for the greatest length of time.
CRP	Conservation Reserve Program. A federal program for seeding down highly erodable land in the farmland areas. Farmers are paid through the ASCS for participation in this program.
Cultivar	A horticulturally developed strain of a plant.
Cut Bank	An exposed vertical bank of sand, soil, gravel, or limestone that is created by excavation or natural erosion.
DNR	Department of Natural Resources. A state agency with the legal mandate for management and protection of the state's natural resources.
Diversity	Variety.
Drumming Log	A fallen log on which a male ruffed grouse performs his courtship display.
Ecology	The study of the relationship between living organisms and their environment.
Environment	The living and non-living components that comprise one's surroundings.
Erosion	The process by which soil is lost by the action of wind or water.
Eutrophication	The process by which soil nutrients, e.g. fertilizers, wash into lakes and marshes and cause excessive growth of aquatic plants that eventually die and fill the wetland at an excessive rate.
Evergreen	A conifer that does not lose its needles in winter.

Glossary Continued

Exotic Species A plant or animal that evolved in another region or on another continent and is not native to the area in question.

Farmstead Shelterbelt An arrangement of trees and shrubs planted around the margin of a farm house and out-buildings that helps prevent unnecessary snow drifting and exposure of livestock to winter winds.

Field Windbreak One or a few rows of trees or shrubs planted along fencelines in cropland areas to reduce the effects of soil erosion by winds and designed to deposit snow evenly across croplands.

Forage Plant material that serves as food for animals.

Forb A non-woody plant that is not a grass. This includes annual, biennial, and perennial flowers.

Germination The process by which a seed sprouts after being dormant.

Grit Fine sand or gravel that is swallowed by birds and retained in their gizzards to grind up their food.

Habitat The place where an animal lives.

Hardiness Zone A horticultural zone which refers to the northern-most areas in which a plant species can be expected to be winter hardy.

Hardwood A type of tree with broad leaves, not needles.

Herb A plant, often aromatic, that has medicinal value or a plant that is used for food seasoning.

Herbaceous Vegetation A plant or plants that are not woody and that die back at the end of a growing season.

Herbicide A chemical used to kill plants.

Insecticide A chemical used to kill insects.

Invertebrate An animal that does not possess a backbone.

Landscape A view or vista of scenery depicting the land.

Landscape Architecture The art and science of designing and arranging a parcel of land by contouring the land and planting flowers, grasses, trees, and shrubs to achieve a healthy relationship between people and their surroundings.

Legume A plant which bears its seeds in pods that split into two halves with seeds attached to the lower edge of one of the halves. Legume roots typically have nodules in which atmospheric nitrogen can be transformed into soluble nitrogen usable by plants.

Mast Nuts or acorns.

Midwest For purposes of this book, the Midwest is defined as Minnesota, Iowa, Wisconsin, Michigan, and northern Illinois, Indiana, and Ohio.

Monoculture An area of farm crops or trees characterized by extensive acreages of a single species.

Native Plant A plant species that originally occurred in an area.

Old Growth	A forest stand which has aged to 1.5 times the age at which the timber is normally harvested.
Perennial	A plant that lives for at least several years.
Persistence	The tendency of a tree or shrub's fruit to remain on the plant through the winter.
Pesticide	A chemical manufactured to kill insect or animal pests.
Predator	An animal that captures, kills, and eats prey.
Prey	An animal that is caught, killed, and eaten by predators.
PFM	Private Forest Management. A program of the DNR's Division of Forestry in which assistance and advice is provided to private landowners regarding forest management.
Rip Rap	A layer of medium to large rocks that is used to stabilize banks along ponds, lakes, rivers, and reservoirs.
Riparian	The area of land that is adjacent to a stream or river.
SCS	Soil Conservation Service. A unit of the federal U.S. Department of Agriculture which conducts soil surveys and maintains county offices to provide advice and assistance to landowners, primarily farmers, regarding land use practices that conserve the soil.
Shelter	A place where an animal can hide from predators or the weather to sleep, rest, or raise its young.
Shrub	A woody plant that typically branches near the ground.
Snag	A dead tree.
Structural Habitat Components	Nest boxes and nest platforms, dust and grit, cut banks, cliffs and caves, dens, snags, downed logs and perches, water, salt and other trace minerals, feeders, rock piles, and brush piles that are used by wildlife.
Sucker	The characteristic by which some trees and shrubs send up new sprouts from their root system as a means of vegetative reproduction, generally resulting in the creation of a thicket.
Suet	Fat generally derived from the body of cattle, hogs, or deer. It often can refer more specifically to the fat that surrounds the kidneys of cattle.
Sugaring	A technique of painting a sweet, partially fermented brew on tree trunks at dusk to attract moths for collection or viewing.
SWCD	Soil and Water Conservation District. A locally managed district established to plan and implement comprehensive soil and water conservation plans on a watershed-by-watershed basis through coordination with rural landowners.
Topography	The relief or lay of the land including surface configuration, contours, slopes, and drainage patterns.
Tree	A perennial plant having a permanent, woody, self-supporting main trunk, and usually developing branches at a distance from the ground.

USDA	United States Department of Agriculture. A federal branch of government with the legal mandate to oversee agricultural programs and policies in the United States.
USDI	United States Department of Interior. A federal branch of government with the legal mandate to oversee natural resource programs and policies in the United States.
USFS	United States Forest Service. A unit of the USDA with the legal mandate to manage the nation's national forests.
Vegetative Habitat Components	Living conifers, legumes, butterfly, bee, and moth plants, hummingbird plants, summer plants, fall plants, winter plants, and nut-and acorn-producing plants that are used by wildlife.
Weed	A plant that is out of place.
Wildlife	Native wild animals including birds, mammals, reptiles, amphibians, fish, and invertebrates.
Winter Hardy	The quality of a plant to survive winter weather in a given region.
Woodlot	A tract of forest.

Appendix A
Plants For Use In Landscaping

This appendix is a listing of plants found to have excellent to fair values for wildlife the Midwest. It is organized according to the eight vegetative habitat components. Within each of the eight tables the plants are listed in descending order of quality. The first plants listed are "excellent" followed by "good", and then "fair." Within some of these catagories, trees and shrubs, annuals, and biennials and perennials have been separated to facilitate understanding.

The information contained in this chapter is based on an extensive review of the literature. References used are indicated by an asterisk in the "Literature Cited" section.

These tables can help you identify plants suitable for use on your land if you understand the code letters in the key. The key is presented inside the fold on the back cover of this book. As you review this section, fold out the back cover so the key is available for reference.

Disease and Insect Problems
Disease and insect problems can drastically affect your planting intentions. If a disease or insect problem is indicated by an asterisk after the common name, see Appendix M and consult with your local ASCS, SCS, DNR forestry, or DNR wildlife representative for further recommendations.

Plant Type
The plant type codes are relatively simple categories that will help you identify different groups of plants. Short shrubs (SS) are those 1' to 10' tall, medium shrubs (MS) are those 10' - 15' tall, and tall shrubs (TS) are 15' to 25' tall.

AN	= Annual Forb		**PG**	= Perennial Grass
AQ	= Aquatic Plant		**PL**	= Perennial Legume
AV	= Annual Vine		**PR**	= Perennial Forb
BA	= Biennial Treated As Annual		**PV**	= Perennial Vine
BI	= Biennial		**SS**	= Short Shrub
CO	= Conifer		**TR**	= Tree
MS	= Medium Shrub		**TS**	= Tall Shrub
PA	= Perennial Treated As Annual		**WS**	= Wet Soil Plant

Origin

A native plant (N) is a species that occurs naturally in the Midwest, and a cultivar (C) is a horticulturally developed strain of a native plant that is adapted to the Midwest. An exotic plant (E) is a species or cultivar that is not native to the Midwest. If you are concerned about using native plants for your landscaping project, this column will identify which plants to use.

C = Cultivar Of A Species Native To The Midwest   **N** = Native To The Midwest
E = Not Native To The Midwest

Wildlife Value

"Wildlife value" refers to what type of benefits are provided by a plant. Cover (C) refers to either summer nesting cover or winter shelter and "F" refers to "food" in the form of fruit, berries, grain, sap, seeds, browse, forage, roots, or tubers that are eaten by wildlife. "A" refers to plants which provide both food and cover. "L" means that a plant is eaten by certain butterfly caterpillars. "B" refers to plants that are preferred by butterflies, and "M" identifies plants that are attractive to moths. Honeybee and bumblebee nectar sources are identified by an "E."

Ruby-throated hummingbirds are attracted to flowers marked by an "N." Some plants, primarily annuals, are attractive to bees, moths, butterflies, or hummingbirds and also produce small seeds that are eaten by goldfinches, juncos and other seed-eating birds in winter. Those plants are marked by an "S." Northern orioles are attracted to plants marked by an "O." These code letters do not correspond to the same code letters used in other columns.

A = Both Food And Cover   **L** = Butterfly Caterpillar Plant
B = Butterfly Nectar Plant   **M** = Moth Nectar Source
C = Mainly Cover   **N** = Hummingbird Nectar Plant
E = Honeybee And Bumblebee Nectar Source   **O** = Oriole Nectar Plant
F = Mainly Food   **S** = Seeds Also Eaten By Finches And Juncos

Landscape Uses

"Landscape uses" refer to the various ways that a plant can be used. The codes are self-explanatory. For example, if you wanted to place a hanging basket on your porch with a plant that would attract hummingbirds, review Appendix A for plant component IV and scan for the letter "H" in the landscape uses column. Plants with a "Z" could be used in an herb garden, and a "D" indicates plants which can be used as foundation plants by a house.

The letters used in this column do not mean the same thing in other columns.

A = Edging/Borders   **M** = Privacy Hedges And Screens
B = Backyard   **N** = Flower Garden/Bedding
b = Border Shrub   **P** = Prairie
C = Grassy Nesting Cover   **Q** = Wetland Or Pond
D = Foundation Plants In Yards   **R** = Rock Garden
E = Erosion Control On Slopes   **S** = Shelterbelt/Windbreak
F = Food Plot   **t** = Small Ornamental Trees/Shrubs For Lawns
G = Ground Cover   **T** = Shade Tree In Yard
H = Hanging Basket   **U** = Tall Annuals/ Perennials — Backdrop To
I = Formal Hedge   Borders
J1 = Tub or 2-5 Gallon Container   **V** = Vegetable Garden
J2 = 8" - 12" Diameter Pot   **W** = Woodland
J3 = 4" - 6" Diameter Pot   **X** = Window Boxes
K = Vines For Trellises And Fences   **Y** = Orchard
L = Boulevard Trees   **Z** = Herb Garden

No. Wildlife Species

"No. wildlife species" refers to the number of wildlife species which have been documented to use a plant for food or shelter. Much of this information has been derived from DeGraaf and Whitman (27), Martin, Zim and Nelson (71), and Opler and Krizek (82).

Landscape Score

The "landscape score" is based on articles by Ray (86, 87) and presents a score for trees and shrubs based on their traditional landscaping qualities. It does not include any consideration of wildlife values. Scores for trees are based on criteria of shape (10 points), fall color (10 points), winter interest (10 points), cleanliness (5 points), disease resistance (10 points), pest resistance (10 points), hardiness (10 points) and life expectancy (5 points). A perfect score is 70.

Shrub scores are based on criteria of foliage quality (10 points), form (10 points), floral display (10 points), fragrance (5 points), autumn color (10 points), winter interest (10 points), hardiness (10 points), and disease and pest resistance (10 points). A perfect score is 75.

Hardiness Zones

"Hardiness zones" refer to the hardiness zones shown in Chapter 3.

Plant Characteristics

Plant Characteristics

"Plant characteristics" are important features of a plant that you need to know to avoid problems with the species. For example, a dioecious species (code "D") has male and female flowers on separate plants, so at least two and probably three plants are needed at a site to ensure pollination. Plants which spread by suckering (code "S") are often undesirable in a yard setting but are highly desirable in shelterbelts and woody cover plantings. Other categories included are relatively self-explanatory.

The letters used in this column do not mean the same thing in other columns.

B	= Plant In Containers And Bring Indoors For Winter	M	= Bird Droppings In Vicinity Can Create Problems On Patios, Sidewalks Or Clothes-lines
C	= Dig Up Bulbs/Corms And Bring Indoors During Winter	P	= Pollution Resistant In Cities
D	= Dioecious (plant 2 or more)	R	= Resistant To Drought
E	= Cover With Snow In Winter	S	= Suckers To Form Thicket
F	= Don't Plant Near Red Raspberry	T	= Tolerant Of Salt
L	= Needs Shelter; Plant In Sheltered Location	W	= Cover With Straw In Winter

Height

"Height," given in feet and/or inches, describes the potential height of a species under optimum conditions.

Sun Exposure Requirement

"Sun exposure" refers to the amount of sunlight needed by a plant for adequate or optimum development. Full (code "F") means that a plant should be located in full sunlight and "P" means that a plant will tolerate shade for a part of the day. Some plants will tolerate all conditions (code "A") and others will grow in full shade (code "S").

The letters used in this column do not mean the same thing in other columns.

A	= All (full sun, partial shade, full shade)	P	= Partial Shade
F	= Full	S	= Full Shade

Moisture Preference

"Moisture preference" refers to the amount of moisture needed by a plant for adequate or optimum growth. "D" means a plant will grow in dry soil, and "M" means that a plant will grow in moist soil. Some plants will grow in wet, or water-logged soil (code "W") and other plants are so adaptable that they will grow in conditions that range from wet to dry (code "A").

The letters in this column do not mean the same thing in other columns.

A	= All (wet, moist, dry)	M	= Moist
D	= Dry	W	= Wet

PH Preference

It is important to know the pH of your soil when you develop a landscaping plan. The codes in this column generally describe the different pH tolerances of plants. The pH scale ranges from 0 to 14. A level of 7.0 is neutral. Values less than 7.0 are acid and values more than 7.0 are alkaline. The specific tolerance of plants is presented when available.

A	= Acid Soils (less than 7.0)	N	= Neutral Soils (about 7.0)
AN	= Slightly Acid (6.5 - 7.0)	NB	= Slightly Alkaline (7.0 - 7.5)
B	= Alkaline Soils (greater than 7.0)	R	= Broad Range Of Tolerance

Soil Types

The codes presented here are very general and are suggested to help you get started in a landscaping plan. The county ASCS or SCS office should be consulted if you wish to develop a conservation plan for a farm, however. They have detailed soil maps for most counties. The soils listed for a species are those in which a plant would be expected to do reasonably well.

The letters used in this column do not correspond to the code letters used in other columns.

B	= Broad Range Of Tolerance	P	= Peat
C	= Clay Types	S	= Sand
L	= Loam		

Soil Characteristics

"Soil characteristics" are those qualities of a soil which are critical to the survival of many plants. For example, some plants require a well-drained soil (code "W") while others need a wet, poorly drained soil (code "P"). Some plants need fertile soils (code "F") and others like black cherry or black walnut grow best in a deep rich soil (code "D") or one high in organic content (code "O").

D	= Deep, Rich	P	= Poorly Drained
F	= Fertile	W	= Well Drained
O	= High Organic Content		

Width

Width refers to the potential width in feet of a tree or shrub when mature if grown in optimum conditions. (Keep the mature width in mind when spacing trees and shrubs in a yard or shelterbelt. There is a tendency to crowd plants too close together.)

Plant Group
I. Conifers

Rating Excellent

PLANT NAME	CULTIVAR	Plant Type	Origin	No. Wildlife Species	Wildlife Value	Landscape Score	Landscape Uses	5	4	3S	3N	Plant Characteristics	Height	Sun Exposure	Moisture Preference	pH Preference	Soil Types	Soil Characteristics	Width (ft.)
										Hardiness Zones									
Abies balsamea Balsam fir		CO	N	21	C		BTW	•	•	•	•	R	60	A	WM	4.0-6.5	SL	WO	20-35
Abies concolor White fir		CO	E		C		BT	•	•			LR	50	FP	MD	4.0-6.5	SL	W	10-20
Chamaecyparis thyoides Atlantic white cedar		CO	E		C		BT	•	•				50	FP	WM	A	S	W	30
Juniperus chinensis Chinese juniper	'Ames'	CO	E		A		BDb	•	•			D	6	FP	MD			W	3-9
Juniperus communis Common juniper		CO	E	15	C		BG	•	•			D	4	FP				S	3-9
Juniperus virginiana* Eastern red cedar		CO	N		A		BSMW	•	•	•	•	TR	20	FP	MD	4.7-7.8	CS	W	10-20
Larix decidua European larch		CO	E		C		SB	•	•	•	•		75	F	A			W	29-39
Larix laricina American larch, tamarack		CO	N		C		BSW	•	•	•	•	TR	50	FP	A	4.8-7.5		WOP	15-25
Picea abies Norway spruce		CO	E		C		BSTM	•	•	•	•		60	F	M			W	24-35
Picea glauca White spruce		CO	N	34	A	56/57	BSMW	•	•	•	•	R	100	FP	MD	4.5-7.5	CSL	W	20-30
Picea glauca densata Black hills spruce		CO	E		C	54/57	SBM	•	•	•	•	R	45	FP	MD	4.5-7.5	CSL	W	27
Picea mariana Black spruce		CO	N		C		BW	•	•	•	•		40	FP	A	3.5-7.0		WOP	15-30
Picea pungens* Colorado blue spruce	'glauca'	CO	E	34	A	56/57	BSMD	•	•	•	•	T	100	FP	MD	4.6-6.5	CS	W	20-30
Picea rubens Red spruce		CO	E	34	A		BS	•	•	•	•		70	FP	WM	A			
Pinus banksiana Jack pine		CO	N		C		SW	•	•	•	•	TR	50	F	MD	4.6-6.5	SL	W	20-30
Pinus nigra Austrian pine	var. austriaca	CO	E		C	51/57	BT	•	•			TR		FP	M	AB	CS		30-50
Pinus ponderosa Ponderosa pine	var. scopulorum	CO	E		C		BSTM	•	•	•	•	R	100	FP	MD	4.9-9.1	CSL	W	25-60
Pinus resinosa Red pine		CO	N	47	C	50/57	BSTMW	•	•	•	•	R	80	F	MD	4.5-6.5	SL	W	20-40
Pinus Strobus* Eastern white pine		CO	N	47	C	57/57	BSTMW	•	•	•	•	TR	100	FP	A	4.5-6.5	CS	WP	50-80
Pseudotsuga menziesii Douglas fir	var. glauca	CO	E		C	50/57	BS	•	•			R	60	FP	M	6.0-6.5	SL	W	15-25
Tsuga canadensis Eastern hemlock		CO	N	26	C		SMWI	•	•	•	•		60	A	WM	6.0-8.0		W	25

*See Appendicies M and N concerning undesirable qualities, disease, or insect problems.

Plant Group
I. Conifers

Rating Fair

PLANT NAME	CULTIVAR	Plant Type	Origin	No. Wildlife Species	Wildlife Value	Landscape Score	Landscape Uses	5	4	3S	3N	Plant Characteristics	Height	Sun Exposure	Moisture Preference	pH Preference	Soil Types	Soil Characteristics	Width (ft.)
										Hardiness Zones									
Pinus sylvestris* Scotch pine	Riga, Belgian	CO	E	1	C	54/57	BS	•	•	•	•	R	60	F	MD	4.0-6.5	SL	W	30-50
Thuja occidentalis Northern white cedar American arborvitae		CO	N	4	C		BSMD	•	•	•	•		60	FP	M	6.0-8.0	CS	DOW	10-20
Taxus canadensis Canada yew		CO	N	7	C		BWL	•	•	•	•	D	6	A	M	A		W	9

*See Appendicies M and N.

PLANT NAME	CULTIVAR	Plant Type	Origin	No. Wildlife Species	Wildlife Value	Landscape Score	Landscape Uses	Hardiness Zones				Plant Characteristics	Height	Sun Exposure	Moisture Preference	pH Preference	Soil Types	Soil Characteristics	Width (ft.)
								5	4	3S	3N								
Amorpha canescens Lead plant		PL	N		C		PECBNZ	•	•	•	•		3	F	MD				
Amorpha nana Dwarf indigo		PL	N		C		PEC	•	•	•			1	F	D				
Andropogon gerardi Big bluestem	native	PG	N		C		PEC	•	•	•	•	R	8	F	A		CS	WF	
Andropogon gerardi Big bluestem	Pawnee	PG	C		C		PEC	•	•	•		R	8	F	A		CS	WF	
Andropogon gerardi Big bluestem	Champ	PG	C		C		PEC	•	•	•		R	8	F	A		CS	WF	
Andropogon gerardi Big bluestem	PM-SD-27	PG	C		C		PEC	•	•	•	•	R	8	F	A		CS	WF	
Astragalus adsurgens Prairie milkvetch		PL	N		C		PEC	•	•	•	•		2	F	D				
Astragalus agrestis Purple milkvetch		PL	N		C		PEC	•	•	•	•		2	F	M				
Astragalus canadensis Canada milkvetch		PL	N		C		PEC	•	•	•	•		4	F	WM				
Astragalus crassicarpus Groundplum milkvetch		PL	N		C		PEC	•	•	•	•		1	F	D				
Bouteloua curtipendula Sideoats grama	native	PG	N		C		PEC	•	•	•	•	R	2	F	MD			W	
Bouteloua curtipendula Sideoats grama	Killdeer	PG	C		C		PEC				•	R	2	F	MD			W	
Bouteloua curtipendula Sideoats grama	Pierre	PG	C		C		PEC	•	•	•	•	R	2	F	MD			W	
Bouteloua curtipendula Sideoats grama	Trailway	PG	C		C		PEC	•	•	•		R	2	F	MD			W	
Bouteloua curtipendula Sideoats grama	Butte	PG	C		C		PEC		•	•	•	R	2	F	MD			W	
Lotus purshianus Deer vetch		PL	N		C		PEC	•	•	•	•		2	F	D				
Oxytropis lamberti Purple locoweed		PL	N		C		PEC	•	•	•	•		1	F	D				
Panicum virgatum Switch grass	native	PG	N		C		PEC	•	•	•	•		5	F	A				
Panicum virgatum Switch grass	Nebraska - 28	PG	C		C		PEC		•	•	•		5	F	A				
Panicum virgatum Switch grass	Summer	PG	C		C		PEC	•	•	•			5	F	A				
Panicum virgatum Switch grass	NDG-965-96	PG	C		C		PEC				•		5	F	A				
Panicum virgatum Switch grass	Pathfinder	PG	C		C		PEC	•	•	•			5	F	A				
Panicum virgatum Switch grass	PM-SD-149	PG	C		C		PEC	•	•	•	•		5	F	A				
Petalostemum candidum White prairie clover		PL	N		C		PECN	•	•	•	•		3	F	MD		BL	W	
Petalostemum purpureum Purple prairie clover		PL	N		C		PECN	•	•	•	•		3	F	MD		BL	W	
Psoralea argophylia Silverleaf scurfpea		PL	N		C		PEC	•	•	•	•		2	F	MD			W	
Psoralea esculenta Indian breadroot		PL	N		C		PEC	•	•	•	•		3	F	MD		SL	W	
Schizachyrium scoparium Little bluestem	native	PG	N		C		PEC	•	•	•	•	R	3	F	MD		LS		

Plant Group
II. Grasses & Legumes — Rating **Excellent**

PLANT NAME	CULTIVAR	Plant Type	Origin	No. Wildlife Species	Wildlife Value	Landscape Score	Landscape Uses	5	4	3S	3N	Plant Characteristics	Height	Sun Exposure	Moisture Preference	pH Preference	Soil Types	Soil Characteristics	Width (ft.)
Schizachyrium scoparium — Little bluestem	Camper	PG	C		C		PEC	•	•	•		R	3	F	MD		LS		
Schizachyrium scoparium — Little bluestem	Blaze	PG	C		C		PEC	•	•	•		R	3	F	MD		LS		
Sorgastrum nutans — Indiangrass	native	PG	N		C		PEC	•	•	•	•	R	6	F	MD			W	
Sorgastrum nutans — Indiangrass	Holt	PG	N		C		PEC		•	•		R	6	F	MD			W	
Sorgastrum nutans — Indiangrass	Nebraska-54	PG	C		C		PEC		•	•		R	6	F	MD			W	
Sorgastrum nutans — Indiangrass	Oto	PG	C		C		PEC		•	•		R	6	F	MD			W	
Vicia americana — American vetch		PL	N		C		PEC	•	•	•	•		2	F	M				

Plant Group
II. Grasses & Legumes — Rating **Fair**

PLANT NAME	CULTIVAR	Plant Type	Origin	No. Wildlife Species	Wildlife Value	Landscape Score	Landscape Uses	5	4	3S	3N	Plant Characteristics	Height	Sun Exposure	Moisture Preference	pH Preference	Soil Types	Soil Characteristics	Width (ft.)
Dactylis glomerata — Orchard grass		GR	E		C		EC	•	•	•	•		4	F	M				
Medicago sativa — Alfalfa	Iroquois	PL	E		A		EC	•	•	•	•		3	F	MD	B	L	W	
Trifolium pratense — Red clover		PL	E		A		EC	•	•	•	•		1½	F	MD		LC	W	
Trifolium repens — White clover		PL	E		F		EC	•	•	•	•		½	F	MD		LC B	W	
Lotus corniculatus — Birdsfoot trefoil		PL	E		A		E NG	•	•	•	•		1½	FP	A				

Plant Group
Trees/Shrubs
III. Butterflies/Bee/Moth — Rating **Excellent**

PLANT NAME	CULTIVAR	Plant Type	Origin	No. Wildlife Species	Wildlife Value	Landscape Score	Landscape Uses	5	4	3S	3N	Plant Characteristics	Height	Sun Exposure	Moisture Preference	pH Preference	Soil Types	Soil Characteristics	Width (ft.)
TREES/SHRUBS/VINES																			
Acer nugundo* — Boxelder		TR	N	5	L	30/58	BSW	•	•	•	•	RD	75	FP	MD	5.0-7.0	B	DF	35-50
Aristolochia durior — Dutchman's pipe (all parts are poison)		PV	E		L		BK	•	•				30	FP	M				
Betula spp. — Birches (characteristics vary)	Several spp.	TR	N	9	L	44/58	BW	•	•	•	•		80	FP	M	5.0-8.0	SL	W	
Ceanothus americanus — New Jersey tea		SS	N	13	B		BbD	•	•	•	•		3		A		S		3
Cephalanthus occidentalis — Buttonbush		AQ	N	11	B		BW	•	•				12	FP	WM				9
Cercis canadensis — Eastern redbud		TS	E	2	E		Bt	•				L	20	FP	MD				24
Clethra alnifolia — Sweet pepperbush, Summersweet clethra		SS	E	8	B		BDb	•	•				6		A				6

Plant Name	Cultivar	Plant Type	Origin	No. Wildlife Species	Wildlife Value	Landscape Score	Landscape Uses	Zone 5	Zone 4	Zone 3S	Zone 3N	Plant Characteristics	Height	Sun Exposure	Moisture Preference	pH Preference	Soil Types	Soil Characteristics	Width (ft.)
Eleagnus commutata — Silverberry		SS	N		E		BSEW	•	•	•	•	SR	9	F		to 7.5		W	3
Ledum groenlandicum — Labrador tea		SS	N	5	B		BWR	•	•	•	•		3	W	A				
Lindera benzoin — Spicebush		MS	N	15	L		BWb	•	•				15	A	M			F	
Philadelphicus coronarius — Sweet mock orange		SS	E		BE		BbDt	•	•	•	•		9	FP	M				9
Populus spp. — Aspens (characteristics vary)	Several spp.	TR	N	10	L		W	•	•	•	•	DS	60	A	MD			W	
Prunus spp. — Plum fam. (characteristics vary)	many species	SS MS	N E	6	B														
Quercus spp. — Oak fam. (characteristics vary)	many species	TR	N	14	L														
Rubus spp. — Blackberry fam. (characteristics vary)	many species	SS	N	12	B														
Salix discolor — Pussy willow		TS	N	10	EB		BW	•	•	•	•	D	21	F	WM	5.5-7.5		PD	14
Salix humilis var. microphylia — Prairie willow		SS	N	10	EL		W	•	•	•	•		4	F	D			W	
Salix nigra — Black willow		TR	N	10	BEL		BSW	•	•			D	50	FP	WM	6.5-8.0			20-40
Salix Pentandra — Laurel willow		TR	E	10	BEL		BSM	•	•	•	•		36	FP	WM	up to 8			
Spirea alba — Narrowleaf meadowsweet		SS	N	8	B		B	•	•	•	•	S	4	F	WM	N			
Spirea latifolia — Broadleaf meadowsweet		SS	N	8	B		Bb	•	•	•	•		6	A	D	N			
Spirea tomentosa — Hard hack		SS		8	B			•	•			S	4	A	WM	A			
Symphoricarpos occidentalis — Wolfberry	species	SS	N		EL	37/64	SPE	•	•	•	•	SR	6	A	MD		SL	W	
Symphoricarpos occidentalis — Wolfberry	White hedge	SS	C		EL	37/64	SE	•	•	•	•	SR	6	A	MD		SL	W	
Symphoricarpos orbiculatus — Coralberry	species	SS	N		EL		BSEW	•	•	•		S	3	A	MD			F	3
Symphoricarpos orbiculatus — Coralberry	Roseum	SS	C		EL		BSE	•	•	•	•	S	3	A	MD			F	3
Syringa x hyacinthiflora — Canadian lilac	Maiden's Blush	MS	E		BE		BbDmt	•	•			RS	16	FP	MD	AN	B	FW	12
Syringa josiflexa — Chinese/Hungarian lilac	Royalty	SS	E		BE		BbDmt	•	•			RS	15	FP	MD	AN	B	FW	15
Syringa meyeri — Dwarf Korean lilac	Palibin	SS	E		BE		BbDmt	•	•			RS	5	FP	MD	AN	B	WF	7
Syringa patula — Miss Kim Korean lilac	Miss Kim	SS	E		BE		BbDmt	•	•			R	4	FP	MD	AN	B	FW	4
Syringa x prestoniae — Preston lilac	Miss Canada	SS	E		BE		BbDmt	•	•	•	•	R	10	FP	MD	AN	B	FW	8
Syringa x prestoniae — Preston lilac	Minuet	SS	E		BE		BbDmt	•	•	•	•	R	8	FP	MD	AN	B	FW	6
Syringa x prestoniae — Preston lilac	James MacFarlane	SS	E		BE		BbDmt	•	•	•	•	RS	10	FP	MD	AN	B	FW	10
Syringa x prestoniae — Preston lilac	Donald Wyman	SS	E		BE		BbDmt	•	•	•	•	RS	10	FP	MD	AN	B	FW	10
Viburnum lantana — Wayfaring bush	Aureum, Rogosum	MS	E		E	43/64	BSb	•	•	•	•		15	A	MD				12

Plant Group
Trees/Shrubs
III. Butterflies/Bees/Moths
Rating **Excellent**

PLANT NAME	CULTIVAR	Plant Type	Origin	No. Wildlife Species	Wildlife Value	Landscape Score	Landscape Uses	Hardiness Zones 5	4	3S	3N	Plant Characteristics	Height	Sun Exposure	Moisture Preference	pH Preference	Soil Types	Soil Characteristics	Width (ft.)
Viburnum lantana / Wayfaring bush	Mohigan	MS	E		E	43/64	BSb	•	•	•	•		6	A	MD				12
Weigela florida / Old-fashioned weigela	Red Prince Bristol Red	SS	E		M E		B	•	•				9						6

Plant Group
Annuals
III. Butterfly/Moth/Bee
Rating **Excellent**

PLANT NAME	CULTIVAR	Plant Type	Origin	No. Wildlife Species	Wildlife Value	Landscape Score	Landscape Uses	Hardiness Zones 5	4	3S	3N	Plant Characteristics	Height	Sun Exposure	Moisture Preference	pH Preference	Soil Types	Soil Characteristics	Width (ft.)
Anethum graveolens / Dill		AN	E		E L		Z	•	•	•	•		3	F	MD		B		
Aster ericoides / Heath aster		AN	N	7	BL E		N, J-2	•	•	•	•		3	F	MD				
Aster spp. / Asters	singles	AN	N		BL E		NPW, J-2	•	•	•	•		4	F	MD	NB		WD	
Borago officinalis / Borage		AN	E		E		Z	•	•	•	•	L	3	FP	M		B	W	
Calendula officinalis / Pot marigold		AN	E		B		NXAU, J-2	•	•	•	•		2	FP	MD			WFD	
Campanula medium / Canterbury bells		BA	E		E		NRA,J-2	•	•	•	•		3	FP	MD			WFD	
Cleome hasslerana / Spider flower		AN	E		ES		NUA	•	•	•	•	R	5	FP	MD		B		
Dianthus barbatus / Sweet William		BA	E		B M		ARNJ-3	•	•	•	•		1½	FP	MD	7.0-7.5		W	
Heliotropium arborescens / Heliotrope		AN	E		B M		NUAX J-2	•	•	•	•		2	FP	M			DW O	
Impatiens biflora or capensis / Spotted touch-me-not / Spotted jewelweed		AN	N		ES		NWX, J-2	•	•	•	•		3	S	WM				
Impatiens pallida / Pale touch-me-not		AN	N		ES		NWX, J-2	•	•	•			3	S	WM				
Lathyrus odorata / Sweet pea		AV	E		E		VNHKA	•	•	•	•		8	FP	M	NB		DW FO	
Marjorana hortensis / (See Origanum marjorana)																			
Mirabilis jalapa / Marvel of Peru, Four O'clock		PA	E		M S		NRA	•	•	•	•	RC	2	FP	M		B	W	
Nicotiana alata / Flowering tobacco		AN	E		M S		NUJ-2	•	•	•	•		3	FP	M		B	FWO	
Origanum marjorana / Sweet marjoram		PA	E		E		NZ	•	•	•	•		1	FP			B	W	
Petroselinum hortense / Parsley		BA	E		E		NZ	•	•	•	•		1	FP	M			DO WF	
Petunia x hybrida / Petunia	singles	AN	E		BE MS		NJ3XHA	•	•	•	•		1½	FP	M	B	S	DW	
Pimpinella anisum / Anise		AN	E		L		Z	•	•	•	•		1½	F				WO	
Rudbeckia hirta / Black-eyed susan	native	PA	N	5	BL		NPUA	•	•	•	•	R	3	FP	MD			ODW	
Rudbeckia hirta / Black-eyed susan	"Goldsturm"	PA	C	5	BL		NUA	•	•	•	•	R	3	FP	MD			ODW	
Rudbeckia hirta / Black-eyed susan	"Gloriosa Daisy"	PA	C	5	BL		NUA	•	•	•	•	R	3	FP	MD			ODW	

III. Butterfly/Moth/Bee

Plant Group *Annuals cont.* **Rating Excellent**

Plant Name / Cultivar	Cultivar	Plant Type	Origin	No. Wildlife Species	Wildlife Value	Landscape Score	Landscape Uses	5	4	3S	3N	Plant Characteristics	Height	Sun Exposure	Moisture Preference	pH Preference	Soil Types	Soil Characteristics	Width (ft.)
Salvia splendens — Scarlet sage, Salvia	several	AN	E		ES		NXAJ2	•	•	•	•		2½	FP	MD			ODW	
Satureja montana — Winter savory		PA	E		E		NZAR	•	•	•	•		1	F	M			WO	
Tagetes erecta — African marigold		AN	E	3	BEL		NAJ2J3	•	•	•	•		3	F	MD			W	
Tagetes patula — French marigold		AN	E	3	BEL		NAJ2J3	•	•	•	•		1½	F	MD			W	
Tithonia rotundifolia — Mexican sunflower	Torch	AN	E		B		NUM	•	•	•	•	R	7	F	MD		BL	W	3
Tropaeolum majus — Nasturtium		AN	E		B		NKMX AH	•	•	•	•	R	10	FP	MD		S	W	
Verbena x hybrida — Garden verbena		AN	E	19	BE		GRN, J-3	•	•	•	•	R	1½	F	MD		S	WF	
Zinnia elegans — Zinnia	singles	AN	E		BS		NXAJ1 J2	•	•	•	•	R	3	FP	MD			OWF	

III. Butterfly/Bee/Moth

Plant Group *Biennials/Perennials* **Rating Excellent**

Plant Name / Cultivar	Cultivar	Plant Type	Origin	No. Wildlife Species	Wildlife Value	Landscape Score	Landscape Uses	5	4	3S	3N	Plant Characteristics	Height	Sun Exposure	Moisture Preference	pH Preference	Soil Types	Soil Characteristics	Width (ft.)
Achilea millefolium — Yarrow	species	PR	N	3	B		BPNZR	•	•	•	•	R	2	F	MD			W	
Achilea millefolium — Yarrow	several	PR	CE	3	B		BNZR	•	•	•	•	R	2	F	MD			W	
Althaea rosa — Hollyhock	singles	BI	E		BLE		NU	•	•	•			6	F	MD		B	WF	
Amorpha canescens — Leadplant		PL	N		B		BPNE CZ	•	•	•	•		2	F	MD		S	W	
Anaphalis margaritacea — Pearly everlasting, cudweed		PR	N		L		W	•	•	•	•		2	F	D				
Apocynum cannabinum — Indian hemp		PR	N	43	B		WNP	•	•	•	•		4	FP	MD				
Apocynum medium — Intermediate dogbane		PR	N	43	B		BN	•	•	•	•		4	FP	MD				
Apocynum sibiricum — Sessile-leaved dogbane		PR	N	43	B		PN	•	•	•	•		4	FP	MD				
Aquilegia canadensis — American columbine	species	PR	N		E		DNBW	•	•	•	•		3	PF	M		B	OWF	
Aquilegia canadensis — American columbine	several	PR	C		E		DNB	•	•	•	•		3	PF	M		B	OWF	
Aquilegia vulgaris — European columbine		PR	E		E		DNB	•	•	•			3	PF	M		B	OWF	
Arabis spp. — Rock cress		PR	E		L		RANG	•	•	•	•		2	FP	MD		B		
Asclepias incarnata — Swamp milkweed		PR	N	20	BEL		BPWN	•	•	•	•		4	FP	WM				
Asclepias speciosa — Showy milkweed		PR	N		BEL		P	•	•	•	•		3	FP	M				
Asclepias sullivantii — Prairie milkweed		PR	N	2	BEL		BP	•	•	•	•		5	F	M				
Asclepias syriaca — Common milkweed		PR	N	42	BEL		BNPW	•	•	•	•		3	FP	MD				

Plant Group
Biennials/Perennials cont.
III. Butterfly/Bee/Moth

Rating Excellent

PLANT NAME	CULTIVAR	Plant Type	Origin	No. Wildlife Species	Wildlife Value	Landscape Score	Landscape Uses	Hardiness Zones 5	4	3S	3N	Plant Characteristics	Height	Sun Exposure	Moisture Preference	pH Preference	Soil Types	Soil Characteristics	Width (ft.)
Asclepias tuberosa Butterflyweed		PR	N	9	B		NW	•	•	•	•	R	3	FP	MD		S	WO	
Aster spp. Asters	many species	PR	N	19	BL		BN,J2	•	•	•	•		4	FP	MD		B	W	
Barbarea vulgaris Winter cress		BI	E	18	B		WZ	•	•	•	•		3	F	WM				
Bidens aristosa Tickseed sunflower		PR	N	10	B		WP	•	•	•	•		4	F	WM				
Campanula medium Canterbury bells		BI	E		ES		NRAJ-2	•	•	•	•		3	F	MD			FW	
Carex spp. Sedges	several species	PR	N	8	L		WP	•	•	•	•		1	F	WM				
Centaurea dealbata Persian centaurea		PA	E		BE		BN	•	•	•	•		1½	FP	M		B		
Centaurea macrocephala Centaurea		PR	E		BE		BN	•	•				4	F					
Centaurea montana Mountain bluet		PR	E		BE		BNA	•	•				2	F	M			WF	
Chelone glabra Turtlehead		PR	N		BE		P	•	•				2	F	WM				
Cirsium flodmanii Prairie thistle		PR	N	18	B		BPN	•	•	•	•		2	F	MD				
Daucus carota Queen Anne's Lace, Wild Carrot		BI	E		BE L		W	•	•	•	•		2	FP	MD				
Digitalis purpurea Foxglove		BI	E		E		NU	•	•				5	A	M	A		FWO	
Echinacea purpurea Purple coneflower	native	PR	N	7	B		BPN	•	•	•	•	R	4	FP	MD		S	W	
Echinacea purpurea Purple coneflower	Bright Star, The King	PR	C	7	B		BN	•	•	•	•	R	4	FP	MD		S	W	
Echinacea purpurea Purple coneflower	White Lustre	PR	C	7	B		BN	•	•	•	•	R	4	FP	MD		S	W	
Echinops spp. Globe thistle	Taplow Blue	PR	E		B		BN	•	•	•	•	R	4	FP	MD			W	
Epilobium angustifolium Fireweed		PR	N		M E		NW	•	•	•	•		4	FP	MD			W	
Erigeron spp. Fleabane		BI	N	8	B		W	•	•	•	•		2	F	M				
Eupatorium maculatum Joe Pye-Weed		PR	N	9	BE		B	•	•	•	•		5	FP	WM			F	
Eupatorium perfoliatum Boneset		PR	N	3	BE		NZ	•	•	•	•		3	FP	MD			W	
Euthamia graminifolia Lance-leaved goldenrod		PR	N	18	BE		NP	•	•	•	•		2	F	MD		S	W	
Gaillardia x grandiflora Gaillardia		PR	E		BE		NUA	•	•	•	•	R	3	F	MD			W	
Gentiana septemfida var. lagondechiana Dwarf blue gentian		PR	E		M		N	•	•				1	A	M				
Gladiolus spp. Gladiolus		PR	E		E		NJ-2	•	•	•	•	C	3	F		AN	S	W	
Helianthus laetiflorus Showy Sunflower		PR	N		B		NPU	•	•	•	•	R	4	F	MD		LS	W	
Helianthus maximiliani Maimillian sunflower		PR	N		B		NPU	•	•	•	•	R	5	F	MD		LS	W	
Helianthus occidentalis Western sunflower		PR	N		B		NPU	•	•	•	•	R	3	F	MD		LS	W	

III. Butterfly/Bee/Moth

Plant Group *Biennials/Perennials cont.*

Rating Excellent

Plant Name / Cultivar	Cultivar	Plant Type	Origin	No. Wildlife Species	Wildlife Value	Landscape Score	Landscape Uses	5	4	3S	3N	Plant Characteristics	Height	Sun Exposure	Moisture Preference	pH Preference	Soil Types	Soil Characteristics	Width (ft.)
Heliopsis helianthoides — Oxeye sunflower		PR	N		B		NWPU	•	•	•	•	R	3	F	M		LS	W	
Hemerocallis fulva — Tawny daylily		PR	E		B		NU	•	•	•	•		6	F	MD		B	W	
Hesperis matronalis — Dame's rocket		PR	E		M		N	•	•	•	•		4	PS	MD		B	W	
Houstonia spp. — Houstonia		PR	N	11	B		NWR	•	•	•	•		⅔	F	MD		S	W	
Hyssopus officinalis — Hyssop		PR	E		BE		NZ	•	•	•	•		2	F	D	B		W	
Lespedeza capitata — Bush clover		PR	N		E		NP	•	•	•	•		4	F	MD		S	W	
Levisticum officinale — Lovage		PA	E		E		Z	•					6	FP	M	NB		DOF	
Liatris aspera — Rough blazing star		PR	N	6	BS		NP	•	•	•	•	R	3	FP	MD		B	W	
Liatris cylindracea — Dwarf blazing star		PR	N	6	BS		NPR	•	•	•	•	R	2	FP	D				
Liatris ligulistylus — Meadow blazing star		PR	N	6	BS		NP	•	•	•	•	R	5	FP	MD		B	W	
Liatris punctata — Dotted gayfeather		PR	N	6	BS		NP	•	•	•	•	R	2	FP	MD		SL	W	
Liatris pycnostachya — Prairie blazing star		PR	N	6	BS		NP	•	•	•	•	R	4	FP	M			DF	
Liatris spicata — Gayfeather	species	PR	N	6	BS		NP	•	•	•	•	R	3	F	WM			OW	
Liatris spicata — Gayfeather	Kobold	PR	N	6	BS		NP	•	•	•	•	R	3	F	WM			OW	
Lilium candidum — Madonna lily		PR	E		M		NAU	•	•	•		L	6	FP	M	B	B	W	
Lupinus perennis — Lupine		PR	N		BL		NWP	•	•	•	•		2	A	MD	N	S	W	
Lupinus russel — Lupine	Russel	PR	E		BL		N	•	•	•	•		5	A	MD	N		W	
Melissa officinalis — Lemon balm		PR	E		E		Z	•	•	•	•		2	FP		B		W	
Mentha piperita — Peppermint		PR	E		E		Z	•	•				2	FP	MD			W	
Mentha spicata — Spearmint		PR	E	9	BE		GZ	•	•	•	•		2	PS	MW			D	
Monarda didyma — Scarlet bergamot		PR	E	2	BM		NZA	•	•	•			3	A	WM			FDO	
Monarda fistulosa — Wild bergamot		PR	N	2	BM		NPZ	•	•	•	•		2	F	MD			O	
Muscari spp. — Grape hyacinth		PR	E		E		NGAR	•	•	•	•		½	F	M	N-B		WF	
Narcissus spp. — Daffodil		PR	E		E		NRJ-2	•	•	•			2	FP	M		L	W	
Oenothera biennis — Common evening primrose		BI	N		MS		NU	•	•	•			5	F	MD			W	
Oenothera speciosa — Showy evening primrose		PR	N		MES		NAR	•				C	4	F	MD			W	
Origanum dictamus — Cretan dittany		PR	E		E		NZH	•	•	•	•	B	1	F	M			W	
Origanum vulgare — Wild marjoram		PR	E		E		NZ	•	•	•	•		2	F	D		B	W	

PLANT NAME / CULTIVAR	Plant Type	Origin	No. Wildlife Species	Wildlife Value	Landscape Score	Landscape Uses	5	4	3S	3N	Plant Characteristics	Height	Sun Exposure	Moisture Preference	pH Preference	Soil Types	Soil Characteristics	Width (ft.)
Paeonia spp — Peony / singles	PR	E		B		NAU	•	•	•	•		3	FP	MD		L	WF	3
Physostegia virginiana — Obedient plant	PR	E	2	E		NGU	•	•	•	•		2½	FP	MD		B	W	
Prunella vulgaris — Selfheal	PR	E	14	B		W	•	•				1	FP	M			W	
Rosemarinus officinalis — Rosemary	PR	E				Z	•	•										
Rumex spp. — Docks	PR	E	7	L		NZ	•	•	•	•		2	FP				WF	
Salvia officinalis — Garden sage	PR	E		E		NXAJ2Z	•	•	•	•		2½	FP	M			DOW	
Sedum alboroseum — Pink live-forever	PR	E		BL		NA	•	•	•	•		2	A	M		B	W	
Sedum spectabile — Sedum / Autumn Joy	PR	E		BL		NA	•	•	•	•		2	A	WM		B	W	
Solidago nemoralis — Gray goldenrod	PR	N		BE		NPW	•	•	•	•		3	F	MD		S	W	
Solidago rigida — Stiff goldenrod	PR	N	18	BE		NP	•	•	•	•		5	F	MD		B		
Solidago rugosa — Rough-stemmed goldenrod	PR	N	18	BE		NWP	•	•	•	•		7	F	MD		B	W	
Solidago speciosa — Showy goldenrod	PR	N		BE		NP	•	•	•	•		3	F	MD		B		
Thymus vulgaris — Thyme	PR	E		BE		GZ	•					1	F	MD		S	W	
Trifolium pratense — Red clover	BI PL	E		BE		EC	•	•	•	•		1½	F	MD		LC	W	
Vicia spp. — Vetches	PR	NE	14	BL		P	•	•	•	•		3	F	MD			W	
Viola spp. — Violets	PR	NE	7	L		AGPW NR	•	•	•	•		1	A	MD			WF	

PLANT NAME / CULTIVAR	Plant Type	Origin	No. Wildlife Species	Wildlife Value	Landscape Score	Landscape Uses	5	4	3S	3N	Plant Characteristics	Height	Sun Exposure	Moisture Preference	pH Preference	Soil Types	Soil Characteristics	Width (ft.)
Campsis radicans — Scarlet trumpet vine	PV	E		M		BK	•				L	30						
Celtis occidentalis — Hackberry	TR	N		B	46/58	BSWL	•	•	•	•	R	50	FP	A	6.6-8.0	B	D	50
Cornus spp. — Dogwoods, Characteristics vary / Several	SS	N		B		BSWE	•	•	•	•	S	8	A	WM				
Crataegus spp. — Hawthorne	TS	C N		E		BS	•	•	•	•	R	20-30	FP	A	6.1-8.0	B	W	15-30
Malus spp.* — Apples, crabapples	TR	E		BE		BS	•	•	•	•		18-30	F	MD	5.0-6.5	L	W	18-36
Myrica pensylvanica — Northern bayberry	SS	E	22	F		BEb	•				LD	5		MD		S	W	3
Rhododendron spp. — Azaleas, Characteristics vary / several	SS	N		B		BW	•	•				4						
Rhus typhina — Staghorn sumac	TS	N	5	B	47/64	BSEW	•	•	•	•	D SR	20	FP	MD			W	9

PLANT NAME	CULTIVAR	Plant Type	Origin	No. Wildlife Species	Wildlife Value	Landscape Score	Landscape Uses	Hardiness Zones				Plant Characteristics	Height	Sun Exposure	Moisture Preference	pH Preference	Soil Types	Soil Characteristics	Width (ft.)
								5	4	3S	3N								
Ribes spp.* Currants, Gooseberries Characteristics vary	Several	SS	N		B		BW	•	•	•	•		5-7						
Rosa spp. Roses - wild varieties		SS	N		B		BSPN	•	•	•	•		6							4-9
Rubus spp. Raspberries		SS	N		B		BESW												
Sambucus spp. Elderberries, Characteristics vary	Several	SS	N		B		BESW	•	•	•	•		12	A	A			F		9
Spirea x arguta Garland spirea		SS	E		B		B	•	•				6	F						4
Spirea trilobata Three-lobed spirea		SS	E		B		B	•	•	•			4	F						3
Spirea vanhoutte Vanhoutte spirea		SS	E		B		B	•	•	•			6	F						6
Syringa vulgaris Lilac	French, May-blooming, varieties	MS	E	4	BE		BS	•	•	•	•	SR	18	F	MD	A		W		8
Vaccinium spp. Blueberries		SS	N	5	L		BW	•	•	•	•		2-5	FP	D	A	S	W		2-6
Viburnum spp. Viburnum, Characteristics vary	Several	MS	N		B		BSEW	•	•	•			6-15	FP	MD			W		

*See Appendicies M and N.

PLANT NAME	CULTIVAR	Plant Type	Origin	No. Wildlife Species	Wildlife Value	Landscape Score	Landscape Uses	Hardiness Zones				Plant Characteristics	Height	Sun Exposure	Moisture Preference	pH Preference	Soil Types	Soil Characteristics	Width (ft.)
								5	4	3S	3N								
Ageratum houstonianum Ageratum		AN	E		BS		J2J3 NAX	•	•	•	•		1½	FP	M		B	WF	
Chrysanthemum spp. Painted daisy or Annual daisy	singles	AN	E		B		NAJ2	•	•	•	•		2	FP	MD			D	
Cosmos bipinnatus Cosmos		AN	E		BE		NU	•	•	•	•	L	6	FP	MD		S	W	
Cosmos sulphureus Cosmos		AN	E		BE		NU	•	•	•	•	L	6	FP	MD		S	W	
Dahlia spp. Dahlia	singles	PA	E		B		NA	•	•	•	•	C	2	FP	M			OWF	
Gilia capitata See Ipomopsis capitata																			
Iberis amara/coronaria Hyacinth-flowered candytuft		AN	E		BES		NRAJ3	•	•	•	•	R	2	FP	MD	NB	L	W	
Iberis umbellata Globe candytuft		AN	E		BES		NRAJ3	•	•	•	•	R	1	FP	MD	NB	L	W	
Impatiens balsamina Garden balsam		AN	E		BS		NXAJ2	•	•	•	•		2	A	MD		S	FO	
Ipomoea purpurea Morning glory		AV	E		B		NMKH	•	•	•	•	R	10	FP	MD		SB	W	
Ipomoea tricolor Morning glory		AV	E		B		NMKH	•	•	•	•	R	10	FP	MD		SB	W	
Ipomopsis capitata Standing cypress		AN	E		M		N	•	•	•	•			F	MD				
Limonium bonduelli superbum Algerian statice or Sea lavender		BA	E		B		NRA	•	•	•	•	RT	3	F	D		S	W	
Limonium sinuatum Notchleaf statice or Sea lavender		BA	E		B		NRA	•	•	•	•	RT	2½	F	D		S	W	

III. Butterfly/Bee/Moth

Plant Group *Annuals cont.* — **Rating Fair**

PLANT NAME / CULTIVAR	Plant Type	Origin	No. Wildlife Species	Wildlife Value	Landscape Score	Landscape Uses	Zone 5	Zone 4	Zone 3S	Zone 3N	Plant Characteristics	Height	Sun Exposure	Moisture Preference	pH Preference	Soil Types	Soil Characteristics	Width (ft.)
Limonium suworowii — Russian statice or Sea lavender	BA	E		B		NRA	•	•	•	•	RT	1	F	D		S	W	
Phaseolus coccineus — Scarlet runner bean	AV	E		E		G	•	•	•	•		10	FP	MD				
Phlox drummondi — Annual phlox	AN	E		BS		GNA J2R	•	•	•	•		1½	FP	M		S	OWF	
Salpiglossis sinuata — Painted tongue	AN	E		B		NU	•	•	•	•		3	F	MD	B	SL	OW FD	
Scabiosa atropurpurea — Pincushion flower	AN	E		B		NA	•	•	•	•		3	F	MD	B		OD WF	
Senecio cineraria — Dusty miller	PA	E		B		NAJ-3	•	•	•	•	R	1½	FP	D		S	WO	

Plant Group *Biennials/Perennial* — **Rating Fair**

PLANT NAME / CULTIVAR	Plant Type	Origin	No. Wildlife Species	Wildlife Value	Landscape Score	Landscape Uses	Zone 5	Zone 4	Zone 3S	Zone 3N	Plant Characteristics	Height	Sun Exposure	Moisture Preference	pH Preference	Soil Types	Soil Characteristics	Width (ft.)
Aconitum napellus — Monkshood	PR	E		E		NA	•	•	•	•		4	P	M		B		
Agastache foeniculum — Blue giant hyssop	PR	N		B		NPWU	•	•	•	•		4	FP	MD			W	
Aster nova-angliae — New England aster	PR	N		B		NWJ2	•	•	•	•		4	A	A		SL	WF	
Aubrieta deltoide — Purple rock cress	PR	E		B		NRA	•	•	•			1	F	MD	B		W	
Baptisia tinctoria — Wild indigo	PR	N		B		NPW	•	•	•	•		3	F	MD		L	WF	
Caltha palustris — Marsh marigold	PR	N		E		F	•	•	•	•		1½	F	W		L	DO	
Chicorium intybus — Chicory	PR	E		B		N	•	•	•	•		4	F	MD			W	
Colchicum speciosum — Showy autumn crocus	PR	E		B		NR	•	•				1	FP	MD			W	
Crocus neapolitanus — Crocus	PR	E		E		NAR	•	•	•			1	F	MD		L	W	
Delphinium spp. — Delphinium	PR	E		E		NU	•	•	•	•		5	F	MD	NB		DO WF	
Echinacea pallida — Pale purple coneflower	PR	N		B		NP	•	•	•	•	R	5	F	MD		SL	W	
Fragaria virginianum — Wild strawberry	PR	N	5	B		GE	•	•	•	•	W	1	F	MD		LS	W	
Fuchsia triphylla — Fuchsia - container plant only	PR	E		BE		HXN					BL	2	PS	M				
Iberis sempervirens — Candytuft (singles)	PR	E		BE		NARE	•	•	•	•		1	FP	M			W	
Iris shrevi — Blue flag iris	PR	N		B		NQ	•	•	•	•		3	F	WM	A			
Iris sibirica — Iris	PR	E		B		N	•	•	•	•		3	FP	A	AN	B	F	
Lobelia cardinalis — Cardinal flower	PR	N		ME		NW	•	•	•	•		4	A	WM		SL	WO	
Lotus corniculatus — Bird's foot trefoil	PL	E		B		NEGX	•	•	•	•		1½	FP	A				

PLANT NAME / CULTIVAR	Plant Type	Origin	No. Wildlife Species	Wildlife Value	Landscape Score	Landscape Uses	5	4	3S	3N	Plant Characteristics	Height	Sun Exposure	Moisture Preference	pH Preference	Soil Types	Soil Characteristics	Width (ft.)
Medicago sativa — Alfalfa	PL	E	5	BL		EC	•	•	•	•		3	F	MD	B	L	W	
Mertensia virginica — Bluebells	PR	N		E		NW	•	•	•	•		2	PS	M			O	
Nepeta cataria — Catnip	PR	E		ES		Z	•	•	•			3	FP	MD		LS	DWF	
Papaver orientale — Oriental poppy	PR	E		E		NR	•	•	•	•		4	FP	M		S	FOW	
Penstemon digitalis — Foxglove penstemon	PR	N		ELS		NP	•	•	•		R	4	FP	D		S	W	
Penstemon grandiflorus — Large-flowered penstemon	PR	N		ELS		NP	•	•	•	•	R	2	F	D		S	W	
Petalostemum candidum — White prairie clover	PL	N		B		NP EC	•	•	•	•		3	F	MD		LB	W	
Petalostemum purpureum — Purple prairie clover	PL	N		B		NP EC	•	•	•	•		3	F	MD		LB	W	
Phlox divaricata — Sweet william phlox	PR	N	3	BS		NWJ2	•	•	•	•		2	PS	M		L	WD	
Phlox paniculata — Summer phlox	PR	N	3	BE MS		NAJ2	•	•	•	•	L	4	FP	M			DFO	
Phlox pilosa — Prairie phlox, Downy phlox	PR	N		BE MS		NPWJ2	•	•	•	•		2	FP	MD		LS		
Potentilla sp. — Cinquefoil	PR	N	9			NW	•	•	•	•		3	FP	MD				
Primula spp. — Primrose (vulgaris, japonica)	PR	E		B		NJ3	•	•	•	•		2	PS	M		B	DOW	
Psoralea esculenta — Indian breadroot	PR	N		B		PE C	•	•	•	•		3	F	MD		SL	W	
Pulsatilla nuttalliana — Pasque flower	PR	N		E		NPR	•	•	•	•	R	1	F	MD	7.0-8.0	LS	W	
Ratibida columnifera — Upright prairie coneflower	PR	N		B		NP	•	•	•	•		3	F	MD		L	W	
Ratibida pinnata — Grayhead prairie coneflower	PR	N		B		NPW	•	•	•			3	F	MD		CL		
Schizachyrium scoparium — Little bluestem	PG	N	5	L		PEC	•	•	•	•	R	3	F	MD		S		
Silphium lacinatum — Rosinweed, Compass plant	PR	N		B		NPU	•	•				8	F	MD		L	W	
Silphium perfoliatum — Cup plant	PR	N		B		NPU	•	•				6	F	MD		L	WF	
Trifolium repens — White clover	PL	E		BE		EC	•	•	•	•		½	F	MD		BLC	W	
Veronica spp. — Speedwell	PE	E		E		NAR	•	•				1	FP	M			W	

Plant Group: Trees/Shrubs — Rating Excellent
IV. Hummingbird/Oriole

Plant Name	Cultivar	Plant Type	Origin	No. Wildlife Species	Wildlife Value	Landscape Score	Landscape Uses	5	4	3S	3N	Plant Characteristics	Height	Sun Exposure	Moisture Preference	pH Preference	Soil Types	Soil Characteristics	Width (ft.)
Campsis radicans — Scarlet trumpet vine		PV	E		N		BK	•				L	30						
Catalpa speciosa — Northern catalpa		TR	E		N		BT	•	•	•		L	75		M				30-50
Lonicera x brownii — Scarlet trumpet honeysuckle	"Dropmore"	PV	E		NO		BK	•	•	•	•		2½	F	MD				
Symphoricarpos orbiculatus — Coralberry	species	SS	N	15	N		BESW	•	•	•		S	3	FP	MD			F	3
Weigela florida — Old-fashioned weigela	Bristol Red, Red Prince	SS	E		N		B	•	•				9						6

Plant Group: Annuals — Rating Excellent
IV. Hummingbird/Oriole

Plant Name	Cultivar	Plant Type	Origin	No. Wildlife Species	Wildlife Value	Landscape Score	Landscape Uses	5	4	3S	3N	Plant Characteristics	Height	Sun Exposure	Moisture Preference	pH Preference	Soil Types	Soil Characteristics	Width (ft.)
Fuchsia riccartoni — Hardy fuchsia		AN	E		N		NAH	•	•	•	•		2	PS					
Impatiens biflora or capensis — Spotted jewelweed or spotted touch-me-not		AN	N		N		NWX, J-2	•	•	•	•		3	S	WM				
Impatiens pallida — Pale touch-me-not		AN	N		N		NJWX, J-2	•	•	•			3	S	WM				
Ipomopsis capitata — Standing cypress or Blue thimble flower		AN	E		N		N	•	•	•	•			F	MD				
Nicotiana sanderae — Sander tobacco		AN	E		N		N, J2	•	•	•	•		3	F			B		
Petunia x hybrida — Petunia	singles	AN	E		N		J3, XNHA	•	•	•	•		1½	FP	M	B	S	DW	
Phaseolus coccineus — Scarlet runner pole bean		AV	E		N		G	•	•	•	•		9	FP	MD				
Phaseolus coccineus — White Dutch runner bean		AV	E		N		G	•	•	•	•		10	FP	MD				
Phaseolus coccineus — Scarlet runner bushbean		AV	E		N		G	•	•	•	•		1½	FP	MD				
Salvia splendens — Scarlet sage	several	AN	E		NS		NXA, J2	•	•	•	•		2½	FP	MD			DOW	

Plant Group: Biennials/Perennial — Rating Excellent
IV. Hummingbird/Oriole

Plant Name	Cultivar	Plant Type	Origin	No. Wildlife Species	Wildlife Value	Landscape Score	Landscape Uses	5	4	3S	3N	Plant Characteristics	Height	Sun Exposure	Moisture Preference	pH Preference	Soil Types	Soil Characteristics	Width (ft.)
Althaea rosa — Hollyhock	singles	BI	E		NO		NU	•	•	•	•		6	F	MD		B	WF	
Amaryllis belladonna — Amaryllis		PR	E		N		NJ-2	•				B	2½	F	MD				
Aquilegia canadensis — American columbine	native	PR	N		N		DNBW	•	•	•	•		3	PF	M		B	FOW	
Aquilegia canadensis — American columbine	several	PR	C		N		DNB	•	•	•	•		3	PF	M		B	FOW	

PLANT NAME	CULTIVAR	Plant Type	Origin	No. Wildlife Species	Wildlife Value	Landscape Score	Landscape Uses	5	4	3S	3N	Plant Characteristics	Height	Sun Exposure	Moisture Preference	pH Preference	Soil Types	Soil Characteristics	Width (ft.)
Aquilegia vulgaris — European columbine		PR	E		N		DNB	•	•	•	•		3	PF	M		B	FOW	
Delphinium cardinale — Delphinium		PR	E		N		N	•	•										
Delphinium nudicale — Delphinium		PR	E		N		N	•	•										
Digitalis purpurea — Foxglove		BI	E		N		NU	•	•				5	A	M	A		FOW	
Epilobium angustifolium — Fireweed		PR	N		N		NW	•	•	•	•		4	FP	MD			W	
Gentiana septemfida var. lagodechiana, Dwarf blue gentian		PR	E		N		N	•	•				1	A	M				
Gladiolus cardinalis — Gladiolus	red colors	PR	E		N		N J-2	•	•	•	•	C	3	F		AN	S	W	
Hemerocallis flava — Daylily		PR	E		NO		N	•	•	•	•		4	A	MD		B	O	
Heuchera sanguinea — Coral bells	several	PR	E		N		N	•	•	•	•		2½	FP	MD			WO	
Hibiscus syriaca — Rose of Sharon	singles, red colors	SS	E		NO		BNJ-1D	•					10	F	M			WF	
Hosta spp. — Hosta		PR	E		N		N	•	•	•	•		2	PS	MD		B	WO	
Liatris spp. — Blazing stars		PR	N		NS		NP	•	•	•	•		4	FP	MD		LS	W	
Lilium michiganense — Turk's cap lily		PR	N		NC		NWU	•	•	•			8	FP	M			DF	
Lilium philadelphicum — Wood lily		PR	N		NC	W	•		•	•	•		2	FP	MD	A			
Lilium tigrinum — Tiger lily		PR	E		NO		NEAU	•	•	•	•		3	F	M	N		WO	
Lobelia cardinalis — Cardinal flower		PR	N		N		NW	•	•	•	•		4	A	WM		SL	WO	
Monarda didyma — Scarlet bergamot	Cambridge Scarlet Garden View	PR	E		N		NZA	•	•	•			3	A	WM			FO D	
Penstemon gloxinoides — Penstemon	Firebird	PR	E		NS		J-2,N,U	•	•				2	F	MD		S	W	
Phlox decussata — Moss pink		PR	E		NS		N,J2	•	•	•	•		4	F	MD				
Phlox divaricata — Sweet William, Wild blue phlox		PR	N		NS		NW,J2	•	•	•	•		2	PS	M		L	WD	
Phlox spp. — Perennial phlox		PR	N		NS		N,J2	•	•	•	•		4	FP	M		L	WD	

PLANT NAME	CULTIVAR	Plant Type	Origin	No. Wildlife Species	Wildlife Value	Landscape Score	Landscape Uses	5	4	3S	3N	Plant Characteristics	Height	Sun Exposure	Moisture Preference	pH Preference	Soil Types	Soil Characteristics	Width (ft.)
Ceanothus americanus — New Jersey tea		SS	N		N		BbD	•	•	•	•		3			A	S		3
Cercis canadensis — Eastern redbud		TS	E		N		Bt	•				L	20	FP	MD				24
Crataegus crus-galli — Cockspur hawthorn	Splendens, inermis	TS	C		N	62/64	BStb	•	•			SR	20	FP	A	6.1-8.0	C	W	24

Plant Group
Trees/Shrubs cont.
IV. Hummingbird/Oriole

Rating Fair

Plant Name	Cultivar	Plant Type	Origin	No. Wildlife Species	Wildlife Value	Landscape Score	Landscape Uses	5	4	3S	3N	Plant Characteristics	Height	Sun Exposure	Moisture Preference	pH Preference	Soil Types	Soil Characteristics	Width (ft.)
Crataegus phaenopyrum — Washington hawthorn		TR	E		N		BStL	•	•			R	20	F	MD	6.1-8.0	B		18
Kolkwitzia amabilis — Beauty-bush		SS	E		N		Bb	•				L	9	FP	MD	B	B		9
Liriodendron tulipifera — Tulip tree		TR	E	9	N		BTL	•				L	100	FP	M			DW	45
Lonicera spp.* — Honeysuckle	several	SS	E		N		BS	•	•	•	•		10	F	MD				3-9
Malus spp. — Apples, crabapples	several	TR	NC		N			•	•	•	•	CB							18-36
Rhododendron spp. — Azaleas	several	SS MS	NE		N		NBW	•	•				2-36						3-6
Ribes sanguineum — Red currant		TS SS	N		N		BSW						5	FP					8
Syringa spp. — Lilacs	many	MS	E		N		BS	•	•	•	•	SR	18	F	MD	A		W	

*See Appendicies M and N.

Plant Group
Annuals
IV. Hummingbird/Oriole

Rating Fair

Plant Name	Cultivar	Plant Type	Origin	No. Wildlife Species	Wildlife Value	Landscape Score	Landscape Uses	5	4	3S	3N	Plant Characteristics	Height	Sun Exposure	Moisture Preference	pH Preference	Soil Types	Soil Characteristics	Width (ft.)
Antirrhinum majus — Snapdragon		AN	E		N		NAU	•	•	•	•		3	FP	MD	NB		DFW	
Begonia x sempervirens-cultorum — Wax begonia		AN	E		N		BNAIH, J3	•	•	•	•		¾	A	M			DFW	
Cleome hasslerana — Spider flower		AN	E		NS		NUA	•	•	•	•	R	5	FP	MD		B		
Consolida regalis — Larkspur		AN	E		N		NU	•	•	•	•		5	FP				WF	
Dahlia spp. — Dahlia	singles	PA	E		N		NA	•	•	•	•	C	2	FP	M			FOW	
Dianthus barbatus — Sweet William		BA	E		N		ARNJ-2	•	•	•	•		1½	FP	MD	7.0-7.5		W	
Dianthus chinensis — China pink	singles	AN	E		N		NRAJ-3	•	•	•	•		1	FP	MD	7.0-7.5		W	
Hibiscus manihot — Sunset hibicus		AN	E		N		N	•	•	•	•		9	F	M			F	
Hibiscus trionum — Flower-of-an-hour		AN	E		N		N	•	•	•	•		2	F	M			F	
Impatiens balsamina — Garden balsam		AN	E		NS		NXA,J2	•	•	•	•		2	A	MD		S	FO	
Ipomoea coccinea — Scarlet star glory		AV	E		N		NMKH	•	•	•	•		10	FP	MD		S	W	
Ipomoea multifida — Cardinal climber		AV	E		N		NMKH	•	•	•	•		20	FP	MD		S	WF	
Ipomoea purpurea — Scarlet morning glory		AV	E		N		NMKH	•	•	•	•	R	10	FP	MD		SB	W	
Ipomoea quamoclit — Cypress vine	Hearts 'n' Honey	AV	E		N		NMKH	•	•	•	•		20	FP	MD		S	WF	
Mirabilis jalapa — Four O'Clock, Marvel of Peru		PA	E		NS		NRA	•	•	•	•	RC	2	FP	M		B	W	
Pelargonium x hortorum — Geranium		PA	E		N		NAH,J1 J2	•	•	•	•		2	FP	MD	AN		DF WO	

Plant Group
Annuals cont.
IV. Hummingbird/ Oriole

Rating Fair

PLANT NAME	CULTIVAR	Plant Type	Origin	No. Wildlife Species	Wildlife Value	Landscape Score	Landscape Uses	Hardiness Zones 5	4	3S	3N	Plant Characteristics	Height	Sun Exposure	Moisture Preference	pH Preference	Soil Types	Soil Characteristics	Width (ft.)
Scabiosa atropurpurea Pincushion flower		AN	E		N		NA	•	•	•	•		3	F	MD	B		DF WO	
Tagetes erecta African marigold		AV	E		N		NAU,J2 J3	•	•	•	•		3	FP	MD		L	W	
Tagetes patula French marigold	singles	AV	E		N		NA,J2, J3	•	•	•	•		1½	FP	MD		L	W	
Tithonia rotundifolia Mexican sunflower		AN	E		N		NUM	•	•	•	•	R	7	F	MD		BL	W	2½
Tropaeolum majus Nasturtium		AV	E		N		HXAN MK	•	•	•	•	R	10	FP	MD		S	W	
Tropaeolum speciosum Flame flower		AV	E		N		NH	•	•	•	•		10	FP	MD				
Verbena x hybrida Garden verbena		AV	E		N		NGRJ-3	•	•	•	•	R	1½	F	MD		S	WF	

Plant Group
Biennials/Perennial
IV. Hummingbird/ Oriole

Rating Fair

PLANT NAME	CULTIVAR	Plant Type	Origin	No. Wildlife Species	Wildlife Value	Landscape Score	Landscape Uses	Hardiness Zones 5	4	3S	3N	Plant Characteristics	Height	Sun Exposure	Moisture Preference	pH Preference	Soil Types	Soil Characteristics	Width (ft.)
Asclepias tuberosa Butterflyweed		PR	N		N		NW	•	•	•	•	R	3	FP	MD		S	WO	
Delphinium elatum Delphinium		PR	E		N		NU	•	•	•	•	F	4	F	MD	NB		WF DO	
Iris spp. Iris	several	PR	E		N		N	•	•	•	•		3	FP	A	AN	B	F	
Mertensia virginica Bluebells		PR	N		N		NW	•	•	•	•		2	PS	M			O	
Oenothera speciosa Showy evening primrose		PR	N		N		NAR	•				C	4	F	MD			W	
Parthenocissus quinquefolia Virginia creeper		PV	N	37	N		NW BK	•	•	•	•		30	A	MD		B		
Silphium perfoliatum Cup plant		PR	N		N		NPU	•	•				6	F	MD		L	WF	
Tulipa spp. Tulip		PR	E		N		NX	•	•	•	•		2	FP	M		L	W	
Zinnia elegans Zinnia		AN	E		NS		NXA,J1 J2	•	•	•	•	R	3	FP	MD		L	DFW O	

Plant Group
Trees/Shrubs/Aquatics
V. Summer Plants

Rating: Excellent

PLANT NAME	CULTIVAR	Plant Type	Origin	No. Wildlife Species	Wildlife Value	Landscape Score	Landscape Uses	Hardiness Zones 5	4	3S	3N	Plant Characteristics	Height	Sun Exposure	Moisture Preference	pH Preference	Soil Types	Soil Characteristics	Width (ft.)
Acer ginnala Amur maple, Ginnala maple		TS	E		C	57/64	BStM	•	•	•	•		18	FP	MD	6-7	SL	W	10 +
Acer ginnala Dwarf ginnala maple		SS	E		C		BStMb	•	•	•	•		10	FP	MD	6-7	SL	W	10 +
Amelanchier alnifolia* Saskatoon berry	species	SS	N	58	F		BSWP	•	•	•	•	DS	6	FP	MD	AB		W	6-8
Amelanchier alnifolia* Saskatoon berry	Regent	SS	C	58	F		BSWP	•	•	•	•	DS	6	FP	MD	AB		W	6-8
Amelanchier arborea Downy serviceberry		TS	N	40	F		TBSWt	•	•	•	•		40	A	MD			DFO	15-18
Amelanchier bartramiana Bartram serviceberry		SS	N	39	F		BWt	•	•	•	•		4	FP	M			F	4
Amelanchier canadensis Shadblow serviceberry		TS	N	26	F		BWt	•	•	•	•		18	A	WM			P	12
Amelanchier x grandiflora Apple serviceberry		TS	N	58	F		BSWt	•	•	•	•	S	25	FP	M				18
Amelanchier laevis Alleghany serviceberry		TS	N	58	F	49/64	BWSt	•	•	•	•	L	30	FP	MD	AN			18-24
Amelanchier stolonifera Running serviceberry		SS	N		F		BW	•	•	•	•	S	6						6
Aralia nudicaulis Wild sarsaparilla		PR	N		F		NW	•	•	•	•		2						2
Chara spp. Musk grass		AQ	N	20	F		Q	•	•	•	•								
Echinochloa spp. Wild millet		AQ	N	29	F		Q	•	•	•	•								
Eleocharis spp. Spike rush		AQ	N	29	F		Q	•	•	•	•								
Equisetum spp. Horsetail		WS	N	6	A		Q	•	•	•	•								
Fragaria spp. Junebearing strawberry	Cyclone	PR	E	31	F		GE	•	•			SLW	1	F	MD		LS	W	
Fragaria spp. Junebearing strawberry	Veestar, Redcoat, Trumpeter, Sparkle, Bounty	PR	E	31	F		GE	•	•	•	•	SLW	1	F	MD		LS	W	
Fragaria spp. Everbearing strawberry	Ogallala, Super-fection, Fort Laramie	PR	E	31	F		GE	•	•	•	•	WSL	1	F	MD		LS	W	
Lemna spp. Duckweed		AQ	N	16	F		Q	•	•	•	•								
Morus alba tatarica* Russian mulberry	full size	TR	E	44	F		BStT	•	•	•	•	DMR	30	FP	M		CS	FD	24
Morus alba tatarica* Russian mulberry	dwarf	SS	E	44	F		BSt	•	•	•	•	DMR	6	FP	M		CS	FD	6
Morus rubra* Red mulberry		TR	N	44	F		BSW	•				M	18	FP	WM		L	FD	30
Myriophyllum spp. Water milfoil		AQ	N	14	F		Q	•	•	•	•								
Najas flexilis Northern naiad		AQ	N	19	F		Q	•	•	•	•								
Phragmites spp. Wild cane		WS	N		C		Q	•	•	•	•								
Polygonum spp. Smartweed		WS	N	66	F		Q	•	•	•	•								
Potamogeton spp. Pondweed		AQ	N	40	F		A	•	•	•	•								

*See Appendicies M and N.

91

PLANT NAME	CULTIVAR	Plant Type	Origin	No. Wildlife Species	Wildlife Value	Landscape Score	Landscape Uses	5	4	3S	3N	Plant Characteristics	Height	Sun Exposure	Moisture Preference	pH Preference	Soil Types	Soil Characteristics	Width (ft.)
Prunus americana — Wild plum		MS	N	16	A	44/58	BSWP	•	•	•	•	SR	18	FP	MD	6.6-7.5	LS	W	15-25
Prunus cerasus — Pie cherry	Meteor	TS	E	81	F		BSt	•	•	•		M	18					W	18
Prunus cerasus — Pie cherry	North Star	SS	E	81	F		Bt	•	•	•			12					W	10
Prunus cerasus — Pie cherry	Mesabi	SS	E	81	F		B	•	•	•	•		8					W	6
Prunus fructicosa — European dwarf cherry, Mongolian cherry	'Scarlet'	SS	E	81	A		S	•	•	•	•	S	6	F	A		SL	FDPW	3
Prunus japonica — Japanese bush cherry		SS	E		F		BS	•	•	•	•		4						24
Prunus maaki — Amur chokecherry		TR	E		F		BSTt	•	•	•	•		40	F	MD		B	W	15
Prunus nigra — Canada plum		MS	N		A		Bts	•	•	•	•	R	15	FP		N			18
Prunus pensylvanica — Pin cherry	species	MS	N	81	F		BWtS	•	•	•	•	M	10-30	FP	MD				18
Prunus pensylvanica — Pin cherry	Stockton	MS	C	81	F		BtS	•	•	•	•		30	FP	MD				40-56
Prunus serotina — Black cherry		TR	N	81	F	37/58	BWST	•	•	•	•	M	60	FP	MD				to 15
Prunus tomentosa — Nanking cherry	Drilea, Orient	MS	E	49	F	48/48	BSltMb	•	•	•	•		15	F	MD	N	SLC	W	15-35
Prunus virginiana — Common chokecherry	species	TS	N	81	A		BSWP	•	•	•	•	SR	20	A	MD	6.5-7.5	SL	WF	
Prunus virginiana — Common chokecherry	Shubert	TS	C	81	A		BStl	•	•	•	•	SR	20	A	MD	6.5-7.5	SL	WF	15-35
Prunus virginiana — Common chokecherry	Canada red	TS	C	81	A		BSt	•	•	•	•	SR	20	A	MD	6.5-7.5	SL	WF	15-35
Prunus spp. — Cherry plum	Sapalta, Compass	SS	E		F		B	•	•	•	•		6						4
Prunus spp. — Cherry plum	Red diamond	SS	E		F		B	•	•	•	•		6						4
Rubus allegheniensis — Highbush blackberry	species	SS	N	49	A		BSW	•	•	•		EWLS	9	F					9
Rubus allegheniensis — Highbush blackberry	thornfree	SS	C	49	A		BS	•				EWLS	9	F					9
Rubus flagellaris — Northern dewberry		SS	N	49	F		BW	•	•				2	F	MD				2
Rubus occidentalis* — Black raspberry	species	SS	N	97	A		BSW	•	•				5	F	MD				9
Rubus occidentalis* — Black raspberry	Dundee, Bristol, Blackhawk*	SS	C	97	A		BS	•	•				5	F	MD				9
Rubus odoratus — Flowering raspberry		SS	E	49	F		BW	•	•				5	PS	M				9
Rubus parviflorus — Thimbleberry		SS	N		F		BW	•	•	•	•	E	6	F	MD				3
Rubus spp. — Purple raspberry	Amethyst, Brandywine	SS	E	97	A		BS	•	•	•	•		5	F	MD				3
Rubus idaeus var. strigosus — Red raspberry	species	SS	N	97	A		BSWE	•	•	•	•		5	F	MD				3
Rubus idaeus var. strigosus — Red raspberry	Heritage	SS	E	97	A		BSE	•	•	•			5	F	MD				3

*See Appendicies M and N.

PLANT NAME / CULTIVAR	Plant Type	Origin	No. Wildlife Species	Wildlife Value	Landscape Score	Landscape Uses	Hardiness Zones 5	4	3S	3N	Plant Characteristics	Height	Sun Exposure	Moisture Preference	pH Preference	Soil Types	Soil Characteristics	Width (ft.)
Rubus idaeus var. strigosus / Red raspberry — Latham, Boyne	SS	E	97	A		BSE	•	•	•	•		5	F	MD				3
Ruppia maritima / Widgeon grass	AQ	N	33	F		Q	•	•	•	•								
Sagittaria spp. / Arrowhead	AQ	N	19	F		Q	•	•	•	•		3	F					
Sambucus canadensis / American elderberry — species	SS	N	79	A	47/48	BSW	•	•	•	•	DS	12	A	A			WF	9
Sambucus canadensis / American elderberry — Nova & Adams #1	SS	C	79	A	47/48	BS	•	•	•		DS	12	A	A			WF	9
Sambucus pubens / Scarlet elder	SS	N	79	A		BSW	•	•	•	•		12	A	MD			DW	12
Sambucus racemosa / Golden elder — Redman Sutherland Golden	SS	E	79	A		BS	•	•	•	•		12						12
Scirpus spp. / Bulrush	AQ	N	52	A		Q	•	•	•	•		6	F					
Sparganium spp. / Burreed	AQ	N	19	F		Q	•	•	•	•			F					
Spartina spp. / Cordgrass	WS	N	15	C		Q	•	•	•	•		8	F	W			P	
Typha spp. / Cattails	AQ	N	17	A		Q	•	•	•	•		6	F					
Vaccinium angustifolium / Lowbush blueberry — species	SS	N	53	F		BWG	•	•	•	•	DSE	2	FP	D	4.3-5.8	SL	WO	2
Vaccinium angustifolium / Lowbush blueberry — Northblue, Northland	SS	C	53	F		BG	•	•	•		DSE	2¼	FP	D	4.3-5.8	SL	WO	2
Vaccinium angustifolium / Lowbush blueberry — Bluetta, Blueray, Bluecrop, Rancocas	SS	C	53	F		BG	•	•			DSE	5	FP	D	4.3-5.8	SL	WO	3
Vaccinium angustifolium / Lowbush blueberry — Northsky	SS	C	53	F		BG	•	•	•	•	DSE	2	FP	D	4.3-5.8	SL	WO	2
Vaccinium corymbosum / Highbush blueberry	MS	E	53	F		BW	•					9	FP	A	AN	L	F	6
Vaccinium myrtilloides / Velvet leaf blueberry	SS			F		W	•	•	•	•	L			D				
Vaccinium vitis-idaea / Cowberry, Lingenberry	SS	N		F		BWG	•	•	•	•	E	1		A				3
Vallisneria spiralis / Wild celery	AQ	N	16	F		Q	•	•	•	•			F					
Vitis aestivalis / Summer grape — species	PV	N	75	F		BSW	•						S					
Vitis riparia / Riverbank grape — species	PV	N	75	F		BSWK	•	•	•	•	X	30	S					
Vitis riparia / Riverbank grape — Beta, Valiant	PV	N	75	F		BSK	•	•	•	•	X	30	S					
Zannichellia palustris / Horned pondweed	AQ	N	12	F		Q	•	•	•	•								
Zizania aquatica / Wild rice	AQ	N	23	F		Q	•	•	•	•		6	F					

Plant Name	Cultivar	Plant Type	Origin	No. Wildlife Species	Wildlife Value	Landscape Score	Landscape Uses	5	4	3S	3N	Plant Characteristics	Height	Sun Exposure	Moisture Preference	pH Preference	Soil Types	Soil Characteristics	Width (ft.)
Acer negundo* Boxelder		TR	N	5	C	30/58	BSW	•	•	•	•	RD	75	FP	MD	5.0-7.0	B	DF	35-50
Acer rubrum Red maple		TR	N		C		BSWT	•	•	•	•	D	45		WM	AN	SL	P	40-60
Acer saccharum Sugar maple		TR	N	18	C		BSWT	•	•	•	•		60	F	M	3.7-7.3	CL	WF	60-80
Gaylussacia baccata Black huckleberry		SS	N	12	F		BWR	•	•	•	•		3	A	D	A	S		2
Gaylussacia brachycera Box huckleberry		SS	E	12	F		BG	•				E	2			A			
Lonicera syringantha Lilac-flowered honeysuckle		SS	E		C		BS	•	•				9						9
Physocarpus opulifolius Ninebark	species	SS	N		C		BS						9	A	MD	R		W	9
Physocarpus opulifolius Ninebark	Golden, Darts Gold	SS	C		C	47-50/64	BS	•	•	•	•		5-9	A	MD	R	B	W	5-9
Prunus armeniaca var. mandshurica Manchurian bush apricot		TS	E		F		BS	•	•	•	•	D	10-20	F					18
Prunus besseyi Western sandcherry		SS	N		A		S	•	•	•	•	SR	6	F	MD			W	6
Prunus padus* European birdcherry	Aberti, Commutata, Grandiflora, Redleaf	TS	E		F		Bt	•	•	•			20	FP	MD				24
Prunus pumila Sandcherry	Besseyi, Depressa	SS	E		F		BS	•	•	•	•	R	3-5	F	MD		S	W	6
Prunus salicina, hybrid Siberian plum		MS	E		F		BS	•	•	•	•	D	12	F					12
Ribes alpinum* Alpine currant	'Tall Hedge' Green mound	SS	E	31	F	42/48	BDI	•	•	•	•	D	7½	F	MD				3
Ribes americanum* American black currant		SS	N	31	F		BWE	•	•	•	•		4		WM				4
Ribes cynosbati* Prickly gooseberry		SS	N	31	A		BW	•	•	•	•		4	A			B		3
Ribes 'Dakota Dwarf' Gooseberry	Dakota Dwarf	SS	C	31	F														
Ribes diacanthum* Siberian currant		SS	E	31	F		BI												
Ribes hirtellum* Gooseberry	species	SS	N	31	F		B	•	•	•	•		5						5
Ribes hirtellum* Gooseberry	Pixwell, Welcome	SS	C	31	F		B	•	•	•	•		5						3
Ribes odoratum* Buffalo currant		SS	N	31	F		BW	•	•	•	•		6						3
Ribes sanguineum splendens* Flowering currant		SS	E	31	F	B							5	FP					3
Ribes sativum* Garden currant	Cascade, Red Lake	SS	E	31	F	B		•	•	•	•		4	FP			B		3
Salix exigua Sandbar willow		TR	N		C		SEW	•	•				15	F	WM				
Salix purpurea Purple osier willow	Lambertiana	MS	E		C		SEW	•	•	•	•		10	F	WM				6

*See Appendicies M and N.

PLANT NAME / CULTIVAR	Plant Type	Origin	No. Wildlife Species	Wildlife Value	Landscape Score	Landscape Uses	5	4	3S	3N	Plant Characteristics	Height	Sun Exposure	Moisture Preference	pH Preference	Soil Types	Soil Characteristics	Width (ft.)
Acer saccharinum — Silver maple	TR	N		C		BSWT	•	•	•	•		75	FP	M	5.5-6.5	B		75
Betula alleghaniensis* — Yellow birch	TR	N				BT	•	•	•	•		70	PS	M				25-50
Betula papyrifera* — Paper birch	TR	N	37	F	44/58	BWT	•	•	•	•	D	80	FP	M	5.0-8.0	SL	W	30-50
Ostrya virginiana — Ironwood	TR	N	9	C	53/58	BSWTt	•	•	•	•		30	A	M		B	F	20-30
Populus deltoides — species — Eastern cottonwood	TR	N	4	C	33/58	BSWT	•	•	•	•	RD	180	F	A	6.6-7.5	B	W	80-100
Populus deltoides — Siouxland — Eastern cottonwood	TR	C	4	C	33/58	BSWT	•	•	•	•	RD	180	F	A	6.6-7.5	B	W	80-100
Tilia americana — American basswood	TR	N		C		BSWT	•	•	•	•		120		A	5.0-7.5	SL	W	80-100

*See Appendicies M and N.

Plant Name / Cultivar	Plant Type	Origin	No. Wildlife Species	Wildlife Value	Landscape Score	Landscape Uses	Hardiness Zones 5	4	3S	3N	Plant Characteristics	Height	Sun Exposure	Moisture Preference	pH Preference	Soil Types	Soil Characteristics	Width (ft.)
Avena spp. / Oats	GR	E	91	A		CE	•	•	•	•		3	F	MD				
Cornus alba / Westenbirt dogwood — Sibirica	SS	E		F		BI	•	•	•	•		9	FP	WM				9
Cornus racemosa / Gray dogwood	SS	N	42	F		BWSE	•	•	•	•	SR	9	A	A		B	W	9
Cornus rugosa / Round-leaved dogwood	SS	N		F		BW	•	•	•	•		9	PS					
Cornus sericea or stolonifera / Red-osier dogwood — species	SS	N	47	F	53/64	BSWEI	•	•	•	•	S	8	A	WM	to 7.5	B	W	6
Cornus sericea or stolonifera / Red-osier dogwood — baileyi, coloradensis, Flaviramea, Isanti, Kelsey	SS	C	47	F	53/64	BSWE	•	•	•	•	S	8	A	WM		B		12
Eleagnus commutata / Silverberry	SS	N		A		BWSE	•	•	•	•	RS	9	F		to 7.5		W	6
Fraxinus americana / White ash	TR	N	8	F		BWTL	•	•			D	100	A	M	5.0-7.5		DFW	50+
Fraxinus nigra / Black ash	TR	N	11	A		SWT	•	•	•	•	D	70	F	A	4.1-6.6		O	30-60
Fraxinus pennsylvanica lanceolata / Green ash — species	TR	N	11	A	49/58	BSWTL	•	•	•	•	RD	50	F	MD	6.1-7.5	SL	W	30-50
Fraxinus pennsylvanica lanceolata / Green ash — Summit	TR	C	11	A	49/58	BSTL	•	•	•	•	RD	50	F	MD	6.1-7.5	SL	W	30-50
Helianthus spp. / Graystripe sunflower — Sundak	GR	E	60	F		F	•	•	•	•		8	F	MD		SL	FW	
Helianthus spp. / Oilseed sunflower	GR	E	60	F		F	•	•	•	•		8	F	MD		SL	FW	
Hordeum vulgare / Barley	GR	E	50	F		FE	•	•	•	•		4	F	MD		SL	FW	
Ilex verticellata / Winterberry — Winter Red	SS	N	48	A	41/64	SBWA	•	•	•	•	D	9	A	WM	5.5 AN		WO	9
Malus spp. / Apples — Beacon, Fireside Haralson, Redwell	TR	E		F		BSQT												18-36
Parthenocissus quinquefolia / Virginia creeper	PV	N	37	A		BK NW	•	•	•	•		30	A	MD		B		
Sheperdia argentea / Silver buffaloberry — Sakakawea	MS	N			35/64	SP	•	•	•	•	DL RS	16	F	A	R		DW	12-18
Sorbus alnifolia* / Korean mountain ash	TR	E	15	F		Bt	•	•				30	FP				W	15-25
Sorbus americana* / American mountain ash	TR	N	15	F		BSWbt	•	•	•	•		30	FP	MD			FD	15-25
Sorbus aucuparia* / European mountain ash	TR	E	15	F	44/58	BSt	•	•	•	•		30	FP	M	A		W	15-30
Sorghum vulgare / Grain sorghum	GR	E	34	A		F	•	•	•	•		5	F	MD		SL	FW	
Sorghum spp. / Sudex, cane sorghum	GR	E	34	A		F	•	•	•	•		7	F	MD		SL	FW	
Triticum spp. / Wheat	GR	E	94	F		F	•	•	•	•		4	F	MD		SL	FW	
Weigela florida / Old-fashioned weigela — Bristol Red, Red Prince	SS	E		ME		B	•	•				9						6
Zea mays / Field corn	GR	E	100	A		F	•	•	•	•		8	F	MD		SL	FW	

*See Appendicies M and N.

Plant Group
VI. Fall Plants — Rating **Good**

Plant Name	Cultivar	Plant Type	Origin	No. Wildlife Species	Wildlife Value	Landscape Score	Landscape Uses	Hardiness Zones 5	4	3S	3N	Plant Characteristics	Height	Sun Exposure	Moisture Preference	pH Preference	Soil Types	Soil Characteristics	Width (ft.)
Amaranthus cruenthus — Grain amaranth	R158	GR	E		FS		BF	•	•	•	•		7	F					
Ampelopsis brevipedunculata — Porcelain ampelopsis		PV	E		F		BK	•					15						
Aralia elata — Japanese angelica		TR	E		F		Bt	•					30						
Arctostaphylos uva-ursi — Bearberry	species	SS	N	4	F		BSWEG	•	•	•	•		1	FP		A	S	W	3
Arctostaphylos uva-ursi — Bearberry	Massachusetts	SS	C	4	F		BSEG	•	•	•	•		1	FP		A	S	W	3
Brassica napus var. napobrassica — Rutabaga		PR	E		F		F	•	•	•	•			F	MD				
Cornus alternifolia — Alternate-leaf dogwood or Pagoda dogwood		TS	N	34	A		BWtD	•	•	•	•		30	A	M			F	18
Cotoneaster acutifolia — Pekin cotoneaster		SS	E		A		BS						6	F	MD				6
Cotoneaster lucidus — Hedge cotoneaster		MS	E		A		BSlb	•	•	•	•		9	FP	MD	R		W	5-7
Cotoneaster multiflorus* — Many-flowered cotoneaster		SS	E		A	52/64	BSGlb	•	•				8	F	MD				12
Fagopyrum esculentum — Buckwheat		GR	E	12	F		F	•	•	•	•		3	F	MD				
Glycine max — Soybean		GR	E	11	F		F	•	•	•	•		3	F	MD		SL	WF	
Ilex glabra — Inkberry		MS	E	9	F		B	•	•			D	10	FP	MD	A	SP		
Lonicera Koralkowii		SS	E		A		bSM	•	•										
Lonciera maaki — Amur honeysuckle	Rem red	MS	E	8	A		S	•	•	•	•		12	FP	MD			W	to 14
Panicum miliaceum — Proso millet	Dawn	GR	E		A		F	•	•	•	•		5	F	MD				
Shepherdia canadensis — Canadian buffaloberry		TS	N		A		SE	•	•	•	•	DR	6	F	MD				6
Viburnum dentatum — Arrowwood viburnum		SS	N	10	A	52/64	BSWDI	•	•	•	•	S	8	FP	WM	R	CS	W	8

*See Appendicies M and N.

Plant Group
VI. Fall Plants — Rating **Fair**

Plant Name	Cultivar	Plant Type	Origin	No. Wildlife Species	Wildlife Value	Landscape Score	Landscape Uses	Hardiness Zones 5	4	3S	3N	Plant Characteristics	Height	Sun Exposure	Moisture Preference	pH Preference	Soil Types	Soil Characteristics	Width (ft.)
Aralia spinosa — Devil's walking stick		TR		10			NW	•				S	30		M			FD	15
Cornus alba — Siberian dogwood, Tatarian dogwood	Spaethii	MS	E		F		Bb	•	•	•	•		10	FP					9
Cornus alba — Siberian dogwood, Tatarian dogwood	Argenteomarginata	MS	E		F		Bb	•	•	•	•		10	FP					9
Cornus alba — Siberian dogwood, Tatarian dogwood	Gouchaultii	MS	E		F		Bb	•	•	•	•		10	FP					9
Cornus canadansis — Unique bunchberry		SS	N	9	F		BWG	•	•	•	•		1	PS	M				

Plant Group
VI. Fall Plants

Rating Fair cont.

PLANT NAME	CULTIVAR	Plant Type	Origin	No. Wildlife Species	Wildlife Value	Landscape Score	Landscape Uses	5	4	3S	3N	Plant Characteristics	Height	Sun Exposure	Moisture Preference	pH Preference	Soil Types	Soil Characteristics	Width (ft.)
Cotoneaster apiculatus Cranberry cotoneaster		SS	E		A		BRE	•	•				3	F	MD				3
Cotoneaster divaricatus Spreading cotoneaster		SS	E		F		BEL	•					8						6
Lonicera caerulea var. edulis Sweetberry honeysuckle		SS	E				BSDb	•	•	•	•		4						3
Lonicera maximowsiczii var. sachalinesis Sakhalin honeysuckle		SS	E				BDb	•	•	•	•		9						9
Lonicera morrowii Morrow honeysuckle		SS	E				BIb	•	•	•	•		6						6
Lonicera tatarica* Tatarian honeysuckle	Freedom	MS	E	18	B	47/64	BSIb	•	•	•	•		14	A	MD		B	W	9

*See Appendicies M and N.

Plant Group
VII. Winter Plants

Rating Excellent

PLANT NAME	CULTIVAR	Plant Type	Origin	No. Wildlife Species	Wildlife Value	Landscape Score	Landscape Uses	5	4	3S	3N	Plant Characteristics	Height	Sun Exposure	Moisture Preference	pH Preference	Soil Types	Soil Characteristics	Width (ft.)
Celastrus scandens Bittersweet		PV	N	15	F		BWKG	•	•	•	•	D	21	FP	MD		B	W	
Celtis occidentalis Hackberry		TR	N	48	A	46/58	BSWL	•	•	•	•	R	50	FP	A	6.6-8.0	B	D	50+
Crataegus spp. Hawthorn	native species	TS	N	29	A		BSW	•	•	•	•	R	20-30	FP	A	6.1-8.0	B	W	15-30
Crataegus crus-galli Cockspur hawthorn	Splendens inermis	TS	C	29	AN	62/64	BStb	•	•			SR	20	FP	A	6.1-8.0	C	W	24
Eleagnus angustifolia* Russian olive		TR	E	50	A	44/64	BSIEbt	•	•	•	•	R	20	F	MD	B	SL	W	15
Juniperus virginiana* Eastern red cedar		TR	N	33	A		BSWEb	•	•	•	•	R	50	FP	MD	7.8-8.6	B	W	10-20
Malus pyrus baccata Siberian crabapple	several	TR	E	31	A		BSIT	•	•	•	•		30	F	MD	5.0-6.5	L	W	30
Malus 'red splendor' 	Red splendor	TS	E	31	F	47/58	BSt	•	•	•	•		18	F	MD	5.0-6.5	L	W	18
Populus tremuloides Quaking aspen		TR	N	11	A		W	•	•	•	•	DSR	60	FP	MD	7.5-8.0		W	30-35
Rhus glabra Smooth sumac		TS	N	50	F		BSEW	•	•	•	•	DSR	20	FP	MD			W	9
Rhus typhina Staghorn sumac		TS	N	50	F	47/64	BSEW	•	•	•	•	DSR	20	FP	MD			W	9
Viburnum trilobum American highbush cranberry	species	MS	N	34	F	56/64	BSWE	•	•	•	•		15	FP	MD		B	WD	to 15
Viburnum trilobum American highbush cranberry	Wentworth, Andrews	MS	C	34	F	56/64	BSE	•	•	•	•		12	FP	M		B	WD	to 12
Viburnum trilobum American highbush cranberry	Bailey compact	SS	C	34	F	56/64	BSED	•	•	•	•		6	FP	M		B	WD	to 6

*See Appendicies M and N.

Plant Group
VII. Winter

Rating: Good

Plant Name / Cultivar	Plant Type	Origin	No. Wildlife Species	Wildlife Value	Landscape Score	Landscape Uses	5	4	3S	3N	Plant Characteristics	Height	Sun Exposure	Moisture Preference	pH Preference	Soil Types	Soil Characteristics	Width (ft.)
Aronia melanocarpa — Glossy black chokeberry	SS	N	7	A	57/64	BDSWb	•	•	•	•	SR	10	FP	A	NB	BS		6
Crataegus phaenopyrum — Washington hawthorn	TR	E	25	BN		BSLt	•	•			R	20	F	MD	6.1-8.0	B		18
Euonymus atropurpurea — Eastern wahoo	TS	N		A		BSW	•	•	•	•		20						18
Euonymus europaea (Aldenhamensis) — European spindle tree, European euonymus	SS	E		A		BSb	•	•				8						12
Euonymus europaea (Red Caps) — European spindle tree, European euonymus	SS	E		A		BSb	•	•				8						12
Malus sp. (Chestnut, Dolgo Profusion) — Crabapple	TS	E		F		BSt	•	•				20	F	MD	5.0-6.5	L	W	18
Myrica pensylvanica — Northern bayberry	SS	E	22	F		BEb	•				LD	5		MD		S	W	3
Phellodendron amurense — Amur corktree	TR	E		F		BST	•	•			D	50					W	30
Phellodendron sachalinense — Sakhalin corktree	TR	E		F		BST	•	•			D	50					W	30
Rosa carolina — Pasture rose	SS	N		F		P	•	•				7	F	D				4
Rosa blanda — Meadow rose	SS	N	18	F		NP	•	•	•	•		4	F			L	WP	2
Rosa rugosa (Hansen's hedge) — Dwarf hedge rose	SS	E	24	A	34/68	BSlb	•	•	•	•	SR	8	F		to 8.0			6
Symphoricarpos albus (species) — Common snowberry	SS	C	8	A	37/64	WSE	•	•	•	•	S	4	A	M	B	C		3
Symphoricarpos albus (laevigatus) — Common snowberry	SS	C	8	A		WSE	•	•	•	•	S	4	A	M	B	C		3
Symphoricarpos occidentalis (species) — Wolfberry	SS	N		A	37/64	SPE	•	•	•	•	SR	6	A	MD		SL	W	3
Symphoricarpos occidentalis (White Hedge) — Wolfberry	SS	N		C	37/64	SPE	•	•	•	•	SR	6	A	MD		SL	W	3
Symphoricarpos orbiculatus (species) — Coralberry	SS	N	27	A		BSEWlt	•	•	•	•	S	5	FP	MD		B	F	3
Symphoricarpos orbiculatus (Roseum) — Coralberry	SS	N	27	A		BSElt	•	•	•	•	S	5	FP	MD		B	F	3
Viburnum lantana (Aureum, Rugosum) — Wayfaringbush	MS	E		A	43/64	BSb	•	•	•	•		15	A	D				12
Viburnum lantana (Mohican) — Wayfaringbush	MS	W		A	43/64	BSb	•	•	•	•		6	A	MD				12
Viburnum lentago — Nannyberry	TS	N	11	A	49/64	BSWbt	•	•	•	•	SR	24	A	MD	6.1-7.5	B	D	6-10
Viburnum opulus (Compactum) — European highbush cranberry	SS	E		F		BSMb	•	•	•	•		6	A	M			W	8
Viburnum opulus (Aureum, Notcutt) — European highbush cranberry	MS	E		F		BSMb	•	•	•	•		10	FP	M			W	12
Viburnum sargenti (Onandaga, calvescens, flavum) — Sargent's highbush cranberry	MS	E		F		BSMEb	•	•	•	•		12	A	M				12

Plant Group VII. Winter — Rating Fair

Plant Name / Cultivar	Plant Type	Origin	No. Wildlife Species	Wildlife Value	Landscape Score	Landscape Uses	Hardiness Zones 5	4	3S	3N	Plant Characteristics	Height	Sun Exposure	Moisture Preference	pH Preference	Soil Types	Soil Characteristics	Width (ft.)
Aronia arbutifolia — Red chokeberry	SS	E	12	C		BSMb	•					8	FP	A				3
Aronia prunifolia — Purple chokeberry	SS	E		C		BSMb	•	•				5	FP	A				6
Euonymus nana (Turkestania) — Dwarf euonymus	SS	E		A		BDb	•	•	•	•	S	3	A	MD				3
Malus 'radiant' (Radiant) — Crabapple	TS			F		BS	•	•				18	F	MD	5.0-6.5	L	W	18
Populus grandidentata — Bigtooth aspen	TR	N	7	A		W	•	•	•	•	DS	60	FP	MD		B	W	20-30
Rhus aromatica (Low grow) — Sweet-scented sumac	SS	N		C		EG	•				D	5						5
Viburnum alnifolium — Hobblebush	SS	E	6	A		B	•	•	•	•	S	10	PS	M				9
Viburnum cassinoides — Witherod	MS	N	9	F		BSWbt	•	•	•	•		6	PS	M				6

Plant Group VIII. Nut & Acorn Plants — Rating Excellent

Plant Name / Cultivar	Plant Type	Origin	No. Wildlife Species	Wildlife Value	Landscape Score	Landscape Uses	Hardiness Zones 5	4	3S	3N	Plant Characteristics	Height	Sun Exposure	Moisture Preference	pH Preference	Soil Types	Soil Characteristics	Width (ft.)
Aesculus glabra — Ohio buckeye	TR	E		AN		BT	•	•	•	•		36	F	M	6.1-6.5	LS	W	30-40
Aesculus sylvatica — Painted buckeye	TR	N		BA		BT	•	•				36	F	M		L		18-24
Castanea dentata* — American chestnut	TR	N	7	A		BT	•	•				90				S	F	45
Castanea mollissima — Chinese chestnut	TR	E	7	A		BT	•				D	40				S		36
Carya cordiformis — Bitternut hickory	TR	N		A		WT	•	•	•	•		60						30 +
Carya ovata — Shagbark hickory	TR	N	34	A		BSWT	•	•				80	FP	MD			FW	80 +
Corylus americana — American hazel, filbert	SS	N	24	F		SWB	•	•	•	•	D	8	FP	M			F	6
Corylus cornuta — Beaked hazel	SS	N	22	F		WB						10	A	M			WF	8
Juglans cinerea — Butternut	TR	N	18	A	38/58	BSWT	•	•	•	•		60	F	MD	6.6-8.0		WFD	50-60
Juglans nigra — Black walnut	TR	N	24	A	44/58	BSWT	•	•	•			90	F	M	6.6-8.0	L	WF	60-100
Quercus alba — White oak	TR	N	75	A	58/58	BSWT	•	•			T	90	A	M	5.5-7.5	SL	WF	50-90
Quercus bicolor (Plant northern strains) — Swamp white oak	TR	N	75	A		BSWT	•	•			T	80	FP	WM	6.0-6.5	CS	OW	40-50
Quercus coccinea (Plant northern strains) — Scarlet oak	TR	N	75	A		BSWT	•	•				80	FP	D	A	S	W	45
Quercus ellipsoidalis* — Northern pin oak	TR	N	75	A		BSWT	•	•	•	•	R	60	F	MD	6.1-7.5	B	W	30-50
Quercus macrocarpa — Bur oak	TR	N	96	A		BSWT	•	•	•	•	T	60	F	MS	4.6-8.0	B	W	40-80
Quercus rubra — Northern red oak	TR	N	75	A		BSWT	•	•	•	•	T	75	A	MD	4.8-6.5	B	WF	40-80
Quercus velutina — Black oak	TR	N	75	A		BSWT	•	•				60	FP	MD		S	WF	60

Appendix B
Planning Checklist

Plants Appropriate For Use In Yards, Listed By Yard Features

This is a list of various plants which you may wish to consider in planning your yard. Appendix A should be consulted to learn additional details about plants that may fill your needs.

Key To Wildlife Value: EX — Excellent   G — Good   F — Fair

BOULEVARD TREES FOR LAWN SITES ADJACENT TO STREETS	WILDLIFE VALUE
WIDE STREETS—More Than 50 Feet Wide	
Sugar Maple	G
Shagbark Hickory	EX
Hackberry	EX
White Ash	EX
Green Ash	EX
White Oak	EX
Swamp White Oak	EX
Basswood	F
MEDIUM STREETS-40 to 50 Feet Wide	
Red Maple	G
Scarlet Oak	EX
Eastern Hophornbeam (Ironwood)	F
NARROW STREETS	
Cockspur Hawthorn	G-EX
Washington Hawthorn	G
Ohio Buckeye	EX
Painted Buckeye	EX

MED.—LARGE SHADE TREES FOR LAWNS	
Red Maple	G
Sugar Maple	G
Silver Maple	F
Ohio Buckeye	EX
Painted Buckeye	EX
River Birch	F
Shagbark Hickory	EX
Hackberry	EX
White Ash	EX
Green Ash	EX
Black Walnut	EX
Butternut	EX
Bitternut Hickory	EX
Amur Corktree	G
Sakhalin Corktree	G
White Oak	EX
Swamp White Oak	EX
Bur Oak	EX
Basswood	F
Amur Chokecherry	EX
Northern Catalpa	EX
Tulip Tree	G
Black Cherry	EX

SMALL ORNAMENTAL LAWN TREES	
Ginnala Maple (Amur maple)	EX
Downy Serviceberry	EX
Apple Serviceberry	EX
Alleghany Serviceberry	EX
Eastern Redbud	G
Pagoda Dogwood	G
Cockspur Hawthorn	G-EX
"Snowbird" Hawthorn	G
"Radiant" Crabapple	F-G
"Red Splendor" Crabapple	EX
"Profusion" Crabapple	G
Siberian Crabapple	EX
Eastern Hophornbeam (Ironwood)	F
Manchurian Apricot	G-EX
Amur Chokecherry	EX
Pin Cherry 'Stockton'	EX
Chokecherry 'Shubert'	EX
Korean Mountain Ash	EX
American Mountain Ash	EX
European Mountain Ash	EX
Showy Mountain Ash	EX

FOUNDATION PLANTS	
Black Chokeberry	EX
Red-osier Dogwood 'Isanti'	EX-G
Chinese Juniper 'Ames'	EX
Sweet Mock Orange 'Aureus'	EX
Alpine Currant	G
Garland Spirea 'Compacta'	G
Snowberry	G-EX
Meyer Lilac	G
Viburnums	G-EX
Coralberry	G-EX
Tatarian Dogwood 'Argenteomarginata'	F-G

FORMAL HEDGES	
Ginnala Maple (Amur Maple)	EX
Black Chokeberry	G
Ninebark 'Golden'	G
Ninebark 'Darts Gold'	G
Hedge Cotoneaster	G
Alpine Currant	G
Arrowwood Viburnum	G

SPREADING GROUND COVERS — **WILDLIFE VALUE**

ANNUALS
Rose Moss	G

PERENNIALS
Sweet William	G-EX
Coral Bells	EX
Plantain Lily (Hosta Spp.)	EX
Dwarf Bearded Iris	G
Moss Pink	EX
Primrose	G

SHRUBS
Bearberry	G
Lowbush Blueberry	EX
Bayberry	G
Sweet-scented Sumac	F
Thimbleberry	EX

EDGES

ANNUALS
Snapdragon	G-EX
Waxleaf Begonia	G
Pot Marigold	EX
Dahlia	G
China Pink	G
Candytuft	G
Flowering Tobacco	EX
Poppy	G
Geranium	G
Annual Phlox	EX
Petunia	EX
Scarlet Sage	EX
Marigolds	G
Nasturtium	G-EX
Garden Verbena	G
Zinnia	EX

PERENNIALS
Yarrow	G-EX
Asters	G
Canterbury Bells	EX
Sweet William	G-EX
Coral Bells	EX
Plantain Lily (Hosta Spp.)	EX
Dwarf Bearded Iris	G
Moss Pink	G-EX
Sedum	EX

TALL FLOWERS FOR BACKGROUND, BACKDROPS OR BORDERS

ANNUALS
Hollyhock	EX
Snapdragon	G
Canterbury Bells	EX
Spider Flower	G-EX
Sunflower	EX
Flowering Tobacco	EX
Sages	EX
Giant Marigold	G
Mexican Sunflower	G-EX
Zinnia, Tall Varieties	G-EX

PERENNIALS
False Indigo	G
Delphinium	G
Sunflower	EX

FLOWERS FOR HANGING BASKETS OR STRAWBERRY JARS
Waxleaf Begonia	G
Impatiens	G-EX
Petunia, Cascade Forms	EX
Nasturtium	G-EX
Garden Verbena	G
Fuchsia	G

WINDOW BOXES
Wax Begonia	G
Impatiens	G-EX
Geranium	G
Petunia	EX
Marigold	G
Nasturtium	G-EX
Button Zinnia	EX

CONTAINER GARDEN PLANTS FOR USE IN TUB OR 2-5 GALLON CONTAINERS (J-1)
Rose of Sharon	EX
Geranium	G
Zinnia	G-EX
African Marigold	G-EX
French Marigold	G-EX

PLANTS FOR USE IN 8" TO 12" DIAMETER CONTAINERS (J-2)
Ageratum	G
Amaryllis	EX
Heath Aster	EX
New England Aster	G
Asters	EX
Pot Marigold	EX
Canterbury Bells	EX
Annual Daisy	G
Oxeye Daisy	EX
Heliotrope	EX
Garden Balsam	G
Spotted Touch-Me-Not (jewelweed)	EX
Pale Touch-Me-Not (jewelweed)	EX
Gladiolus	EX
Daffodil	EX
Flowering Tobacco	EX
Sander Tobacco	EX
Geranium	G
Moss Pink	EX
Sweet William Phlox	G-EX
Annual Phlox	G
Summer Phlox	G
Prairie Phlox	G
Garden Sage	EX
Scarlet Sage	EX

PLANTS FOR USE IN 4" TO 6" DIAMETER CONTAINERS (J-3)	WILDLIFE VALUE
Ageratum	G
Wax Begonia	G
Sweet William	EX
China Pink	G
Hyacinth-Flowered Candytuft	G
Globe Candytuft	G
Petunia	EX
Primrose	G
Dusty Miller	G
African Marigold	G
French Marigold	G-EX
Garden Verbena	EX

VINES FOR STONE OR BRICK WALLS

Virginia Creeper	EX

VINES FOR FENCES, TRELLISES & SCREENS

WOODY VINES

American Bittersweet	EX
Scarlet Trumpet Honeysuckle "Dropmore"	EX
Riverbank Grape	EX
'Beta' Grape	EX

ANNUAL VINES

Moonflower Vine	G
Cardinal Climber	G
Cypress Vine	G
Morning Glory	G
Sweet Pea	EX
Nasturtium, If Trained	G-EX
Scarlet Runner Bean	EX

PLANTS FOR SHADY AREAS

ANNUALS

Snapdragon	G
Wax Begonia	G
Pot Marigold	EX
Canterbury Bells	EX
Spider Flower	G-EX
Larkspur	G-EX
Impatiens Wallerana*	G-EX
Flowering Tobacco	EX
Phlox	G
Scarlet Sage	EX
* Tolerates Deep Shade	

PERENNIALS

Crocus	G
Columbine	EX
Foxglove	EX
Daylily	EX
Coral bells	EX
Plantain Lily (Hosta Spp.)	EX
Siberian Iris	G
Cardinal Flower	G-EX
Virginia Bluebells	G
Scarlet Bergamot	EX
Wild Bergamot	EX
Violets	EX

SHRUBS

Juneberry (Saskatoon Serviceberry)	EX
Dogwoods	EX
Pin Cherry	EX
Scarlet Elder	EX
Canada Yew	EX
Arrowwood Viburnum	G
Wayfaring Bush	G
Nannyberry	G
European Highbush Cranberry	G
Sargent's Highbush Cranberry	G
American Highbush Cranberry	EX

PLANTS FOR MOIST SOILS

ANNUALS

Pot Marigold	EX
Spider Flower	G-EX
Sweet Pea	EX
Flowering Tobacco	EX
Annual Phlox	G
Nasturtium	G-EX

PERENNIALS

Marsh Marigold	EX
Blue Flag Iris	G
Cardinal Flower	G-EX
Virginia Bluebells	G
Scarlet Bergamot	EX
Wild Bergamot	EX
Japanese Primrose	

TREES/SHRUBS

Red Maple	G
Paper Birch	F
Red-osier Dogwood	EX
Black Ash	EX
Winterberry	EX
Tamarack	EX
Black Spruce	EX
Cottonwood	F
Swamp White Oak	EX
Rhodora	G
Willows	EX
Northern White Cedar	EX
Nannyberry	G
American Highbush Cranberry	EX

PLANTS FOR ACID SOILS

TREES/SHRUBS

Bearberry	G
Box Huckleberry	G
Winterberry	EX
Rhododendron	G
Blueberries	EX

PLANTS FOR SANDY/DRY SOILS

ANNUALS

Dwarf Morning Glory	G
Spider Flower	G-EX
Cosmos	G

(continued)

PLANTS FOR SANDY/DRY SOILS

ANNUALS CONTINUED	WILDLIFE VALUE
Gaillardia	EX
Sea Lavender	G
Four O'Clock (Marvel of Peru)	EX
Scarlet Sage	EX
Black-eyed Susan	EX
Sunflowers	EX
Mexican Sunflower	G-EX
Zinnia	EX

PERENNIALS	
Yarrow	G-EX
Butterflyweed	EX
Common Milkweed	EX
Plains Wild Indigo	G
Sweet William	G-EX
Globe Thistle	EX
Little Bluestem	EX
Big Bluestem	EX
Sideoats Grama	EX
Switch Grass	EX
Indiangrass	EX
Daylily	G-EX
Blazing Stars	EX
Black Eyed-susan	EX
Stonecrop	EX
Goldenrods	G-EX

DECIDUOUS SHRUBS	
Ginnala Maple (Amur Maple)	EX
Leadplant	EX
Bearberry	G
New Jersey Tea	G
Black Huckleberry	EX
Northern Bayberry	G
Western Sandcherry	EX
Sandcherry	G-EX
Sumacs	EX
Prickly Gooseberry	G
Roses	G
Buffaloberry	EX
Coralberry	G-EX
Lowbush Blueberry	EX

DECIDUOUS TREES	
Boxelder	G
Aspens	EX
Black Cherry	EX
Scarlet Oak	EX
Hackberry	EX
Green Ash	EX
Northern Pin Oak	EX

CONIFEROUS SHRUBS	
Bearberry	G
Inkberry	G
Common Juniper	EX

CONIFEROUS TREES	
Eastern Red Cedar	EX
White Spruce	EX
Red Pine	EX
White Pine	EX
Scotch Pine	F
Jack Pine	EX

HERB GARDEN

SHRUBS	
Lavender	EX

ANNUALS	
Anise	EX
Garden Sage	EX
Dill	EX

PERENNIALS	
Yarrow	EX
Leadplant	EX
Winter Cress	EX
Boneset	EX
Borage	EX
Chicory	G
Hyssop	EX
Lovage	EX
Lemon Balm	EX
Peppermint	EX
Spearmint	EX
Bergamot	EX
Catnip	G
Cretan Dittany	EX
Sweet Marjoram	EX
Wild Marjoram	EX
Parsley	EX
Selfheal	EX
Rosemary	EX
Winter Savory	EX
Thyme	EX

PRAIRIE FLOWER GARDEN

BIENNIALS/PERENNIALS	
Yarrow	G-EX
Leadplant	EX
Intermediate Dogbane	EX
Indian Hemp	EX
Prairie Milkweed	EX
Prairie Thistle	EX
Purple Coneflower	EX
Boneset	EX
Oxeye Sunflower	EX
Showy Sunflower	EX
Maximillian Sunflower	EX
Western Sunflower	EX
Blazing Stars	EX
Wild Bergamot	EX
Stiff Goldenrod	EX
Plains Wild Indigo	G
Pasque Flower	G
Large-flowered Penstemon	G
Foxglove Penstemon	G
Prairie Phlox	G
Purple Prairie Clover	G

	WILDLIFE VALUE		
White Prairie Clover	G	Tickseed Sunflower	EX
Prairie Turnip	G	Queen Anne's Lace	EX
Upright Prairie Coneflower	G	Fireweed	EX
Grayhead Prairie Coneflower	G	Oxeye Sunflower	EX
Compass Plant	G	Houstonia	EX
Cup Plant	G	Lupine	EX
Gray Goldenrod	G	Gray Goldenrod	EX
Showy Goldenrod	G	Rough-Stemmed Goldenrod	EX
Bird's Foot Violet	G	Violets	EX
		Dogwoods	G
WOODLAND SHRUBS & WILDFLOWERS		Azaleas	G
Buttonbush	EX	Staghorn Sumac	G
Silverberry	EX	Currants/Gooseberries	G
Labrador Tea	EX	Elderberries	G
Spicebush	EX	Blueberries	G
Pussy Willow	EX	Viburnum	G
Coralberry	EX	Giant Blue Hyssop	G
Aster Spp.	EX	New England Aster	G
Spotted Touch-Me-Not (jewelweed)	EX	Wild Indigo	G
Pale Touch-Me-Not (jewelweed)	EX	Cardinal Flower	G-EX
American Columbine	EX	Bluebells	G
Indian Hemp	EX	Sweet William Phlox	G-EX
Swamp Milkweed	EX	Downy Phlox	G
Common Milkweed	EX	Grayhead Prairie Coneflower	G
Butterflyweed	G-EX	Turk's Cap Lily	EX
Winter Cress	EX	Wood Lily	EX
		Nasturtium	G
		Virginia Creeper	G

Appendix C

Commonly Used Field Guides For Midwestern Wildlife

BIRDS

Bull,   John, Edith Bull, and Gerald Gold. 1985. Birds of North America, eastern region. Macmillan Publ. Co. New York. 157 pp.

Bull,   John and John Farrand, Jr. 1977. The Audubon Society field guide to North American birds - eastern region. Alfred A Knopf. New York. 784 pp.

Janssen,   Robert B. 1987. Birds in Minnesota. Univ. of MN Press. Mpls. 352 pp. (Not a field guide; Use in conjunction with a field guide).

Peterson,   Roger, Tory. 1980. A field guide to the birds east of the Rockies. 4th Edition. Houghton Mifflin Co. Boston. 384 pp.

Robbins,   Chandler S., Bertell Bruun, and Herbert S. Zim. 1983. A guide to field identification. Birds of North America. Expanded, revised edition. Golden Press. New York. 360 pp.

BUTTERFLIES

Heitzman,   J. Richard and Joan E. Heitzman. 1987. Butterflies and Moths of Missouri. Missouri Dept. of Conservation. Jefferson City. 385 pp.

Milne,   Lorus and Margery. 1984. The Audubon Society field guide to North American insects and spiders. Alfred A. Knopf. 989 pp.

Pyle,   Robert M. 1981. The Audubon Society field guide to North American butterflies. Alfred A. Knopf. New York. 924 pp.

————,   1984. The Audubon Society handbook for butterfly watchers. Charles Scribner's Sons. New York. 274 pp.

MAMMALS

Burt,   W.H. and R.P. Grossenheider. 1976. A field guide to the mammals. 3rd ed. The Peterson field guide series. Houghton Mifflin Co. Boston. 289 pp.

Hazard,   Evan B. 1982. The mammals of Minnesota. Univ. of MN Press. Mpls. 280 pp.

PHENOLOGY

Gilbert,   James R. 1983. Jim Gilbert's nature notebook. Minnesota Landscape Arboretum. Mpls. 357 pp.

————,   1987. Through Minnesota's Seasons with Jim Gilbert. Univ. of MN. Press. Landscape Arboretum. Mpls. 198. pp.

REPTILES AND AMPHIBIANS

Behler,   John L. 1979. The Audubon Society field guide to North American reptiles and amphibians. Alfred A. Knopf. New York. 743 pp.

Breckenridge,   Walter J. 1970. Reptiles and amphibians of Minnesota. The Univ. of MN Press. Mpls. 202 pp.

Conant,   Roger. 1975. A field guide to the reptiles and amphibians of eastern North America. 2nd Edition. Houghton Mifflin Co. Boston. 429 pp.

Johnson,   Tom R. 1987. Amphibians and Reptiles of Missouri. Missouri Dept. of Conservation. Jefferson City. 368 pp.

Vogt,   Richard C. 1981. Natural history of amphibians and reptiles in Wisconsin. The Milwaukee Public Museum. Milwaukee. 205 pp.

WILDLIFE PHOTOGRAPHY

Freeman,   Michael. 1984. The wildlife photographer's field guide. Writers Digest Books, Cincinnati, Ohio.

Rue,   Leonard Lee III. 1984. How I photograph wildlife and nature. W.W. Norton and Co. N.Y.

Shaw,   J. 1984. The nature photographer's complete guide to field techniques. Amphot. Watson-Gupstill. Publications. N.Y.

Time-Life Books.   Life library of photography. Time-Life Books. N.Y.

Wooters,   J. and J.T. Smith. 1981. Wild images: a complete guide to outdoor photography. Peterson Publ. Co. Los Angeles, California.

Appendix D

Observation Blinds

To facilitate wildlife observation, a blind can be constructed which will allow a person or group of persons to watch from concealment without disturbing wildlife. An approach path can be designed so that people are screened from sight when they enter the blind. This screened path can be constructed in different ways; a dense hedge may be planted on both sides of the approach path; the approach path may enter the blind via a ravine; or an approach path may be constructed through an already existing dense thicket. Terrain and vegetation will suggest other types of screening.

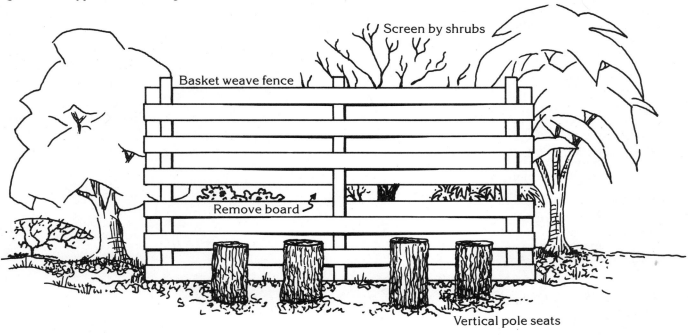

Appendix E

Space Needs For Some Midwestern Wildlife Species

Species	Home Range, Acres/Pair	Minimum Area for Population (Acres)
Birds		
Northern flicker	40	
Eastern bluebird	5	
Pileated woodpecker	100	
Yellow-bellied sapsucker	10	
Hairy woodpecker	25	
Downy woodpecker	10	
Black-backed woodpecker	75	

Appendix E
Space Needs For Some Midwestern Wildlife Species Continued

Species	Home Range, Acres/Pair	Minimum Area for Population (Acres)
Birds cont.		
Three-toed woodpecker	75	
Yellow-headed blackbird		1 - 5
Great horned owl	3000	
Barred owl	595	
Red-shouldered hawk		250
Red-bellied woodpecker		10
Great crested flycatcher		25
Acadian flycatcher		80
Eastern wood pewee		10
Blue jay		10
Tufted titmouse		10
Wood thrush		250
Yellow throated vireo		250
Red-eyed vireo		250
Black and white warbler		750
Prothonotary warbler		250
Worm-eating warbler		750
Northern parula warbler		250
Ovenbird		6550
Pine warbler		80
Louisiana waterthrush		250
Kentucky warbler		80
Scarlet tanager		250
Hooded warbler		80
Reptiles and Amphibians		
Tiger salamander		2
Leopard frog		2
Ringneck snake		20
Gopher (Bull) snake		50
Common garter snake		25
Mammals		
Snowshoe hare		160
White-tailed jackrabbit		160
Least chipmunk		80
Red squirrel	100	640
Northern flying squirrel		360
Northern pocket gopher		40
Deer mouse	3 - 4	40
Northern grasshopper mouse		80
Red-backed vole		40
Porcupine	250-360	6400
Red fox	640-1920	
Black bear	1024-2496	
Raccoon	1110	
Marten	640	
Fisher	2560-3200	
Long-tailed weasel	640	
Striped skunk	43-95	640

Appendix F

Pattern For A Falcon Silhouette

Cut out silhouette to scale, color it black and place on outside of window pane with head angled downward as if bird diving at prey.

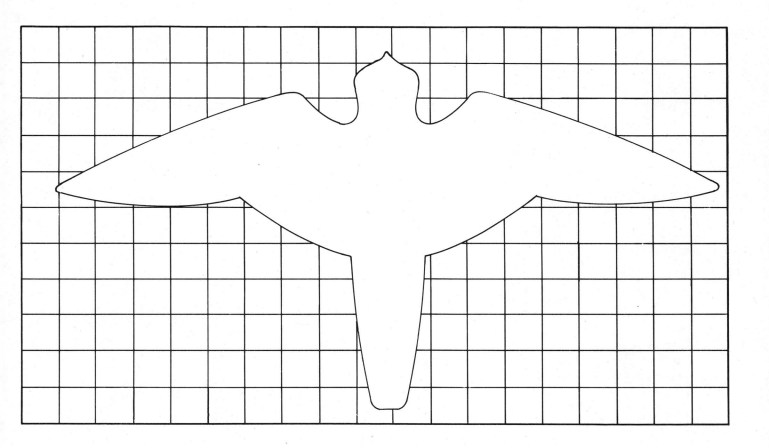

1"

Appendix G

Information on Weed and Pest Control
For Gardens, Yards, and Tree Plantings

SAFER'S ORGANIC INSECT CONTROL
(Insecticidal Soap)

Safer's Organic Insect Control is a safe, non-chemical, contact insecticide made from naturally occurring fats and oils found in the cells of all living things. It is biodegradable and leaves no harmful residue so it can be used right up to the day of harvest. It is not harmful to people, birds, animals, ladybugs, or honeybees.

It can be used on flowers and vegetables in the garden, greenhouse and in the house and on fruit trees. It has no harmful odors. For best results, spray first thing in the morning or evening.

Safer's Insecticidal Soap is available in ready to use spray bottles or in the liquid concentrate form. For most applications, mix 6 tablespoons of concentrate per 1 gallon of water. For whitefly control, only use 3 tablespoons per 1 gallon.

If You Grow	Safer Controls
Beans	Bean Aphid
Cucumbers	Apple Wooly Aphid
Collards	Rose Aphid
Broccoli	Red Spider Mite
Peas	2 Spotted Mite
Tomatoes	White Mite
Squash	Mealy Bugs
Canteloupes	White Fly Adults
Radishes	and Nymphs
Eggplants	Earwigs
Peppers	Milkweed Bug
Watermelons	Boxelder Bug
Grapes	Stink Bug
Fruit Trees	Squash Bug
Ornamental	Leaf Hoppers
Trees & Shrubs	Harlequin Bug
Most House Plants	Blossom Thrips
and Flowers	Rose Slug
Cabbages	Pear Psylla
Brussel Sprouts	Soft Brown Scale
Cauliflower	

DIPEL CROP SAVER
(Bacillus thuringiensis)

Dipel Crop Saver is not a harmful chemical. Unlike chemical insecticides, Dipel kills only leaf-eating caterpillars. Dipel is one of the safest insecticides in use today. It is a biological insecticide containing a naturally occurring disease organism which is fatal to the larval stage. Birds, bees, fish, wildlife and beneficial insects are not affected by it. Dipel is easy to use ... simply mix the Dipel powder with water, apply by sprayer, spraying top and underside of the foliage (leaves). Dipel dust is also available.

In addition to garden use, Dipel is very effective against the gypsy moth. It may be used on flowers too. Non-toxic Dipel is not harmful to dogs, cats, or humans. It is environmentally safe and E.P.A approved.

If You Grow	Dipel Controls
Tomatoes	Tomato Hornworm
Beans	Tomato Fruitworm
Peas	Cabbage Looper
Cabbage	Imported Cabbageworm
Lettuce	Webworm
Cucumber	Beet Armyworm
Squash	Velvetbean Caterpillar

If You Grow	Dipel Controls
Pepper	Melonworms
Cantaloupe	Cutworm
Watermelon	Leafroller
Pumpkin	Cankerworms
Broccoli	Tent Caterpillar
Brussels Sprouts	Cloverworm
Potatoes	Diamondback Moth
Egg Plant	Gypsy moth
Cauliflower	
Beets Greens	
Celery Apples	

ROTENONE PRODUCTS

Rotenone is an extract from roots of two related legumes (bean family) plants grown in the Caribbean islands and South America. The extract is utilized in dusts, wettable powders, and liquid concentrates. It helps control aphids, various beetles, caterpillars, squash bugs and vine borers. Rotenone is relatively non-toxic to bees, people and pets. It is often used in flea powders. It has a shelf life of at least 1 year; keep cool and dry.

ROTENONE 1% DUST

The standard, low concentration dust is for use on vegetables and ornamentals. Usage rate is approximately 1 pound per 2,000 sq. ft. when applied with a standard duster.

ROTENONE 5% WETTABLE POWDER DUST
(commercial strength)

This is a special product with increased concentration. It is labeled to be mixed with water at an average of 2 oz. per gallon, and sprayed at a rate of 400 sq. ft. per 1 gallon (12 lbs. in 100 gallons water per 1 acre), although significantly greater dilutions are usually effective. It may also be used as a dust. It can be effective on hard-to-control insects such as potato beetles, flea beetles, onion thrips, and cucumber beetles.

PYRETHRUM PRODUCTS

This botanical insecticide is from the blossoms of the dalmatian daisy, **Chrysanthemum cinearaefolium.** The raw product is mostly imported. It causes rapid debilitation of a wide variety of garden pests and is similar to rotenone in its low toxicity to people, pets and bees. The effectiveness of pyrethrum is usually enhanced by mixing with piperonyl buloxide, a synergist, extracted from Brazilian sassafras. While not insecticidal, it bolsters the effects of pyrethrum and rotenone.

PYRENONE CROP SPRAY

Pyrenone crop spray is a more potent pyrethrum liquid concentrate for commercial growers. It is an effective botanical alternative to less safe chemicals. Formulated with 6% pyrethrum, 60% piperonyl buloxide and 24% aromatic oils. Labeled for use up to the day of harvest of for almost all common vegetable crop pests, including cornborers and earworms. Usage is 2-6 oz. per acre in enough water for coverage.

RED ARROW Botanical Insect Spray

Red Arrow botanical insect spray is a pyrethrum-rotenone liquid concentrate for spraying. It is a popular, easy-to-mix and use product for effective control of a wide range of insect pests. Average use is 1 tbs. (½ oz.) per gallon of water. (Red Arrow contains 0.5% pyrethrum, 1.5% rotenone, 3% other cube resins, 3% piperonyl buloxide, 24% soybean oils, 60% aromatic oils, and 7% inert ingredients.) It is used by both commercial and home gardeners.

WEED CONTROL FOR TREE AND SHRUB SEEDLINGS
Excerpted and modified from a pamphlet by the Forestry Section, Iowa Department of Natural Resources.
ARE WEEDS REALLY A PROBLEM?

Weeds are a problem because they grow faster and often taller than young seedlings. They compete with your seedlings for the limited moisture, nutrients, light, and space available. Grasses and broadleaf weeds may kill your seedlings. At the very least, they will keep your seedlings from growing as quickly and vigorously as they would without competition.

In addition, a thick stand of weeds next to your seedlings provides habitat for rabbits and rodents which can girdle or cut off your plants.

The only way to avoid these problems is to control the weeds that cause them.

WHAT DOES CONTROLLING WEEDS MEAN?

Controlling weeds means keeping them from growing in a 2'-4' zone around your seedlings. This gives your plants and their roots room to get started and keep growing without competition.

Even though it's important to keep the area around your plants weed-free, you shouldn't leave the entire planting site bare and unprotected. The remaining area should be planted with something shallow-rooted like oats or timothy. By keeping the area around your seedlings weed-free and protecting the remaining soil with a cover crop, you can control weeds effectively. This method will also prevent soil erosion, improve water penetration, and limit excessive sun, heat, and wind. On sites where rabbits or rodents are a problem, this area between rows should be mowed in the fall to reduce populations that may girdle your seedlings during the winter.

HOW DO YOU GET STARTED?

Begin weed control before your seedlings are planted. To prepare for planting, remove all vegetation in strips or circles 2'-4' wide. (The width will depend on the size of your seedlings, the size of competing weeds and the erosion potential of your site.) Scalping the soil is a good technique for doing this.

If you use herbicides to remove vegetation, it's probably best to spray during the fall before planting if perennial or biennial weeds or grasses are a problem. (Annual weeds will die in the fall anyway.) Roundup is a good herbicide to use.

Growing weeds can also be removed in the spring by using a pre-emergent herbicide, Princep, or a post-emergent herbicide like Roundup.

There should be no vegetation growing in the strips or circles at the time of planting. If there is, treat again just prior to planting.

WHAT DO YOU DO AFTER PLANTING?

Weed control will be needed for the first 3-5 years after your seedlings have been planted! While weed control efforts can decrease as your seedlings become established, some control will be necessary until your plants are tall or dense enough to suppress competition.

There are several ways to control weeds, including cultivating, mowing, mulching, and chemical control. You can decide which method or methods will work best for you.

CULTIVATING — Mechanical or hand cultivation usually does not effectively control weeds because it doesn't eliminate weed roots in the immediate vicinity of a tree's or shrub's roots. You'll also need to allow adequate space for cultivation equipment between seedlings when planting.

To avoid root damage, don't try to get closer than 6'-12' to the seedlings or deeper than 3' when mechanically cultivating the 2'-4' strips or circles. Mechanical cultivation should be supplemented with hand cultivation or herbicide treatment to control weeds close to your seedlings.

Cultivation will be required three to five times per season!

MOWING — Mowing is a poor alternative for controlling weeds. Although it controls competition for light and space, weed roots still compete with your seedlings for moisture and nutrients. Weeds and grass must still be controlled around each tree and shrub. There is also the potential for mechanical damage to the seedling when trying to mow too close. Hitting seedling stems while mowing provides a place for disease or decay to start.

If you do decide to mow, you'll need to allow adequate space for equipment between seedlings when planting. Mowing should be done often enough to keep seedlings clearly visible.

MULCHING — Mulch can be used around your seedlings to control weeds and reduce moisture loss. It can be difficult and expensive to obtain mulch and spread it on a large scale, so this method of weed control is probably best for small plantings and gardens. However, it is preferable to cultivating or mowing!

Many materials can be used as mulch, including sawdust, clean ground corn cobs, wood chips, and bark. Straw isn't good unless you can rake it away from the seedlings in the fall. Otherwise, rodents may overwinter there and girdle the seedlings; and weed seeds may be introduced.

You'll need to remove weeds before applying mulch. Apply a pre-emergent herbicide like Princep or Simazine prior to mulching. The mulch must be thick enough to keep weeds from reappearing — 6' to 8' deep.

CHEMICAL CONTROL — Herbicides do a good job of controlling weeds when applied **in the proper amount at the right time.** They are available from most distributors of agricultural supplies. You can use a variety of equipment to apply herbicides, from boom sprayers suitable for large areas of level land to backpack sprayers for smaller areas or on irregular terrain. Specific mixing and application instructions are given on the manufacturer's labels.

Apply herbicides only when needed and handle with extreme care. Follow label directions and heed all precautions. Pesticides are especially dangerous when improperly handled, applied or disposed of. They can injure humans, domestic animals, desirable plants, wildlife and fish, and they can contaminate water supplies.

Two general types of herbicides are effective in controlling grasses and broadleaf weeds. These are (1) pre-emergent, soil- applied chemicals which are put on before weeds emerge to prevent weed growth, and (2) post-emergent chemicals which are applied to the foliage of established weeds to kill them.

For the latest information on recommended chemical weed control for use in tree plantings, contact your county agricultural extension service office or local DNR forester. In Minnesota ask for Forestry Fact Sheet Number 13-1979 "Chemical Weed Control in Shelterbelts and Forest Plantations" by Marvin E. Smith.

WEED CONTROL IS WORTH THE EFFORT

The survival and growth of your seedlings can be increased significantly by controlling weed competition. In fact, weed control may be the most important single factor in establishing successful tree and shrub plantings.

Remember, establishing a wood-producing timber or wildlife area won't be accomplished simply by planting your seedlings.

IF YOUR SEEDLINGS ARE WORTH PLANTING, THEY ARE WORTH TAKING CARE OF. Additional printed information about Princep, Surflan, Goal, and Roundup is available from your county extension office, area wildlife manager, or area forester.

Appendix H

Seeding Rates and Suggested Mixes For Establishment of Grasses and Legumes

AREAS OF ADAPTATION AND PERFORMANCE STANDARDS FOR SELECTED SPECIES AND VARIETIES OF PRAIRIE GRASSES

| | | Area and degree of adaptation in specific Major Land Resource Areas in the prairie pothole region (See accompanying map)* | | | | | |
| | | Major Land Resources Area | | | | | |
Species and Variety	Origin	56	57	90-91	102A	102B	103
Warm-season, Native Grasses							
Big bluestem							
Pawnee	Pawnee County, Nebraska	5-7	5-7	5-7	3-5	1	1
Champ	Iowa, southeast Nebraska	7-0	5-7	5-7	3	1	1

AREAS OF ADAPTATION AND PERFORMANCE STANDARDS FOR SELECTED SPECIES AND VARIETIES OF PRAIRIE GRASSES (CONTINUED)

Species and Variety	Origin	Area and degree of adaptation in specific Major Land Resource Areas in the prairie pothole region Major Land Resources Area					
		56	57	90-91	102A	102B	103
Bonilla							
(PM-SD-27)	Beadle County, South Dakota	3-5	5	5	1	1	3
NDG-4	Morton County, North Dakota	3	3	3	5-7	9	9
Rountree	Iowa	5-7	5-7	5-7	1	1	1
Sand bluestem							
Goldstrike	Western and north-central Nebraska	5-7	5-7	5-7	3	1	1-3
Garden	Nebraska	5-7	5-7	5-7	3	1	3
Indiangrass							
Oto	Kansas, Nebraska	7	7	7	3-5	1	1-3
Holt	Nebraska	3-5	5-7	5-7	3	1	1-3
Nebraska 54	Nebraska	5-7	7	7	3-5	1	1-3
PM-ND-444	North Dakota & South Dakota	1-3	3	3	1	3	5
Switchgrass							
Pathfinder	Kansas, Nebraska	5-7	5-7	5-7	3-5	1	1-3
Nebraska 28	Holt County, Nebraska	3-5	5	3-5	1-3	1	1-3
Summer	Otoe County, Nebraska	3-5	5	5	1-3	1	1
Forestberg							
(PM-SD-149)	Sanborn County, South Dakota	3	3	3	1	1-3	1-3
NDG-965-98	Morton County, North Dakota	1	1-3	1-3	3	5	5
Sunburst	Yankton, South Dakota	3-5	5	5	1-3	1	1
Little Bluestem							
Camper	Kansas, Nebraska	5	5-7	5-7	3	1	3
Blaze	Kansas, Nebraska	3-5	3-5	3-5	3	1	1
Prairie Sandreed							
Goshen	Wyoming	7	7	9	3	5	5
Sideoats grama							
Trailway	Nebraska	5-7	5-7	5-7	1-3	1	1-3
Butte	Nebraska	5	5	5	1	1	1-3
Pierre	South Dakota	3	3-5	3-5	1	1	3-5
Killdeer	North Dakota	3	3-5	3-5	5	5-7	
Cool-season, Native							
Western wheatgrass							
Flintlock	Nebraska	5	5	7	3	1	3
Mandan-456	North Dakota	3	3	5	5	7	9
Green needlegrass							
Green Stipa	North Dakota	3	5	5	5	7	9
Lodorm	North Dakota	3	5	5	5	7	9

* Codes for adaptation are defined as follows: 1-Climatically adapted with optimum level of performance; 3-Good adaptation within 250-300 miles of origin; 5-Moderately adapted within 300-500 miles of origin; 7-Poorly adapted. Southern sources that are moved north-northwest are subject to severe winter injury during establishment, mature late, and will not make seed within normal growing season. Northern sources that are moved southeast mature early, have poor vegetative production, and are less disease resistant; 9-Very poor, use is not recommended: and 0-Not adapted.

Visit your SCS office for advice if you wish to plant prairie grasses outside of the prairie region on the map that accompanies this table.

New Conservation Reserve Program (CRP) practices include seeding down cropland with approved mixtures of grasses and legumes. These approved mixtures may vary from state to state and from year to year. Consult with your local SCS office for the latest information on approved CRP practices if you wish to participate in that program. Following is a variety of seed mixes that can be used to seed down areas for wildlife nesting cover or erosion control. Because of their invasive characteristics, sweet clover and red canarygrass are not recommended.

EXOTIC SPECIES

a. For soils classified as moderately well, well or excessively drained:
    1) Alfalfa 6 lbs/ac, Smooth Bromegrass 8 lbs/ac
    2) Alfalfa 6 lbs/ac, Smooth Bromegrass 6 lbs/ac, Orchardgrass 3 lbs/ac
    3) Alfalfa 4 lbs/ac, Intermediate Wheatgrass 14 lbs/ac
    4) Alfalfa 4 lbs/ac, Intermediate Wheatgrass 7 lbs/ac, Tall Wheatgrass 7 lbs/ac
    5) Birdsfoot Trefoil 5 lbs/ac, Timothy 2 lbs/ac, or Orchard Grass 2 lbs/ac

NOTE: Use mixtures 3 and 4 only in areas where soil ph exceeds 7.0. If the area is for use as pasture, reduce the intermediate wheatgrass to 3 lbs. and increase the tall wheatgrass to 11 lbs. Seeding rates are based on pounds of pure live seed.

b. For soils classified somewhat poorly drained or where soil ph is below 6.5 and the cost of liming materials is deemed excessive:
    6) Birdsfoot Trefoil 5 lbs/ac, Red Clover 2 lbs/ac, Timothy 2 lbs/ac
    7) Birdsfoot Trefoil 6 lbs/ac, Red Clover 2 lbs/ac, Orchardgrass 2 lbs/ac
    8) Smooth Bromegrass 10 lbs/ac, Red Clover 6 lbs/ac, Alsike Clover 1 lb/ac

c. For soils classified as poorly drained and very poorly drained:
    9) Garrison Creeping Foxtail 5 lbs/ac, Red Clover 6 lbs/ac, Alsike Clover 1 lb/ac

NOTE: Use mixture 9 only on wet site conditions.

d. For soils where ph is below 5.5 and the cost of liming materials is deemed excessive:
    11) Red Top 5 lbs/ac, Alsike Clover 3 lbs/ac

NATIVE PRAIRIE SPECIES

Most prairie plantings use a total of 12# - 15# of grass seed per acre, with more seed being used on heavier soils. Following are some possible mixes;

a. For deep well drained, moderately well drained soils and somewhat poorly drained soils:
    1) Switchgrass 5 lbs/ac
    2) Big Bluestem 10 lbs/ac
    3) Switchgrass 1 lb/ac, Big Bluestem 5 lbs/ac, Indiangrass 3 lb/ac

b. For shallow and/or excessively drained soils:
    4) Little Bluestem 1.5 lbs/ac, Big Bluestem or Sand Bluestem 2 lbs/ac, Sideoats Grama 4 lbs/ac, Switchgrass 1 lb/ac, Indiangrass 1.5 lbs/ac

c.   For specific sites or special situations to develop habitat for ground-nesting prairie songbirds. Well adapted to dry or sandy areas in western Minnesota and western Iowa:
   5)   Buffalo Grass 6 lbs/ac, Little Bluestem 4 lbs/ac, Blue Grama 2 lbs/ac

NOTE: Slender wheatgrass and green needlegrass may be added to mixtures 3 and 5 at 2-4 lbs/ac each. Western wheatgrass at 2-4 lbs/ac may be added to mixture 3. These options will be applicable in areas where soil ph exceeds 7.0. This option will prevent use of Atrex during the stand establishment period. Seeding rates must be based on pounds of pure live seed.

For information on planting a more balanced composition of grasses, legumes, and forbs in prairie plantings, consult Prairie Restorations, Inc., of Princeton, Minnesota or the Prairie Moon Nursery at Winona, Minnesota. Following are some grass mixtures you may wish to consider for wet, mesic and dry sites.

WET SITES
   Big Bluestem
   Indian Grass
   Switch Grass
   Blue Joint Grass
   Cordgrass
   Canada Wild Rye

MESIC SITES
   Big Bluestem
   Little Bluestem
   Indian Grass
   Canada Wild Rye
   Needle Grass
   Prairie Dropseed

DRY SITES
   Little Bluestem
   Sideoats Grama
   Kalm's Brome
   June Grass

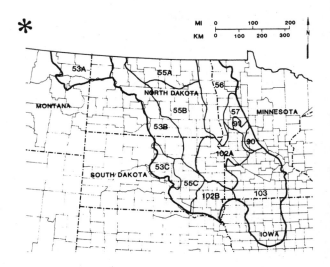

Appendix I

Best Butterfly Nectar Sources in Minnesota

Plant Species	Approximate Number Of Butterfly Species Using Each Plant Species	Plant Species	Approximate Number Of Butterfly Species Using Each Plant Species
Dogbanes	43	Buttonbush	13
Common Milkweed	42	Blackberry	12
Red Clover	21	White Sweet Clover	12
Swamp Milkweed	20	Houstonia	11
Asters	19	Tickseed Sunflower	10
Thistles	18	Butterflyweed	9
Goldenrods	18	Joe-Pye-Weed	9
Winter Cress	18	Ironweed	9
Vetches	14	Peppermint	9
Selfheal	14	Vervain	9
New Jersey Tea	13		

Appendix J

MIDWESTERN BIRDS WHICH USE SNAGS

Species	Create Cavities	Use Cavities
Wood Duck		•
Goldeneye		•
Bufflehead		•
Hooded Merganser		•
Common Merganser		•
Red-Breasted Merganser		•
Turkey Vulture		•
Merlin (pigeon hawk)		•
American Kestrel (sparrow hawk)		•
Peregrine Falcon		•
Barn Owl		•
Northern Hawk Owl		•
Eastern Screech-Owl		•
Barred Owl		•
Long-eared Owl		•
Northern Saw-Whet Owl		•
Chimney Swift		•
Common Flicker	•	
Pileated Woodpecker	•	
Red-Bellied Woodpecker	•	
Red-Headed Woodpecker	•	
Yellow-Bellied Sapsucker	•	
Hairy Woodpecker	•	
Downy Woodpecker	•	
Black-Backed Woodpecker	•	
Three-Toed Woodpecker	•	
Great Crested Flycatcher		•
Tree Swallow		•
Purple Martin		•
Black-Capped Chickadee	•	
Boreal Chickadee	•	
Tufted Titmouse		•
White-Breasted Nuthatch		•
Red-Breasted Nuthatch	•	
Brown Creeper	(occasionally)	•
House Wren		•
Winter Wren		•
Bewick's Wren		•
Carolina Wren		•
Eastern Bluebird		•
European Starling		•
Prothonotary Warbler		•
House Sparrow		•

Use Cavities 12   Create Cavities 31   TOTAL Species 43

MIDWESTERN MAMMALS WHICH USE SNAGS

Animals	Importance of Snags To Animals		
	High	Medium	Low
Squirrels			
Fox	•		
Gray	•		
Red	•		
Northern Flying	•		
Southern Flying	•		
Bats			
Little Brown		•	
Big Brown		•	
Pipistrelle		•	
Silver-Haired	•		
Red	•		
Hoary	•		
Others			
Porcupine	•		
Raccoon	•		
Opossum		•	
Long-Tailed Weasel		•	
Ermine		•	
Short-Tailed Shrew			•
Masked Shrew			•
Arctic Shrew			•
Least Shrew			•
White-Footed Mouse		•	
Pine Marten	•		
Fisher	•		
Least Chipmunk	•		
Eastern Chipmunk	•		

Appendix K

Wildlife Feeder Designs

Part 1. Diagram and instructions for the pop bottle sunflower seed feeder.

Materials Needed: Three 2-liter plastic soft-drink bottles, a 7-inch dessert topping lid, a baby food jar lid, a coping saw, a single-edged razor blade or "X-acto" knife, all-weather rubber sealant, 8 inches of wire or monofilament fishing line, a small nail or 7/16-inch bit and hand drill, and a metal or wood screw.

Soak a 2-liter bottle in warm, soapy water to clean inside and remove label. Pull off the colored plastic base, but save it for use as a measuring device when cutting the feeding holes.

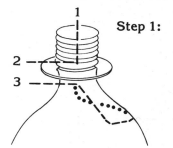

Step 1: Using a second 2-liter bottle, make a perpendicular cut with the coping saw at the bottle's mouth down to the point at which the neck collar begins. Make a second cut at, and slightly above the collar perpendicular to the first cut. Discard the cut piece. Cut the remaining section of the neck and collar away from the bottle, leaving at least a 1-inch flange of plastic beneath the collar. Using a third 2-liter bottle, repeat these same steps. The two spouts that result will be used as feeding holes, with their neck pieces preventing seed spill-out.

Step 2: Cut two 1-inch diameter circular holes across from each other in the sides of the first bottle. The top of the plastic base that was removed earlier will serve as a guide — the top of each cut should be made at the same point as the top of the plastic base.

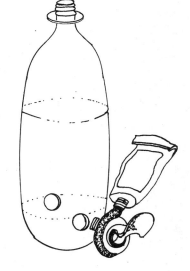

Step 3: Apply sealant around the outside of each feeding hole. Insert spouts into the bottle, flange end outward. The collar on each spout and the sealant will form a watertight "gasket." Secure with a rubberband until dry.

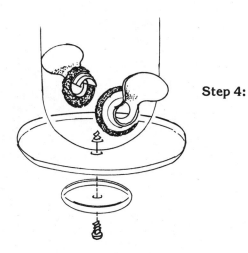

Step 4: Using a drill or small nail, make small holes in the bottom of the bottle and the dessert topping and baby food lids. Attach the two lids, with the baby food lid on the bottom, to the bottom of the bottle with the metal or wood screw. The topping lid will form the perch that the baby food lid will stabilize.

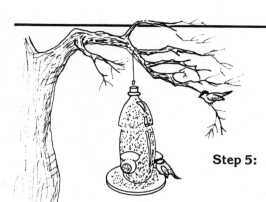

Step 5: Drill or punch two small, parallel holes in the bottle top. String wire or monofilament line through the holes and tie. Once the bottle is filled with sunflower seeds, screw the top onto the bottle.

Part 2. Diagram and instructions for a pop bottle thistle seed feeder.

Materials Needed: 1-liter plastic soft-drink bottle; three or four 3/16-inch wide, 5-inch long wooden dowels (straight, hardwood sticks will do): a single-edged razor blade or "X-acto" knife: 8 inches of wire or monofilament fishing line, a metal eye screw, a hand drill and small bit.

Soak the bottle in warm, soapy water to clean inside and remove label. Pull off the colored plastic base and discard.

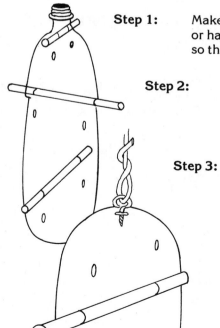

Step 1: Make small parallel cuts in each side of the bottle with the razor blade, "X-acto" knife, or hand drill. Insert the dowels as perches. Alternate the radial alignment of each perch so that all sides of the bottle can be used.

Step 2: At points about 1-inch below each dowel, make small ¼-inch long, 1/8-inch wide incisions through the bottle for feeding holes. Don't make the cuts too large — the correct size will allow birds to pick out individual seeds yet prevent spillage. (A wood-burning needle will also make the right-sized feeding holes).

Step 3: Bore a 7/16-inch hole in the bottom of the bottle and insert the eye screw. When suspended, the bottom becomes the top of the feeder. Affix wire or monfilament line to the eye screw and tie.

Gas line antifreeze plastic bottles provide an easy way to fill both feeders with seed. Cut a funnel from a 12-ounce bottle with a coping saw about half-way up. The necks of this funnel and both feeder bottles will mate, providing a convenient way to fill them without spillage.

119

Part 3.   **Instructions for making the Olson deer feeder.**

1. Select two 55-gallon barrels which have not been used for storage of flammable material like gasoline. Cutting barrels which have held flammable materials can cause the barrel to explode!! Cut one barrel in two with an acetylene torch. These two halves will each be usable as tops for the feeders. Cut an 8"x 10"hole in the end of each half. This hole is used for filling the feeder with shelled corn. A 1"x 10"x 12"board can be used as a cover for the hole. Bend out with a hammer the bottom edge of each top to facilitate slipping the top over the other barrel. Set the top aside.

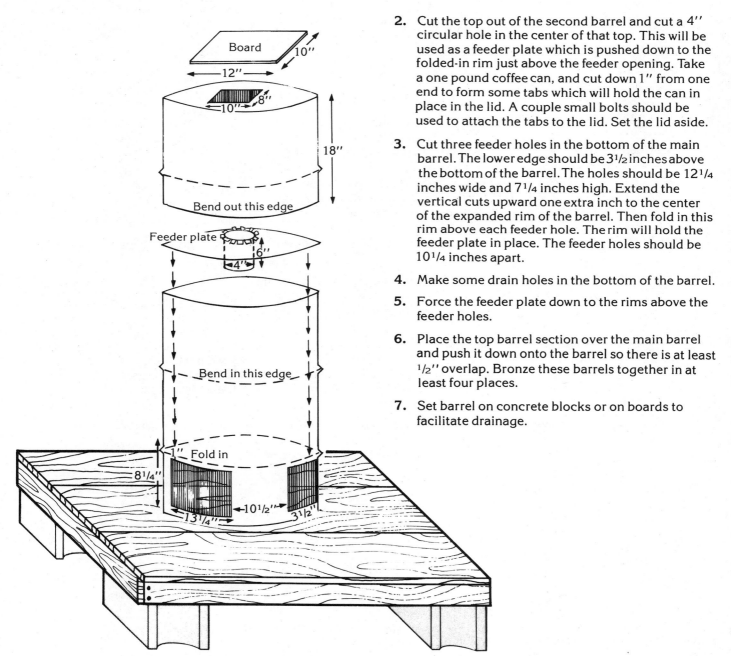

2. Cut the top out of the second barrel and cut a 4" circular hole in the center of that top. This will be used as a feeder plate which is pushed down to the folded-in rim just above the feeder opening. Take a one pound coffee can, and cut down 1" from one end to form some tabs which will hold the can in place in the lid. A couple small bolts should be used to attach the tabs to the lid. Set the lid aside.

3. Cut three feeder holes in the bottom of the main barrel. The lower edge should be 3½ inches above the bottom of the barrel. The holes should be 12¼ inches wide and 7¼ inches high. Extend the vertical cuts upward one extra inch to the center of the expanded rim of the barrel. Then fold in this rim above each feeder hole. The rim will hold the feeder plate in place. The feeder holes should be 10¼ inches apart.

4. Make some drain holes in the bottom of the barrel.

5. Force the feeder plate down to the rims above the feeder holes.

6. Place the top barrel section over the main barrel and push it down onto the barrel so there is at least ½" overlap. Bronze these barrels together in at least four places.

7. Set barrel on concrete blocks or on boards to facilitate drainage.

Appendix L

Sheltered Bird Feeder Designs

There are several rules of importance in building winter feeding shelters for upland birds. The shelter must be protected from prevailing stormy winds, usually north and west. It must be sufficiently open so that feeding birds may escape the attacks of predators—it should not act as a baited trap. It must be built so that heavy snowfall will not break it down or hinder its accessibility. It should be constructed so that frequent visits to replenish the food supply will not be necessary in case of a protracted spell of stormy weather.

The side hill shelter is pictured in Figure a. It should be placed on a hill having a south or east exposure. After the lean-to framework has been erected it should be given a top covering of hay, straw, corn stalks or evergreen boughs, allowing the ends to extend over the three open sides. This type shelter is of value in areas frequented by quail and pheasants.

The open field shelter in Figure b is useful where gray partridge, pheasant and prairie chicken will benefit from a winter food supply. It should face the south and be covered with hay, straw or cornstalks.

The brush shelter, shown in Figure c, is similar and should be placed so the front and sides are free from obstructions which would hinder the birds' escape from predators. This shelter should be of value to pheasants and bobwhite quail.

The hopper feeder, depicted in Figure d, is the most complex and possibly the most efficient. It is simply a sturdy platform of saplings that is 10 to 14 feet square. It is held up at the four corners, and if need be, near the center, with posts or convenient tree trunks. The height may vary from three to four feet depending largely on the average snowfall. It is covered with a snow-protecting roof of hay, straw or evergreen branches.

At the center is placed the food supply hopper, holding a bushel or more of feed, the spout of which rests on a large flat stone. This spout is square, with a notch on each side through which the grain flows out as it is consumed by the feeding birds. The flat stone keeps the feed out of the drifting snow and also prevents the spout from being pressed down into the ground by weight of snow.

Figure a. Side hill shelter

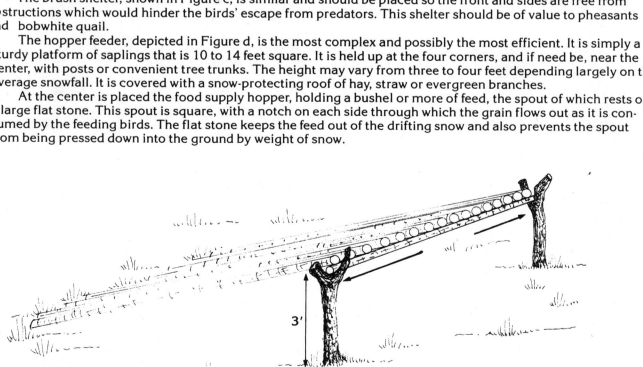

Figure b. Open field shelter

Appendix L
Sheltered Bird Feeder Designs Continued

Inside all these feeding shelters it is advisable to place a layer of hay siftings, chaff or fine-cut hay, to provide additional shelter and food. Also, hay-barn siftings will furnish a good quantity of food in itself, especially where quail are feeding. This carpet will also have a tendency to prevent drifted-in snow from packing hard.

Cracked corn, oats, wheat, cow-peas, millet, buckwheat, broom corn, sunflower seeds and grain screenings can all be used in these feeders. In feeding quail and gray partridges, ground grain and grain screenings are preferable.

Shelters should be placed in spots known to be frequented by birds. Permanency is highly desirable; after several years of use the birds use the established feeding centers as soon as natural food becomes scarce. Several small shelters are preferable to one large one because it makes the birds less vulnerable to predation.

Figure c. Brush shelter

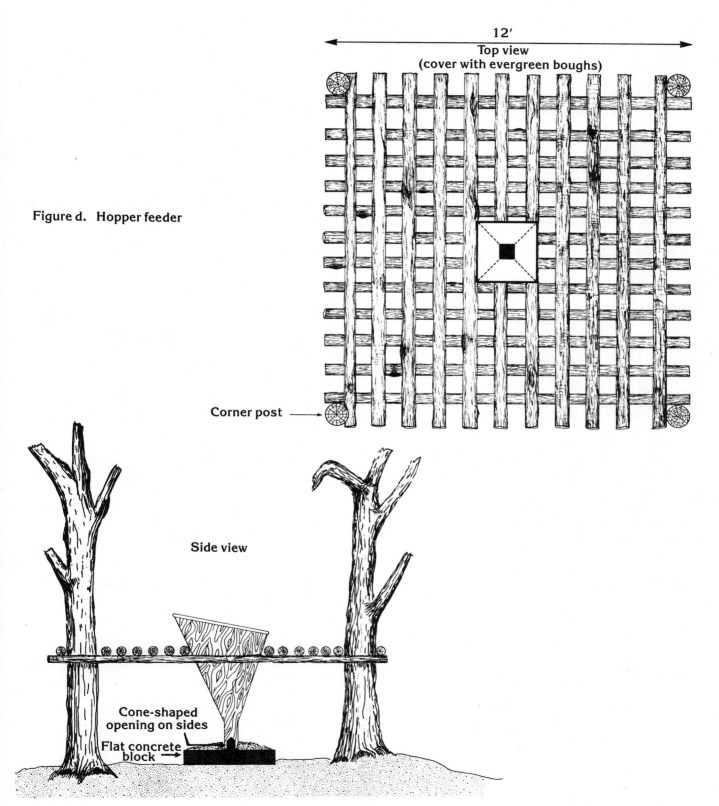

12'

Top view
(cover with evergreen boughs)

Figure d. Hopper feeder

Corner post

Side view

Cone-shaped
opening on sides

Flat concrete
block

Appendix M

Significant Disease and Insect Problems of Midwestern Trees and Shrubs

Discretion should be used when these species are considered for use. Local plant experts should be consulted for further information (101).

Acer negundo (Boxelder)
Boxelder bugs are a nuisance on female trees. Do not plant female trees in yards.

Berberis spp. (Barberry)
Some species are alternate hosts for the black stem rust of wheat and should not be used in regions where wheat is grown. Berberis koreana and Berberis thunbergii are resistant to this disease.

Betula papyrifera (Paper birch), **Betula alleghaniensis** (Yellow birch), and **Betula pendula** (European birch). Short lived due to bronze birch borer. **Betula populifolia** (Gray birch) and **Betula nigra** (River birch) are more resistant to the bronze birch borer. Leaf miners also defoliate trees. Not recommended for hot and dry sites.

Castanea dentata (American chestnut)
Susceptible to chestnut blight which is caused by fungus "Endothia parasitica." Not recommended for planting at this time. Resistant strains are under development.

Cotoneaster integerrimus (European cotoneaster) and **Cotoneaster multiflorus** (Many-flowered cotoneaster)
Fire blight can affect these species.

Crataegus mollis (Downy hawthorn) and **Crataegus punctata** (Dotted hawthorn)
Susceptible to hawthorn rust. **C. crus-galli** (Cockspur hawthorn) **C.x. mordensis** and **C. phaenopyrum** (Washington hawthorn) are resistant. Subject to fire blight.

Euonymus atropurpurea (Wahoo)
Powdery mildew can affect this species in the fall.

Fraxinus pennsylvanica (Green ash)
There is a relatively new disease called "Ash yellows" that appears to be spreading north into Minnesota from Iowa. This could threaten extensive ash plantings in urban areas. Check with your extension office or forester for more details.

Juniperus virginiana (Eastern red cedar) and **Juniperus scopulorum** (Rocky Mountain Juniper)
Susceptible to cedar-apple rust. Don't plant where apples or crabapples are planted.

Lonicera tatarica (Tatarian honeysuckle 'Zabelli')
Very vulnerable to "witches broom" which is caused by aphids. Not recommended for planting at this time. Other varieties are more resistant: 'Freedom' and amur honeysuckle.

Malus spp. (Apples, crabapples)
Many apples are vulnerable to cedar-apple rust and should not be planted where eastern red cedars are common or desired in a planting. Resistant species or cultivars are *Malus baccata* (Siberian crabapple), profusion crabapple, and red splendor crabapple. Apple scab is also a common problem and probably more damaging.

Picea pungens (Blue spruce)
Cystospora canker is a problem. Trees tend to die after reaching 20-25 years of age. Black Hills spruce would be a better choice in yard plantings where spruce is desired.

Pinus strobus (Eastern white pine)
Very susceptible to white pine blister rust. The alternate host is *Ribes* spp. (gooseberries and currants). Don't plant Ribes spp. where white pines are a priority. White pine weevil can cause problems. Deer can also eat seedlings.

Prunus padus (European bird cherry)
  Black knot disease creates swollen black growths on branches.

Quercus ellipsoidalis (Northern pin oak)
  Not recommended for planting because of vulnerability to oak wilt disease, but acceptable if planted in hardiness zone 3N.

Quercus rubra (Red oak)
  Not recommended for planting because of vulnerability to oak wilt disease, but more acceptable if planted in hardiness zone 3N.

Ribes spp. (Currants, gooseberries)
  Most species are alternate hosts for white pine blister rust. Do not plant where white pine is a priority.

Rubus occidentalis (Black raspberry)
  Susceptible to anthracnose disease and should not be planted near red raspberries.

Ulmus americana (American elm)
  Severely affected by Dutch elm disease. No longer recommended for landscaping purposes.

Appendix N

Plants Which Have Undesirable Landscape or Wildlife Qualities

Berberis spp. (Barberries)
  These exotic species are beneficial for wildlife, but can be invasive in places where they are not wanted.

Campsis radicans (Trumpet vine)
  Excellent for hummingbirds where naturalizing is possible, but spreads rapidly in yards.

Caragana spp. (Peashrubs)
  These exotic species are beneficial for wildlife, but can be invasive in places were they are not wanted.

Eleagnus angustifolia (Russian olive)
  It does best in western Minnesota rather than eastern Minnesota and can be invasive on prairies and in pastures.

Euphorbia esula (Leafy spurge)
  Invasive noxious exotic weed.

Fraxinus pennsylvanica (Green ash - "Marshall")
  This cultivar has no seeds for the birds.

Lonicera spp. (Honeysuckles)
  These exotic species are excellent for wildlife, but can be invasive in places where they are not wanted.

Lythrum salicaria (Purple loosestrife)
  An undesirable invasive aquatic weed that chokes out desirable native vegetation. Under no circumstances should it be planted.

*Melilotus spp. (*White and yellow sweet clover)
  These exotic legumes are commonly mixed with grass seed for use in hayfields and for nesting cover. However, it is invasive in prairies and is difficult to eradicate. Consult with local resource people for native legume alternatives.

Morus alba (White mulberry) and ***Morus rubra*** (Red mulberry)
Berries are excellent for birds, but the seeds are readily spread in bird droppings. This causes it to be it to be invasive in some cases. Red mulberry is a native species in some portions of the Midwest, however.

Populus nigra (Lombardy poplar)
Negligible food or cover value for wildlife. Subject to cytospora canker.

Rhamnus cathartica (Common buckthorn) and ***Rhamnus frangula*** (Upright glossy buckthorn). Berries are good for birds, but these exotic species have become invasive in native woodlands.

Robinia pseudoacacia (Black locust)
Native from Pennsylvania to Iowa. Suckers freely and can be very invasive. Affected by the locust borer.

Toxicodendron radicans (Poison ivy)
Berries are used by many wildlife species, but because of its toxic effects on humans it should not be used in landscape plans. A noxious weed.

Phalaris arundinacea (Reed canarygrass).
This exotic grass is frequently planted in low wet areas and in grassy waterways. However, it is invasive where not wanted and mats down in winter-leaving little cover. Prairie cordgrass, big bluestem and switchgrass are better alternatives.

Appendix O

Sources of Seeds, Plants and Garden Catalogs

1. **Caution:** When ordering "native" species of prairie or woodland flowers, grasses, shrubs, or trees, find out the origin of the plants. If they originate more than 200 miles south, 100 miles north or 250 miles east or west of your location, don't order them.

Albert Lea Seed House, Inc.
P.O. Box 167
Albert Lea, MN 56007
A wholesale/retail outlet for a variety of cool season and warm season grasses and forage legumes. Has both certified and uncertified seed available. Will sell in 50 lbs bag lots with United Parcel Service

Arrowhead, Inc.
4001 15th Avenue N.W.
Fargo, ND 58102
Native priarie grass, cool season grass, including the wheatgrasses

Bachman's
6010 Lyndale Avenue South
Minneapolis, MN 55419
Trees, shrubs, flowers, house plants, wildlowers

Blegen, Robert
Star Route, Box 20
Churchs Ferry, ND 58325
Native prairie grass - NDG965 - 98 Switchgrass and NDG4 big bluestem

Breck's
P.O. Box 1758
Peoria IL 61656
Flower bulbs

Burgess Seed and Plant Company
905 Four Seasons Road
Bloomington, IL 61701
Flowers, vegetables, fruits, house plants

Busse Garden Center
635 East 7th Street
Cokato, MN 55321

Cenex Seed
Wilton, ND 58579
Native prairie grass

Cenex Seed Representatives in Minnesota Are:
Arvid Behrene
Rt. 1, Box 39B
Elysian, MN 54028

Chestnut Hill Nursery, Inc.
Route 1, Box 341
Alachua, FL 32615
Dunstan hybrid chestnut, oriental persimmons, figs and
cold hard citrus

C.A. Cruickshank Limited
1015 Mount Pleasant Road
Toronto, Ontario, Canada M4P 2MI
(Catalog $1.00) Flower bulbs and seeds, vegetables,
herbs

Country Wetlands, Nursery and Consulting
S. 75W 20755 Field Drive
Muskego, WI 53150
Excellent source of native aquatic and moist soil plants

DNR, Foresty
Box 44
500 Lafayette Road
St. Paul, MN 55155-4044
Trees and shrubs, wildlife shrub packets

Dundee Nursery
4225 County Road 42
Savage, MN 55378
Trees, shrubs, fruit trees, perennials and wildflowers

Dundee Nursery
16800 Highway 55
Plymouth, MN 55446
Trees, Shrubs, Fruit Trees, Perennials

Dutch Gardens, Inc.
P.O. Box 200
Adelphia, NJ 07710
Flower bulbs

Farmer Seed and Nursery
818 NW 4th Street
Faribault, MN 55021
Trees and shrubs - including native hardwoods

Ferndale Nursery and Greenhouse
P.O. Box 27
Askov, MN 55704
Producer of native wildflowers and ferns

Forest Farm
990 Tetherow Road
Williams, OR 97544-9599
(Catalog $2.00)

Franks Nursery and Crafts
Stores throughout the Midwest.
Trees, shrubs, perennials, annuals

Grand Forks Seed Company
Hwy 81 North
Grand Forks, ND 58201
Native prairie grass, cool season grasses and forage
legumes

Gurney's Seed and Nursery
Yankton, SD 57079
Fruit trees, shrubs, vegetables, flowers, native shade
and nut trees

Hansmeier and Son
Briston, SD 57219
Native prairie grass, many species

Harris Seeds, Garden Trends, Inc.
961 Lyell Avenue
Rochester, NY 14606
Vegetables, annual and perennial flowers, wildflowers,
garden accessories

Haugrud Seed Plant
Route 1, Box 129
Rothsay, MN 54579
Buckwheat seed

Henry Field's Seed and Nursery Co.
Shenendoah, IA 61602
Fruit trees, shrubs, vegetables, flowers, wildflowers,
native shade and nut trees

House of Wesley, Nursery Division
1704 Morrisey Drive
Bloomington, IL 61704
Flowers, fruits, shrubs, trees, vegetables, vines

Inter-State Nurseries
P.O. Box 208
Hamburg, IA 51640
Flowers, fruits, shade trees

Jackson and Perkins Company
Medord, Oregon 97501
Trees, flowers, fruits, vegetables

Ole Jallo
2101 Ridgewood
Alexandria, MN 56308

Cenex Cooperative has many local outlets. They have or can access most varieties of domestic cool season grasses and forage legumes. These listed seed marketing staff people can be contacted for detailed information of special seed requests.

Johnny's Selected Seeds
310 Foss Hill Road
Albion, ME 04910
Vegetables, flowers, wildflowers, alfalfa, grains

J.W. Jung Seed Company
Randolph, WI 53957
Fruit trees, shrubs, vegetables, flowers, native shade and nut trees

Paul Kaste
Fetile, MN 54540
Producer of 'Bison' big bluestem, 'Dacotah' switch-grass, and 'Tomahawk' Indiangrass

Kelly Brothers Nurseries, Inc.
P.O. Box 800
Dansille, NY 14437-0800
Perennials, shrubs, trees, etc. for total landscaping needs.

Kesters Wild Game Food Nurseries, Inc.
P.O. Box 516, 4582 Hwy 116 E
Omro, WI 54963
(Catalog $2.00) Aquatic and marsh plants

Lafayette Home Nursery, Inc.
Lafayette, IL 61449
Prairie forbs

Lakeland Nurseries Sales
Unique Bldg. Mart., Bldg 4
Hanover, PA 17333
Flowers, grasses, fruits, trees

Landscape Alternatives, Inc.
1465 N. Pascal St
St. Paul, MN 55108-2337
Excellent source of native prairie and woodland wild-flowers and grasses

Lee Nursery
Fertile, MN 56490
Wholesale trees and shrubs

Lincoln-Oaks Nursery
Box 1601
Bismarck, ND 58502
Native grasses

Linder's Garden Center
270 West Larpenteur
St. Paul, MN 55117
Excellent variety of trees, shrubs, perennials, and wildflowers.

Little Valley Farm
Route 3, Box 544
Spring Green, WI 53588
(Please send 25¢ for list)

Arthur Lonegran Nursery
Paradise Drive
West Bend, WI 53095
(Does not ship) Native wildflowers

Meyer Seed Company
600 South Caroline Street
Baltimore, MD 21231

Miller Grass Seed Co., Inc.
P.O. Box 81823
Lincoln, NE 68501
Large established seed company for all types of grasse and legumes including many native grass varieties

Minn - Dak Growers Ass'n
P.O. Box 1276
Grand Forks, ND 58206
Buckwheat seed

Michigan Bulb Company
1950 Waldorf
Grand Rapids, MI 49550
Flowers, vegetables, fruit trees

Midwest Wildflowers
Box 64
Rockton, IL 61072
(Catalog: 50¢, seeds only) Native wildflowers

J.E. Miller Nurseries
5060 West Lake Road
Canadaigua, NY 14424
Fruits, trees, flowers

Musser Forests
P.O. Box 340 M.
Indiana, PA 15701-0340
Shrubs, native shade and nut trees

Nandor of the North
HC05
Park Rapids, MN 56470
Container-grown evergreens

Nichols Garden Nursery
Herb and Rare Seed Catalog
1190 North Pacific Hwy
Albany, OR 97321
Herbs, vegetables, flowers, wildflowers

Norfarm Seeds, Inc.
Box 725
Bemidji, MN 56601
Native prairie grass, cool season grass and forage legumes

L.L. Olds Seed Company
2901 Packers Avenue
P.O. Box 7790
Madison, WI 53707
Flowers, vegetables, turf seeds and prairie seeds

Olson, John
Route 1, Box 130
Elsie, NE 69134
Native prairie grasses, 'Goldstrike' sand bluestem

Olson, Wendell
Box 161A
Glyndon, MN 56547
Native prairie grasses

Orchid Gardens
2232-139th Av., NW
Andover, MN 55304
Collector, propagator and vendor for a wide range of native wildflowers and other plants, does not deal in grass seed. (Catalog 25¢).

Richard Owen Nursery
2300 East Lincoln
Bloomington, IL 61701
Fruit trees, shrubs, vegetables, flowers, wildflowers, native shade and nut trees, ginseng

Oxcart Seed Company
Rt #3, Box 226
Hawley, MN 56549
Producer/vendor for northern origin seed of switchgrass, Indian grass, big bluestem, and prairie species mix

Park Nursery
8400 - 60th Street North
Stillwater, MN 55082
Landscape plants, Perennials, Annuals

Park Seed Company
P.O. Box 31
Greenwood, SC 29648-0031
Flowers, vegetables, and herbs

Peavy Seed Company
Bismarck, ND 58502
Native prairie grass

Pine Cone Nursery Inc.
9900 Foley Boulevard Northwest
Coon Rapids, MN 55433

Pinetree Garden Seeds
New Gloucester, ME 04260
Vegetables, (inc. runner beans), flowers

Prairie Moon Nursery
Route 3, Box 163
Winona, MN 55987
Native plants and seeds (wetland, prairie and woodland) from the unglaciated region of SE Minnesota, SW Wisconsin, NE Iowa, and NW Illinois. Seed mixes for different habitats available. Catalog $1.00

Prairie Nursery
P.O. Box 306
Westfield, WI 53964
Prairie grasses, prairie wildflowers

Prairie Restoration Inc.
P.O. Box 327
Princeton, MN 55371
Prairie, woodland, and wetland plants and seeds. Consulting and restoration services available. Catalog 50¢

Prairie Ridge Nursery
9738 Overland Road
Rt #2
Mr. Horeb, WI 53572
Prairie, woodland, and wetland plants and seeds. Consulting and restoration services available. Catalog: 50¢

Putney Nursery, Inc.
Box M
Putney, VT 05346
Wildflowers, perennial, alpine, herb and annual seeds

Reuter Seed Company
320 North Carrolton Ave.
New Orleans, LA 70119

Rogne-Schumacker Seed Farm
Kindred, ND 58051
Native Prairie Grass — 'Roden' western wheatgrass,
'Lodorm' green needlegrass, 'Mandan 759' pubescent
wheatgrass, and NDG 965-98 switchgrass

Sargent's Nursery
3352 North Service Drive
Red Wing, MN 55066
Excellent variety of native shrubs and hardwoods

Schumacher's Berry Farm
Heron Lake, MN 56137
Wholesale only. Excellent variety of shrubs and trees
for wildlife plantings, including Siberian and
Manchurian crabapples

The Sexauer Seed Company
P.O. Box 675
West Fargo, ND 58078
Native and introduced grass species — all kinds.

Sharp Brothers Seed Co.
Healy, KS 67850
Native prairie grass

Sharp Bros. Seed Co. of Missouri
P.O. Box 665
Clinton, MO 64735
Specializing in native grasses and wildflowers for use in
wildlife plantings, habitat restoration, and reclamation
of disturbed land. Several varieties suitable for
Minnesota are included.

Cotton Sheldon
Volga, SD
Native prairie grass

R.H. Shumway Seedsman, Inc.
P.O. Box 1
Graniteville, SC 29829
Full line of vegetable, flower, herb, farm and field seeds
as well as a full nursery line. Catalog $1.00.

Spring Hill Nurseries
110 West Elm Street
Tipp City, OH 45371
Small fruit trees, shrubs, vines, perennial flowers, wildflowers, roses, bulbs, trees and groundcovers.

Stark Brothers Nurseries and Orchards
Highway 54 West
Louisiana, MO 63353

Stock Seed Company
Rt 1, Box 112
Murdock, NE 68407
Native prairie grasses, all types, wildflowers

Stokes Seeds, Inc.
P.O. Box 548
Buffalo, NY 14240
Free catalog on request

Superior View Farms
Bayfield, WI 54814
Plants only

Sunshine Seeds
Wyoming, IL 61491
(Catalog: stamped, addressed envelope) Prairie plants

T.E.C.
The Environmental Collaborative
P.O. Box 539
Osseo, MN 55369
Native trees, shrubs, hardwoods and conifers

Thompson and Morgan Inc.
P.O. Box 1308
Jackson, NJ 08527
Flowers, vegetables (Large catalog)

Otis Twilley Seeds Company
P.O. Box 65
Trevose, PA 19047
Vegetables and flowers

W.J. Unwin Ltd.
P.O. Box 9
Farmingdale, NJ 07727

Van Bourgondien Brothers
P.O. Box A
245 Farmingdale Road
Rt 109
Babylon, NY 11702
Flower bulbs, perennials, wildflowers, and ferns

Vandenberg
Black Meadow Road
Chester, NY 10918
Flowers and other plants

Veldheer Tulip Gardens
12755 Quincy and U.S. 31
Holland, MI 49423
Flower bulbs

Vermont Bean Seed Company
Garden Lane
Bosmoseen, VT 05732
Vegetables (including runner beans), flowers, wildflowers

Vesey's Seeds LTD.
Box 9000
Charlottetown, Prince Edward Island
Canada C1A 8K6
Vegetables, (including runner beans), flowers, seeds for short growing seasons.

W. Atlee Burpee & Co.
300 Park Avenue
Warminster, PA 18991
Fruit trees, shrubs, vegetables, flowers, wildflowers

Wayside Gardens
Hodges, SC 29695-0001
Flowers, shrubs, trees, herbs, fruits

Mason W. Wheeler
Wheeler Farm, Inc.
Aurora, SD 57002
Native prairie grass - "Pierre" sideoats grama, SE-149 switchgrass and garrison creeping foxtail

White Flower Farm
Litchfield, CT 06759-0050
Perennials, bulbs and shrubs

Wildlife Habitat Seed Co.
Rt 3, Box 178
Owatonna, MN 55060
Native prairie grasses: switchgrass, big bluestem, Indiangrass and sideoats grama

Wildlife Nurseries
P.O. Box 2724
Oshkosh, WI 54903
Wetland plants for wildlife and plants for upland birds

Woodlanders, Inc.
1128 Colleton Avenue
Aiken, SC 29801

Zeller Seed Farm
Bird Island, MN 55310
Native prairie grass - cool season

Appendix P

WILDLIFE FOUND IN MIDWESTERN SUMMER HABITATS

KEY
Cmn bkd: Common backyard
Occ bkd: Occasional backyard
Frmstds/Fmwdlts/Fncrows: Farmsteads/Farm woodlots/Fencerows
Rwcps: Rowcrops
Prs & Grslds: Prairies and Grasslands

Ag Wtlds: Agricultural Wetlands
Frst Wtlds: Forest Wetlands and Rivers
Dec Frst: Deciduous Forest
Con Frst: Coniferous Forest

	Cmn bkd	Occ. bkd	Frmstds Fmwdlts Fncrows	Rwcps	Prs & Grslds	Ag Wtlds	Frst Wtlds	Dec Frst	Con Frst
Common loon							•		
Western grebe						•			
Red-necked grebe							•		
Eared grebe						•			
Pied-billed grebe						•	•		
White pelican						•			
Double-crested cormorant						•	•		
Trumpeter swan						•	•		

Appendix P
Wildlife Found in Midwestern Summer Habitats Continued

	Cmn bkd	Occ. bkd	Frmstds Fmwdlts Fncrows	Rwcps	Prs & Grslds	Ag Wtlds	Frst Wtlds	Dec Frst	Con Frst
Canada goose		•				•	•		
Mallard		•				•	•		
Black duck						•	•		
Pintail						•			
Gadwall						•			
American wigeon						•			
Northern shoveler						•			
Blue-winged teal						•			
Wood duck		•				•	•	•	
Redhead						•			
Canvasback						•			
Ring-necked duck							•		
Lesser scaup							•		
Common goldeneye							•	•	•
Ruddy duck						•			
Common merganser							•		•
Red-breasted merganser							•		•
Hooded merganser						•	•	•	•
Turkey vulture								•	•
Northern goshawk								•	•
Cooper's hawk								•	•
Sharp-shinned hawk								•	•
Northern harrier					•	•			
Red-tailed hawk			•		•			•	
Red-shouldered hawk				•				•	
Swainson's hawk			•		•				
Broad-winged hawk								•	•
Bald eagle							•	•	•
Osprey							•	•	•
Peregrine falcon									•
Merlin									•
American kestrel		•	•		•		•	•	
Turkey								•	
Spruce grouse									•
Ruffed grouse								•	•
Sharp-tailed grouse					•				
Greater prairie chicken					•				
Bobwhite			•	•	•				
Ring-necked pheasant		•	•	•	•	•			
Gray partridge			•	•					
Great egret						•	•		
Snowy egret						•	•		
Cattle egret						•	•		
Great blue heron						•	•		
Little blue heron						•	•		
Green-backed heron			•			•	•		
Black-crowned night heron			•			•	•	•	
Yellow-crowned night heron						•	•	•	
American bittern						•	•		
Least bittern						•	•		
Sandhill crane						•	•		

	Cmn bkd	Occ. bkd	Frmstds Fmwdlts Fncrows	Rwcps	Prs & Grslds	Ag Wtlds	Frst Wtlds	Dec Frst	Con Frst
Virginia rail						•	•		
Sora						•	•		
King rail						•	•		
Common moorhen						•	•		
American coot						•	•		
American avocet						•			
Piping plover						•	•		
Killdeer		•	•	•	•	•	•	•	•
Marbled godwit					•				
Upland sandpiper					•				
Spotted sandpiper						•	•		
Wilson's phalarope						•			
American woodcock			•		•		•	•	
Common snipe					•	•	•		•
Herring gull							•		
Ring-billed gull							•		
Franklin's gull						•			
Common tern							•		
Forster's tern						•			
Black tern						•	•		
Rock dove		•	•						
Mourning dove	•		•	•	•			•	•
Yellow-billed cuckoo		•	•					•	•
Black-billed cuckoo		•	•					•	•
Eastern screech-owl		•	•					•	
Great horned owl		•	•		•			•	•
Long-eared owl		•	•					•	•
Short-eared owl					•	•			
Barn owl			•					•	
Barred owl		•	•					•	•
Great gray owl								•	•
Burrowing owl					•				
Boreal owl									•
Northern saw-whet owl								•	•
Whip-poor-will								•	•
Common nighthawk		•	•	•	•			•	
Chimney swift		•							
Ruby-throated hummingbird	•		•					•	
Belted kingfisher		•				•	•		
Northern flicker	•		•	•	•			•	
Pileated woodpecker		•	•					•	•
Red-bellied woodpecker	•		•					•	•
Red-headed woodpecker	•		•					•	•
Yellow-bellied sapsucker		•	•					•	•
Hairy woodpecker	•		•					•	•
Downy woodpecker	•		•					•	•
Black-backed woodpecker									•
Three-toed woodpecker									•
Eastern kingbird		•	•	•	•			•	•
Western kingbird		•	•	•	•				
Great crested flycatcher	•		•					•	•

Wildlife Found in Midwestern Summer Habitats Continued

	Cmn bkd	Occ. bkd	Frmstds Fmwdlts Fncrows	Rwcps	Prs & Grslds	Ag Wtlds	Frst Wtlds	Dec Frst	Con Frst
Eastern phoebe	•		•				•	•	•
Yellow-bellied flycatcher									•
Acadian flycatcher		•					•	•	
Least flycatcher		•	•					•	•
Eastern wood pewee	•		•					•	•
Olive-sided flycatcher		•						•	•
Horned lark			•	•	•				
Barn swallow	•		•						
Cliff swallow		•	•						
Tree swallow	•		•			•	•	•	
Rough-winged swallow		•	•			•	•		
Purple martin	•		•						
Blue jay	•		•					•	•
Gray jay									•
Black-billed magpie			•		•				
Common raven									•
American crow	•		•	•				•	•
Black-capped chickadee	•		•					•	•
Boreal chickadee									•
Tufted titmouse		•	•					•	
White-breasted nuthatch	•		•					•	
Red-breasted nuthatch		•						•	•
Brown creeper		•						•	•
House wren	•		•					•	
Winter wren								•	•
Bewick's wren	•		•					•	
Carolina wren	•		•					•	
Marsh wren						•	•		
Sedge wren					•	•	•		
Mockingbird	•		•					•	
Gray catbird	•		•					•	
Brown thrasher	•		•					•	
American robin	•		•					•	
Wood thrush		•						•	
Hermit thrush								•	•
Swainson's thrush									•
Veery								•	•
Eastern bluebird		•	•		•			•	
Blue-gray gnatcatcher		•	•					•	
Golden-crowned kinglet									•
Ruby-crowned kinglet									
Sprague's pipit					•				
Cedar waxwing	•		•					•	•
Loggerhead shrike			•		•				
European starling	•		•	•				•	
Solitary vireo								•	•
Bell's vireo		•						•	
Yellow-throated vireo		•	•					•	•
Red-eyed vireo		•	•					•	•
Philadelphia vireo								•	
Warbling vireo	•		•					•	
Black-and-white warbler								•	

	Cmn bkd	Occ. bkd	Frmstds Fmwdlts Fncrows	Rwcps	Prs & Grslds	Ag Wtlds	Frst Wtlds	Dec Frst	Con Frst
Prothonotary warbler							•	•	
Golden-winged warbler								•	
Blue-winged warbler								•	
Tennessee warbler								•	•
Nashville warbler								•	•
Parula warbler								•	•
Yellow warbler	•		•					•	•
Magnolia warbler									•
Cape May warbler									•
Yellow-rumped warbler									•
Black-throated green warbler								•	•
Black-throated blue warbler								•	•
Cerulean warbler								•	
Yellow-throated warbler								•	•
Blackburnian warbler									•
Chestnut-sided warbler								•	
Bay-breasted warbler									•
Blackpoll warbler									•
Pine warbler									•
Kirtland's warbler									•
Palm warbler									•
Ovenbird								•	•
Northern waterthrush							•		•
Louisiana waterthrush							•	•	
Yellowthroat	•		•		•	•	•	•	•
Yellow-breasted chat		•	•					•	
Kentucky warbler								•	
Mourning warbler								•	•
Connecticut warbler									•
Hooded warbler								•	
Wilson's warbler								•	
Canada warbler								•	•
American redstart		•	•				•	•	
House sparrow	•		•						
Bobolink			•		•				
Eastern meadowlark		•	•		•				
Western meadowlark		•	•		•				
Yellow-headed blackbird						•			
Red-winged blackbird	•					•	•		
Brewer's blackbird		•							
Common grackle	•		•					•	•
Brown-headed cowbird		•	•					•	•
Orchard oriole		•	•					•	
Northern oriole	•		•					•	
Scarlet tanager		•	•					•	
Northern cardinal	•		•					•	
Rose-breasted grosbeak	•		•					•	
Evening grosbeak									•
Blue grosbeak			•						
Indigo bunting	•		•					•	
Purple finch		•	•						•
American goldfinch	•		•						

Appendix P
Wildlife Found in Midwestern Summer Habitats Continued

	Cmn bkd	Occ. bkd	Frmstds Fmwdlts Fncrows	Rwcps	Prs & Grslds	Ag Wtlds	Frst Wtlds	Dec Frst	Con Frst
Pine grosbeak									•
Dickcissel					•				
Rufous-sided towhee	•		•					•	•
Savannah sparrow			•		•				
Grasshopper sparrow			•		•				
Baird's sparrow					•				
Henslow's sparrow					•				
LeConte's sparrow						•	•		
Sharp-tailed sparrow						•	•		
Lark bunting					•				
Vesper sparrow			•	•	•				
Dark-eyed junco									•
Bachman's sparrow			•						
Chipping sparrow	•		•					•	•
Clay-colored sparrow			•		•				
Field sparrow			•						
White-throated sparrow									•
Swamp sparrow						•	•		
Song sparrow		•	•			•	•		
Chestnut-collared longspur					•				
Virginia opossum		•	•					•	
Masked shrew		•	•		•			•	•
Water shrew							•		
Arctic shrew									•
Pygmy shrew									•
Short-tailed shrew		•	•		•			•	•
Least shrew			•		•			•	
Eastern mole	•		•		•				
Star-nosed mole							•		
Little brown bat		•	•					•	•
Keen's myotis								•	•
Silver-haired bat								•	•
Eastern pipistrelle								•	
Big brown bat		•	•					•	•
Red bat		•	•					•	•
Hoary bat		•	•					•	•
Eastern cottontail	•		•	•	•		•		•
Snowshoe hare							•		•
White-tailed jackrabbit			•	•	•				
Eastern chipmunk	•		•					•	
Least chipmunk									•
Woodchuck		•	•		•				
Richardson's ground squirrel					•				
Thirteen-lined ground squirrel		•	•	•	•				
Franklin's ground squirrel			•		•				
Gray squirrel	•		•					•	
Fox squirrel	•		•					•	
Red squirrel	•		•					•	•
Southern flying squirrel		•	•					•	
Northern flying squirrel		•	•					•	•
Northern pocket gopher		•	•	•	•				
Plains pocket gopher	•		•	•	•				

	Cmn bkd	Occ. bkd	Frmstds Fmwdlts Fncrows	Rwcps	Prs & Grslds	Ag Wtlds	Frst Wtlds	Dec Frst	Con Frst
Plains pocket mouse			•		•				
Beaver						•	•		
Western harvest mouse			•		•				
Deer mouse		•	•	•	•			•	•
White-footed mouse		•						•	
Northern grasshopper mouse					•			•	
Southern red-backed vole			•					•	•
Heather vole									•
Meadow vole		•			•			•	
Rock vole									•
Prairie vole					•				
Woodland vole			•						
Muskrat		•				•	•		
Southern bog lemming							•		
Northern bog lemming							•		•
Norway rat		•	•			•			
House mouse		•	•						
Meadow jumping mouse			•		•	•	•		•
Woodland jumping mouse								•	•
Porcupine								•	•
Coyote			•		•				•
Gray wolf									•
Red fox			•	•	•	•	•		•
Gray fox		•						•	•
Black bear								•	•
Raccoon		•	•	•	•	•	•	•	•
Pine marten								•	•
Fisher								•	•
Short-tailed weasel		•	•						•
Least weasel			•	•	•	•	•		•
Long-tailed weasel			•	•	•	•	•	•	•
Mink			•			•	•	•	•
Wolverine									•
Badger				•	•				
Eastern spotted skunk		•	•	•	•			•	
Striped skunk		•	•	•	•				•
River otter							•		
Bobcat								•	•
White-tailed deer		•	•	•	•	•	•	•	•
Moose								•	•
Blue-spotted salamander							•	•	•
Spotted salamander							•	•	•
Eastern tiger salamander						•	•		
Central newt						•	•		
Four-toed salamander						•	•		
Red-backed salamander						•	•		
Mudpuppy						•			
American toad	•		•	•	•	•	•	•	•
Great plains toad		•			•	•			
Canadian toad		•			•	•			
Blanchard's cricket frog						•	•		
Chorus frog		•				•	•	•	•

Wildlife Found in Midwestern Summer Habitats Continued

	Cmn bkd	Occ. bkd	Frmstds Fmwdlts Fncrows	Rwcps	Prs & Grslds	Ag Wtlds	Frst Wtlds	Dec Frst	Con Frst
Northern spring peeper		•				•	•		
Cope's gray treefrog		•				•	•	•	
Eastern gray treefrog							•	•	•
Bullfrog						•	•		
Green frog						•	•		
Pickerel frog							•		
Northern leopard frog	•					•	•		
Mink frog							•		•
Wood frog		•				•	•	•	•
Common snapping turtle						•	•		
Stinkpot turtle						•	•		
Wood turtle							•		
Blanding's turtle						•	•		
Ornate box turtle					•				
Western painted turtle		•				•	•		
Map turtle							•		
Ouachita map turtle							•		
False map turtle							•		
Smooth softshell							•		
Spiny softshell							•		
Western slender glass lizard					•				
Six-lined racerunner					•			•	
Five-lined skink			•					•	
Northern prairie skink		•		•			•		
Western worm snake								•	
Ringneck snake					•			•	
Eastern hognose snake							•	•	
Western hognose snake							•	•	
Smooth green snake					•			•	
Blue racer					•				
Rat snake			•					•	
Fox snake			•					•	
Bull snake					•			•	
Milk snake					•			•	
Butler's garter snake		•			•	•			
Plains garter snake	•				•			•	
Western ribbon snake						•	•		
Northern ribbon snake							•		
Red-bellied snake			•					•	•
Common garter snake	•		•		•	•	•	•	
Dekay's snake		•			•			•	
Lined snake					•				
Queen snake								•	
Northern water snake						•	•		
Massasauga						•	•		
Timber rattlesnake					•			•	

Index